# IDEOLOGY
# CULTURE
# & THE PROCESS OF
# SCHOOLING

# IDEOLOGY CULTURE & THE PROCESS OF SCHOOLING

Henry A Giroux

 **Temple University Press**

First published 1981 jointly by Temple University Press, Philadelphia 19122, U.S.A., and Falmer Press Ltd, London WC1N 2ET, U.K.

**Library of Congress Cataloging in Publication Data:**

Giroux, Henry A.
Ideology, culture, and the process of schooling.
Includes bibliographical references. 1. Education—United States—
Philosophy—History. 2. Educational research—United States.
3. Curriculum planning—United States. 4. Positivism. I. Title.
LA212.G48   370$^1$.973   81-1732
ISBN 0-87722-228-2   AACR2
ISBN 0-87722-370-X (pbk.)

## Dedication

To Jeanne F. Brady whose passion and love provide a model for a better world.

To the memory of my father, Armand Giroux, who taught me something about the dignity of working-class struggle; to my mother, Alice Giroux, for her support and courage.

To John Di Biase, Jerry Di Biase, Bill Reynolds, and Moe LaMarre who took the long 'march through institutions' with me, and who taught me a great deal about Marx, Jack Kerouac, solidarity.

To those teachers and students everywhere who are struggling for a more decent and just society.

## Acknowledgements

To some very special friends for their intellectual insight, dialogue, and support: Tony Penna, Stanley Aronowitz, William F. Pinar, Maxine Greene, Jean Anyon, Jerry Di Biase, Bill Reynolds, Moe LaMarre, Art Berger, Donaldo Macedo, Paul Breines, Dick Dyro, Peggy Dyro, Kathleen Weiler, Lisa Jackson, A. D. Van Nostrand, David Purpel, Vic Kestenbaum, Ralph Page, Jean Brenkman, Steve Ellenwood, Linda Barberry, Geoff Whitty, Roger Simon, Mal, Cleo Cherry-Holmes, Pat Auborn, Dick Lednicky.

Over the years I have learned a great deal from the critical and often brilliant intellectual tradition set forth in *Telos* under the editorship of Paul Piccone. My intellectual indebtedness to Stanley Aronowitz is enormous. Most importantly, I am indebted to Paulo Freire for the insight he provides and the courage he displays in fighting for social justice. Of course, the final responsibility for the contents of this book rests with me.

# Contents

# Preface

*Stanley Aronowitz*

Until the last decade, the history and philosophy of American education was written in hyperbole. Since the United States had become the leading imperial power in the world and certainly the most powerful of all western capitalist countries, schooling helped Americans avoid the sense of boundaries shared by most Europeans. For even as socialism was sinking deep roots in the continental soil at the turn of the 20th century, Americans became convinced that education was the great democratic institution that enabled even the most humble of its citizens to enjoy the chance for self-improvement. As new generations of immigrants from all over the world followed those from western Europe who had imbibed the religion of educational opportunity, schools remained the hope of the hopeless. Once here, any American with the brains and initiative could become a professional. In effect, the road to intellectual labor replaced the frontier as the sustaining myth of American capitalist democracy.

Certainly there were critics who argued that American education was no more a route to social mobility than the family and farm had been. Just as Sterling Hayden's romantic trek in the film, *Asphalt Jungle,* from the city to the country seemed an anachronism in 1950 when the yeoman farmer had all but disappeared from the American landscape, a new coterie of social critics claimed that schooling was little more than a sophisticated way to transmit the value systems of the dominant society. Against those like Lawrence Cremin and John Dewey whose faith in education went beyond the conventional shibboleths of the enlightenment to assert that schooling was the great leveler of social and economic differences, critics like Michael Katz, Clarence Karier and Colin Greer produced a spate of evidence showing that schools failed to obliterate class inequality. Their argument, that schools were socializing instruments rather than democratic vistas, became the conventional wisdom for many intellectuals in the 1960s, an era when the fight for democracy appeared to be waged in the streets rather than the classroom.

Less than a decade later, Samuel Bowles and Herbert Gintis amplified the critique of schooling by arguing that schools were inextricably linked to the industrial order. Schools were more than ideological apparatuses, according to the authors of

*1*

*Schooling in Capitalist America.* For Bowles and Gintis the humanistic ideals upon which educational systems purportedly rested were little more than legitimations for the most practical function: to provide a steady stream of workers trained in accordance with the social and technical division of labor. Schools, then, were instruments for the social reproduction of the labor force. Thus, the critique of American education acquired a political economy.

The degradation of labor in the 20th century by scientific management had its concomitant in the transformation of schools into the functional equivalent of the old apprenticeship system. However, workers did not acquire a true craft in schools, only a series of credentials that were synchronous with the labor supply: the tighter the job market, the higher the credentials required to perform the most menial tasks. Since labor had become systematically dequalified by technological change and industrial organization, most workers regardless of their diplomas or degrees, possessed few skills except the ability to fit into the disciplinary canon of the industrial order for which they were prepared by schools.

Critical research on schools in the United States, has, for the most part, been a reaction to the euphoric tones sounded by earlier liberal celebrants. Where liberal theory and history has emphasized schools as a means by which the disadvantaged and dispossessed may gain access to status, if not political and economic power, in American society, the 'critical' writers have been equally insistent that schools are institutions that reproduce dominant ideology as well as the labor force. While the two sides of the debate differ as to the role of schools in the social order, they both embody similar functionalist assumptions. That is, education within the institutional matrix of contemporary capitalist societies is, finally, a servant of power. The liberal side tends to abstract the inequality inherent in capitalist property relations from the evidence that a substantial portion of the educated labor force in American society succeeds in obtaining employment and status that compares favorably with that of previous generations of their own social class. The critical side focusses almost exclusively on the fact that schools cannot and do not intend to transform social relations, and that they are essentially subordinate to the prevailing social/political and economic order. The real debate between the two sides is whether this subordination is good for the country and especially those who are the students.

Henry Giroux's work is, in part, a critique of the functionalist assumptions of both liberal publicists and radical critics of American education. He is among the few outstanding scholars who has tried to break from the reductionist descriptions and analyses offered by earlier writers. In this sense, he is a leading figure in the emerging movement of those within the critical school who refuse to reduce schooling to its functions within the dominant society. He is neither an economic determinist nor an ideological determinist. The essays in this volume are convincing evidence that he has begun to find a way out of all determinism by trying to discover how the curriculum functions as an internal discourse as well as a powerful force for social integration.

What constitutes Giroux's major contribution to educational theory? First, he focusses on curriculum as a discourse that may either embody the elements of domination or liberation. By interrogating the functionalism of most educational theory, he emerges with a non-functionalist theory of education and particularly the curriculum as its principal language by which it makes its ideology intelligible to itself. This approach is a far cry from the insistence of all previous theory that schooling is either good or evil. Instead, he performs the difficult but fecund work of *immanent critique*. That is, he takes the categories of learning seriously and thereby takes teachers and students as legitimate subjects of educational practice. This is his second important contribution.

At first glance, the unsuspecting would not necessarily see this move as especially remarkable. After all, can the study of education be anything else than an inquiry into the processes of learning? Surely, many psychologists, learning theorists and educators have tried to understand how people acquire knowledge. Giroux's uniqueness consists in the way in which he approaches these issues. Like Paulo Freire, he probes deeply into the conditions of pedagogy, tries to understand how it is possible that education can be a force for democracy, not by asserting its levelling influence within the social hierarchy because he has comprehended the critique of those who argue for the reproductive functions of education; rather, Giroux takes the pedagogy of the schools as an effort to transmit cultural tradition and ideology as knowledges of hegemonic groups in society. But he leaves room for the possibility that the conditions of learning – the classroom, textbooks, and other spaces where people try to gain power through understanding – may be *counterhegemonic*. Giroux's work is a continuing exploration of how education may contribute to the emancipation of human beings whom, he believes, are in the thrall of ideology. At the same time, he has succeeded in avoiding the entrapment of the hegemonic ideology itself which has plagued most radical critics. This ideology asserts its own power without disruption.

For Giroux schools are institutions of cultural and social reproduction that embody what Pierre Bourdieu calls 'cultural capital'. But, just as workers contend with their employers for shares of social capital through struggles for higher wages, more control over the work place, and social benefits, students and members of the community, including teachers, wage a constant battle for a portion of society's cultural capital through the curriculum and pedagogy. Contrary to both celebrant and reductionist critiques, Giroux proceeds on the basis of the principle of hope according to which the school is a terrain of contestation rather than an ideology machine. In this respect, he goes further than many of his contemporaries such as Michael Apple and Paul Willis who grasp the contradictory character of schooling but have not conceptualized the moment when the classroom becomes open to change. And there lies the absolutely singular breakthrough of Giroux's work. For alone among Americans, he has offered his critique of schooling within a framework of making pedagogy an emancipatory activity. In this sense, there is a definite continuity with the best side of John Dewey's aspiration to make education a democratic laboratory, to promote citizenship through education. However, the similarity of aspiration should not be confused with the method by which democracy may be achieved. Giroux wishes to empower students and teachers by enlivening their critical sensibilities and their options for social change. His project is to overcome the narrow ideological objectives of contemporary education, implicitly to offer a counterhegemonic program that sees schools as a site where cultural capital may be wrested from those who hold it under lock and key.

Beyond his specific contribution to the critical theory of education, social theory as a whole has much to learn from Giroux. His contributions to our growing comprehension of mass culture, of the theory of the state, and of the theory of ideology are no less provocative than his specific work in curriculum studies and pedagogy. He stands in the front rank of those who are trying to decipher the form of hegemony in late capitalism. By showing us a luminous mastery of such historical figures as Marx, Gramsci and Lukacs as well as a deep understanding of the major writers of today, Giroux's synthetic work can be read by virtually any sociologist, American historian and educator. Thus, we must see the present work as both a series of trenchant commentaries on one of our most important social institutions, and as an incipient theory of American culture.

# Introduction

Since the early part of the twentieth century, the educational field has struggled to establish itself as a discipline with a firm scientific foundation. Drawing heavily upon a positivist rationality that had become the dominant theoretical underpinning of allied disciplines such as sociology, psychology, and the natural sciences, American educational theory and research became firmly entrenched within an instrumentalist tradition that defined progress as technological growth and learning as the mastery of skills and the solving of practical problems.[1]

Lost from this perspective were the critical social and political categories necessary for it to perceive either the limited nature of its own theoretical horizons or to question the relationship between schools and other powerful political and economic institutions in the larger society. Reduced to a perspective that gave priority to questions of efficiency, management and prediction, educational research surrendered its capacity to question and challenge the basic imperatives of the dominant society to a functionalist ideology fuelled by the politically conservative principles of social harmony and normative consensus. Within the functionalist perspective there was little room for educators to raise questions concerning the relationship between critical concepts such as ideology, power, and class struggle and their relationship to the process of schooling. But if these concepts went unexplored so did any sustained attempt to provide an account of the reflexive subject. As Walter Feinberg has clearly argued, traditional views of history, institutions, and socialization in American education emphasized 'habit formation and fixed belief systems',[2] and in doing so dissolved the subject in a learning psychology that reduced theory to an afterthought and elevated methodology to the status of an unquestioned truth. History became intelligible only to the degree that one could discover its 'universal laws'. Anyone who saw history not as some abstract social process but 'as the product of concrete struggles for power',[3] found themselves outside of the sanctified reasoning of traditional educational and mainstream social theory. Questions regarding the school's role in social and cultural reproduction as well as the meaning of intentionality itself were subsumed beneath the exclusive focus given in educational research to the merely technical aspects of schooling.[4]

Needless to say the legitimacy of such a rationality was not to be found in the proclaimed *a priori* superiority of its self-evident truths. Instead it was developed and sustained within the context of a unique set of historical and social experiences that buttressed an economic and political order which, in part, legitimated itself through the medium of a relatively uncritical world view and intellectual tradition. Since both the educational field and liberal and radical traditions of critique developed amidst this historical landscape, it would seem worthwhile to mention briefly some of its more salient characteristics.

In the absence of a long standing feudal tradition, American society did not pass through the shift and struggle for power that results when one set of social relations and mode of production is challenged and replaced by another. Unlike many European nations, the United States did not have the benefit of an historical tradition that made visible the category of social class and the underlying dynamic of class struggle that informed such social relations. Likewise, the absence of such a tradition found parallel support in the violent and ongoing legal repression designed to prevent a radical social movement from developing in the United States.[5] In part, this refers to the institutionalized violence waged against the American labor movement, particularly its more radical wing such as the Industrial Workers of the World. Such repression also found expression in the legal, administrative, and legislative witch-hunts directed against political dissidents and groups such as the American Communist Party, which was actually outlawed for a considerable period of time in the United States. In addition, the development of a radical tradition in the United States was further hindered by the success capitalist development, which in the first half of the twentieth century found itself at an historical juncture in which the conditions for its progress and success appeared beyond doubt. For instance, the logic of capital was faced with ample opportunities for developing domestic and foreign markets, an abundance of cheap labor fuelled by waves of European immigrants, and the opportunity to integrate the major labor unions into the mainstream of American politics. With the introduction of scientific management in the 1920s, the socialization of production was supplemented by socialization of reproduction.[6] Knowledge was placed in the hands of management and the separation of conception from execution in the labor process began to appear as a 'fact of life.' The monopolization of institutionalized power and knowledge in the work place was extended into the realm of everyday life, and the colonization of leisure and consciousness provided a new solution to the problems of overproduction and social conflict.[7] The effects of these changes in production and in society at large on the American working class has been captured by Stanley Aronowitz. He writes:

> In the United States . . . mass consumption has been elevated to the level of ideology as well as material practice, so that the traditional barriers offered by craft and labor-intensive industries were smashed not only by force but also by the profound changes in mass psychology made possible by the productivity of labor itself. For two generations American workers were persuaded that the condition for their own progress was tied

umbilically to the accumulation of capital, an ideological stance abetted by the depth of the American depression, the decentralization of industry which destroyed the historical bonds of working class solidarity, and the rise of mass mediated culture that progressively replaced the bar-room and other traditional centers of working class conviviality.[8]

Finally, it is important to note that the failure of a deep-rooted critical tradition and social movement to develop in opposition to capitalist social relations and ideology must also be linked to the appeal of a legitimating liberal democratic ethos which successfully silenced its radical critics by pointing to the rise of Stalinism and fascism.

It is within the context of this historical tradition that both orthodox and radical views of schooling have emerged. Moreover, it is only within the last two decades that the conservative and conformist theoretical pillars of American social theory have been sharply challenged by a growing amount of radical criticism that has taken the school as the center of its focus. Much of this criticism has helped to increase our knowledge of the role that schools play in supporting the ideology and social relations that legitimate the dominant society, but it carries with it a scarred history, in which its intellectual and ideological pursuits remain tied to one-sided forms of social determinism or to over-idealized models of individual emancipation.

The purpose of this introductory chapter is to extend and enlarge upon the theoretical project that has influenced the essays that make up the rest of this book. At the core of this project is an attempt to lay bare the ideological and political character of the dominant rationality on which the basic premises of the educational field have been developed, particularly in the sociology of education and curriculum studies. On the one hand, these essays reveal the ideological underpinnings of the dominant rationality by detailing how they have expressed themselves in: (1) the form and content of the overt curriculum; (2) the ideological commitments embedded in classroom social relations; (3) the covert messages and structuring concepts embodied in classroom cultural artifacts; (4) the meanings rooted in the commonsense assumptions and life experiences of teachers and students. In adddition, the purpose behind these essays is to examine whether existing radical critiques have made good on their claims to provide the theoretical building blocks for a radical theory of pedagogy.

Taken collectively, these essays attempt to move beyond the abstract negation characteristic of many radical critiques, i.e., critiques that expose the political nature of schooling but do so at the cost of propping up a number of false dualisms that fail to link structure and intentionality, content and process, ideology and hegemony, domination and resistance, and so on. In different ways each of these essays also critiques the over-determined models of socialization and abstract celebration of subjectivity that underlie much of the false utopianism or Orwellian pessimism that is supported in many radical perspectives on schooling. Finally, the political project that shapes these essays also lays the theoretical groundwork for developing a radical pedagogy that connects critical theory with the need for social action in the interest of both individual freedom and social reconstruction. This introduction attempts to draw together the basic issues that are presented in the essays in the rest of the book. In doing so I will first identify the modes of rationality and basic problematics that characterize three prominent modes of educational scholarship in the United States. Second, I will focus on the shortcomings of these problematics and identify those intellectual forces that have shaped my criticisms of them. Similarly, I will draw upon the latter intellectual traditions to expand upon a number of concepts central to the reconstruction of a radical theory of pedagogy, particularly the concepts of ideology, hegemony, culture and power. Finally, I will focus on some theoretical concepts that permeate the essays in this book but need to be further developed, and in doing so I will analyze their theoretical and practical applicability for teachers, students, and other educational workers who are concerned with developing a more radical mode of pedagogy.

## Rationality and Problematic in Educational Scholarship

Any attempt to reformulate the diverse approaches that characterize educational theory and practice must take as its central task a considered appraisal of those interests that structure both the basic assumptions and the nature of the questions that such approaches raise and attempt to resolve. Not to do so results in the use of descriptive categories and labels that fail to link such approaches to the broader economic, political, and historical forces which provide the conditions for their existence. Categories such as traditional, conservative, liberal, and radical, among others, hide more than they reveal. If we are to make the various approaches to educational theorizing transparent to the role they play in the process of social and cultural reproduction, we will have to define and situate their respective underlying rationalities within a problematic that illuminates their relationship to the dominant rationality, or to what H.T. Wilson has, on the one hand, called 'the American Ideology',[9] and what I, on the other hand, have called in Chapter One the 'culture of positivism'. This methodological approach is crucial because it illuminates the interconnections that exist between a dominant rationality and the institutions that function in a given society to reproduce it. Such interconnections politicize the notion of rationality by calling into question how its ideology supports, mediates, or opposes the configuration of existing socio-political forces that use the dominant rationality to legitimate and sustain their existence.

Central then to the notion of critique as it is used here are the concepts of rationality and problematic. By rationality, I mean a specific set of assumptions and social practices that mediate how an individual or group relates to the wider society. Underlying any one mode of rationality is a set of interests that defines and qualifies how one reflects on the world. This is an important epistemological point. The knowledge, beliefs, expectations, and biases that define a given rationality both condition, and are conditioned by, the experiences into which we enter. Of crucial importance is the notion that such experiences only become meaningful within a mode of rationality that confers intelligibility on them.

Modes of rationality 'bind' in a non-mechanistic way. As Althusser points out, 'it is not the material reflected on that characterizes and qualifies a reflection . . . but the modality of that reflection, the actual relation the reflection has with its objects'.[10]

All modes of rationality contain a problematic. 'Problematic', in this case, refers to a 'definite theoretical structure' characterized by a dialectical interplay of structuring concepts that serve to raise some questions while suppressing others.[11] That is, the problematic represents a conceptual structure whose meaning is to be found not only in the questions that command the range of answers provided, but also in the questions that are *not* asked. Thus, the problematic defines both the field of the visible as well as the boundary of the invisible. In one sense, the problematic serves as a valuable heuristic tool because it renders questionable the explicit and implicit messages in a theoretical structure; it also reveals the ideological source that lies beneath the choice of what is considered important or unimportant in a mode of thinking. As Brian Henderson notes:

> The problematic of a text is not only the questions that it asks, but the questions that it does not ask. Specifically, it is the relationship between these, for a text raises certain questions only at the price of not asking others. The relationship between questions asked and questions suppressed is always ideological.[12]

It should be stressed that the problematic of a given mode of rationality represents a response not only to its internal logic, but also to the objective struggles, tensions and issues posed by the historical times in which it operates. Thus, the notion of problematic cannot be reduced to a mode of analysis 'conditioned by purely internal criteria';[13] it also serves as a mode of theorizing that articulates a particular relationship between individuals and classes, and the social, political and economic interests that govern the dominant society. In other words, the problematic represents more than the internal logic that governs a text, cultural artifact, or mode of reasoning; it is also the medium and the outcome of constituted and constituting social practices and, as such, must be viewed in terms of its particular relationship to those structural and ideological mechanisms that serve to reproduce an unjust social order.

The three models of rationality that, I believe, presently dominate the field of education are roughly analogous to those used by Habermas in his categorization of science according to the relationship between cognition and specific human interest.[14] I have labelled them: (1) technocratic (2) interpretive and (3) reproductive.

### Technocratic Rationality

Technocratic rationality takes as its guiding interest the elements of control, prediction, and certainty. Reduced to the latter principles of technical control and certainty, its constitutive view of knowledge is mediated through its proclaimed goal of 'controlling the objectified environmental world'.[15] Moreover, as a result of its strong support of the methodological procedures associated with the natural and physical sciences it upholds an epistemology in which 'knowledge starts from the concrete and is raised to general propositions through a process of abstraction/generalization'.[16] Another general feature of this perspective is its strong dependence on the assumption that theoretical categories are independent of observational categories. Not only does such a position reduce theory to the level of being the result of evidence gathering and 'fact' collecting, but it denies the very notion of a determinate theoretical problematic.

Since the beginning of the twentieth century, technocratic rationality has been the major constitutive interest that has governed the underlying principles in educational theory, practice and research in the United States. Its major assumptions have been developed around the search for monological knowledge, the linking of explanation with mathematically demonstrated claims of universal certainty, and the notion that theory is the product of operational research designed to gather 'scientific facts'. The assumptions underlying the technocratic rationality tradition have dominated such areas as the sociology of education,[17] curriculum studies,[18] and educational psychology and research.[19] The manner in which these assumptions are translated into pedagogical theory and practice are spelled out in detail in Chapter One.

In each of the sub-areas of the educational field mentioned above, a managerial model of schooling took precedence. That is, schools in the early part of the century were viewed as factories, students as raw material, and educational issues concerning knowledge, values, and social relationships were reduced to the language of neutrality, technique, and strict means–ends reasoning. As theory was replaced by methodology in these fields, questions regarding moral values and ethics were framed within a logic that celebrated 'scientific' knowledge and bureaucratic organization. Values were seen as important, but 'their effect [could] be contained and neutralized through the adoption of more refined technical methods'.[20] Thus, questions as value-laden as those that centered around the issue of equality could be reduced to studying differences in the 'successful acquisition of school knowledge',[21] rather than analyzing how such differences, for instance, might serve to maintain capitalist relations of production.

Though the language used by mainstream educators has changed in the last few decades, the technocratic rationality that informs their work has not; it has been simply recycled and repackaged. The belief that the interpenetration of science and technology represents progress, that quantitative and mathematical methods should be accorded status as the highest mode of reasoning, and the notion that social progress finds expression in the search for more sophisticated forms of social engineering still permeate the thinking of American schools. Despite a number of different orientations, the historical unfolding of the educational field from its curricular roots in the scientific management movement of the 1920s through its development in the progressive and structural-functionalist stages in the 1940s and 1950s to its present domination by the systems management perspective, one finds an ideological commonality. That is, during each of these 'periods' schools and the pedagogical process itself are seen as relatively neutral phenomena governed, in the last instance, by the technical imperatives of rational engineering. As such, both intentionality and questions regarding the ethical and political nature of schools have been either ignored or dealt with reductively. William Lowe Boyd in his study of curriculum policy-making captures the essence of this stance with his observation:

> . . . since, the reformers believed that there was 'no Republican or Democratic way to pave a street, only a right way' the business of running a city or a school system was viewed as just that, a business matter and not something appropriate for politics. The prompt, business-like despatch of the decision making tasks facing school boards . . . was facilitated by their view that a wide range of educational questions were essentially technical matters beyond the capacity of the laity to decide.[22]

Technocratic rationality has exercised an enormous influence even on those movements that seemed to renounce its logic. As Aronowitz points out, even the progressive venture in American education renounced 'seeking, much less achieving, a coherent world view, a concept of German philosophy. Dewey taught us to be task oriented . . . Having severed means and ends we . . . stressed skills development under the belief that concepts are valuable to the extent they help us solve practical problems, both with respect to social reproduction and to personal well-being'.[23]

### Interpretative Rationality

I think it is accurate to argue that every rationality has within it another problematic struggling to get out. In this case, the 'caged' problematic that represents the Achilles heel of technocratic rationality is the very notion of meaning itself. For it is in the struggle to unshackle the concepts of 'meaning' and 'experience' from the fossilized notion of objectivity that interpretative rationality is grounded.

Interpretative rationality does not take as its starting point the production of monological knowledge; instead, it has a deep-seated interest in understanding the communicative and symbolic patterns of interaction[24] that shape individual and intersubjective meaning. Rather than focusing on or taking for granted the *a priori* forms of knowledge, its constitutive interest lies in understanding how the forms, categories, and assumptions beneath the texture of everyday life contribute to our understanding of each other and the world around us.

Meaning in this mode of rationality is not removed from the worlds of the social actors themselves who constitute, shape, and live within its definitions. Instead, it is seen in its most crucial form as something which is constantly negotiated and renegotiated by human beings as they mutually produce and define the constitutive rules which shape their interactions. Central to this form of rationality are the concepts of appropriation, intentionality and intersubjectivity. Human beings are never seen as passive recipients of information. Interpretative rationality is sensitive to the notion that through the use of language and thought human beings constantly produce meanings as well as interpret the world in which they find themselves. Therefore, if we are to understand their actions we have to link their behavior to the intentions that provide the interpretative screen they use to find meaning in the world. Thus, as Geoff Whitty has argued, this form of rationality rejects the wider culture of positivism and is based on an epistemology in which:

> truth and objectivity are seen as nothing but human products and man rather than nature is seen as the ultimate author of 'knowledge' and 'reality'. Any attempt to appeal to an external reality in order to support claims for the inferiority of one way of seeing over another is dismissed as ideological. Knowledge is inexplicably linked to methods of coming to know and any supposed dichotomy between them is therefore false.[25]

With its constitutive interest in intersubjective consensus, understanding, and communicative discourse, interpretative rationality has provided the organizing principle for a number of pedagogical approaches that have emerged in the United States during the last two decades. These include approaches as diverse as the free school 'movement' of the 1960s,[26] the enthnomethodology and symbolic interactionism movements that became fashionable in the 1970s,[27] and the recent 'new' sociology of education movement.[28] In spite of their differences, all of these approaches were united in opposition to the traditional canons of technical/ instrumental research, linear notions of causation, the primacy of statistical regularities, and the relegation of experience to the realm of *only* the observable. 'Disinterested' educational theory seemed to raise the wrong questions and pursue equally fallacious problems. Moreover, schools appeared, in the technocratic perspective, as 'black boxes'. That is, as institutions bleached of all forms of subjectivity and humanity.

The interpretative pedagogical approaches attempted to promote a recovery of both the subject and intentionality in their pursuit of an alternative mode of educational theory and practice.[29] Instead of seeing school knowledge as objective and value free, it was seen as a social construction tied to the interests, perceptions, and experiences of those who produced and negotiated its meaning. Instead of teachers and students acting as agents of received values and truths, they were now viewed as producers of values and truths. As knowledge became relativized, modes of pedagogy developed that stressed experiences and interpersonal relations. Classroom practice seemed to disengage itself from the larger world as subjectivity and consciousness escaped from the objectivism of technocratic rationality.

In spite of the pointed criticisms that developed around the use of these approaches, pedagogical accounts that were based on an interpretative rationality generated a number of incomplete but important concerns for educational theory and practice. First, they challenged many of the common sense assumptions that teachers, students, and other educational workers use to guide, structure and evaluate their day-to-day classroom experiences. Second, they refocussed attention on the normative and political dimensions of teacher–student classroom relationships. Third, they established a relationship between epistemology and intentionality, on the one hand, and learning and classroom social relationships on the other. In other words, knowledge is treated as a specific social act mediated by different social relationships. Finally, interpretative rationality has played a significant role in helping educators unravel the latent and manifest dimensions of classroom knowledge and classroom relationships.

Unfortunately, praise represents only one side of the picture. If technocratic accounts of schooling lacked any notion of the subject, interpretative accounts equally lacked an adequate notion either of institutions or history. Consequently, the questions raised in the latter tradition ignored the structural landscape against which meanings were formed, negotiated, or sustained. Moreover, the overburdened phenomenological focus on intentions and human activity neglected the issue of precategorical conditioning. Subjectivity thus became falsely viewed as transparent to itself, and questions concerning power, ideology and the ethical nature of the existing society disappeared in a metaphysical mist fuelled by a rather naive optimism in the power of consciousness to change social reality.

### Reproductive Rationality

One way to view reproductive rationality is to posit what it is not. If interpretative rationality takes as its starting point the nature of intentionality and communicative discourse, reproductive rationality begins from the opposite direction. That is, it focusses its attention upon macro-structural relationships and how these relations in the form of structural determinations shape, as well as limit, the actions of human beings. Unlike traditional functionalist accounts, which are also concerned with the ways institutions shape society, reproductive positions reject consensus as the normative glue of a social system; instead, they focus on the way in which dominant classes are able to reproduce existing power relations in an unjust and unequal society. The central question guiding these perspectives is how do institutions such as schools function to reproduce a class-stratified society. Moreover, reproductive rationality is based upon the principles of critique and reconstruction. Its guiding interests are linked to questions of power and political emancipation. Its theoretical project develops around an attempt to expose, criticize and change the way in which class-specific societies reproduce unequal power relationships *behind* the backs of human beings.

The importance of this form of criticism in education in recent years has been considerable.[30] It has helped to illuminate the shortcomings of modes of interpretative pedagogy that were tied too closely to the concerns of immediate practice, and it further demonstrated the importance of looking at schools within the nexus of other more powerful social and economic institutions, particularly the school's relationship to the workplace and the family. Moreover, by providing a relational analysis of schooling, reproductive accounts raised fundamental questions about the way relations of power and repression in schools limit and distort the nature of intentionality and social practice. Reproductive-based perspectives did more, though, than raise questions about 'how power relations at work outside educational institutions penetrate the structure of authority relations and the organization of knowledge within those institutions'.[31] They also revealed the limits of an interpretative view of epistemology that lacked the criteria to render judgement about the *value* of social constructions. Holly sums up the nature of this critique well:

> A satisfactory social epistemology cannot be derived from a subjective relativism of this kind for two reasons. First, a phenomenological analysis cannot, by definition, penetrate beyond the immediately present conditions, the competing definitions avowed or implied by actors in a given situation. We are, therefore, debarred from considering wider social factors, more or less distant in time or space. Secondly, even in the case of the immediate situation, the subject's perceptions or 'constructions of reality' is clearly not the only factor determining the differential status being accorded to various types of knowledge. A viable theory of knowledge needs, on the one hand, to take account of the historical character of objectivied knowledge and, on the other, the nature of social relations temporarily determining a given stratification.[32]

Informed by a variety of Marxist perspectives, reproductive approaches have helped to make the concept of class a central category in critiques of schooling. But unlike what Richard Johnson has called 'culturalist' versions of class analysis,[33] which limit class relations to interpersonal relations, proponents of the reproductive position, such as Althusser, argue that class cannot be reduced to anthropological terms.[34] That is, in this view class relations are seen as essentially relations *over* the distribution of power and the ownership of capital. In part, educational critics have not developed an adequate conception of class because of their failure to account for 'determinations that don't show up in the experience of actors'.[35] Reproductive approaches have been particularly influential in the United States in stressing the determinate nature and primacy of political economy in educational theory and practice. For example, a number of theorists, such as Bowles and Gintis, have attempted to demonstrate how the reproduction of class relations occurs through a correspondence between the social relations of production and education. By insisting on the primacy of production relations as a determinate force in social and cultural reproduction, these critics have focussed attention on how unjust, class-specific forms of tracking, sorting, and selection mechanisms in schools can be traced back to the political and economic structures that govern them.

Accounts of schooling based on the reproductive rationality have been decidedly helpful in correcting some of the political and ideological shortcomings inherent in functionalist as well as interpretative views of the process of schooling. However, in the final analysis, there are serious deficiencies in the reproductive problematic. Some of the most glaring include its *one-sided* determinism, its simplistic view of the mechanisms of social and cultural reproduction in schools, its ahistorical view of human agency and, finally, its profoundly anti-utopian stance toward radical social change.

For instance, in both Althussarian and political economy positions, the reproduction of society appears to occur without the benefit of the subjects it oppresses. Teachers and students are presented as simply value receivers, cultural dupes who play a passive role in constituting the school system they tread through day-by-day. It is assumed in these perspectives that human agents are simply role bearers. The notion that 'the ideology appropriate to the role performance and the actual ideology of the role bearers could fly apart',[36] causing resistance or outright refusal on the part of students or teachers, is lost in these accounts. Thus, it is not surprising that reproductive theories pay little attention to the way human actors organize their behavior, in individual or class terms, through their own set of constituted meanings and discourse. One result has been the refusal to analyze the ways in which pedagogy within the formal and informal instructional context is mediated by social practices and forms of discourse which serve to transmit and reproduce ethnic, sexist, and class-based attributes. Another problem with reproductive accounts of schooling is that they 'greatly exaggerate the impact of dominant symbol systems or ideologies upon those in subordinate classes'.[37]

In a nutshell, the dialectic of domination and resistance, the notion that schools are *neither the exclusive locus* of domination nor of resistance but a combination of both, is lost in the reproductive position. One result is that human experience is simply reduced to a passive reflex of the ideological imperatives of the logic of capital and its institutions. However, schools are more than merely ideological reflections of the dominant interests of the wider society. They are also relatively autonomous institutions that have a particular relationship to the wider society, one which is marked not only by domination and docility, but also by contestation and resistance. Put another way, schools are social sites whose particularity is characterized by an ongoing struggle between hegemonic and counter-hegemonic forces. Reproductive theories not only ignore the contradictory nature of what goes on in schools but also reduce important categories, such as class and ideology, to vulgar misrepresentations. It is one thing to argue that various dimensions of the form and content of schooling are organized along class principles, a notion that contains a great deal of truth,[38] but another thing to assume that they generate unproblematic determinate effects. As one observer notes, a more reasonable approach would be to argue that 'educational knowledge and practices are organized on class principles, but the transmission process is mediated by the cultural field of the classroom in such a way that determinate effects cannot be guaranteed'.[39] A similar failing that reinforces the rest of this perspective is the simplistic notion that *ideology itself* is simply the determinate instance of a given mode of production. Such a characterization recycles the classical Marxist base-superstructure argument and reduces ideology to mere phenomena.

Finally, if reproductive theories 'forget' that structures not only constitute the subject but are themselves shaped by human action, there is little room in this perspective to provide a historical account of the genesis of consciousness or, for that matter, the transformation of structure itself. The result has been a bracketing of history that separates diachronic (historical) from synchronic (static) accounts. What emerges here is an ahistorical position that lacks the possibilities for discovering its own grounding and genesis. Not surprisingly, reproductive accounts leave little room for historical transformation and change. The mechanisms of structural domination appear so powerfully entrenched in these perspectives, and the possibility of human resistance so remote, that the message that finally emerges contains little hope for social action and radical reconstruction. Writing about the pessimism that comes out of Althusserian positions, E.P. Thompson observes:

> . . . they are marked by their very heavy emphasis upon the ineluctable weight of ideological modes of domination – domination which destroys every space for the initiative or creativity of the mass of the people; a domination from which only the enlightened minority of intellectuals can struggle free . . . why bother to try to communicate, to educate, agitate, and organize since the reason is powerless to penetrate the mists of 'ideology'? In this way, a 'revolutionary' and 'Marxist' critique, which despairs of communication and which has only a fictional political cor-relative, and which, moreover, reveals that all social evils are insoluble within capitalism, ends up as 'the ideological husk of passivity', in which the proclaimed need for 'revolution' becomes a license for intellectual withdrawal . . . If this is all that Althusserianism is . . . it is actively rein-forcing and reproducing the effective passivity before 'structure' which holds us all prisoners. It is enforcing the rupture between theory and practice.[40]

The notion that all of the traditions, formulated within the basic rationalities analyzed in this essay thus far, contained serious theoretical deficiencies has been at the center of my own work. While it was clear to me that only the interpretative and reproductive rationalities contained the elements of necessary critique for developing a radical theory of pedagogy, neither one of these rationalities proved adequate on its own. Thus, interpretative rationality responded to positivist theory and practice by attempting to reinstate consciousness and subjectivity at the core of its problematic, but in doing so it lapsed into subjectivism. Similarly, reproductive rationality politicized the meaning of structure only to do away with an account of either the reflexive subject or the way in which human agents con-stitute the social practices underlying the reproduction of the existing society. In both rationalities, there is a failure to overcome the false dualism of subject and object in the analysis of cultural and social reproduction. Neither account links ac-tion and structure so as to illustrate how they interpenetrate and affect each other in a non-reductive fashion. Consequently, it appeared to me that at the heart of these two rationalities was a failure to provide a dialectical linkage between social change, power relations, and forms of resistance, on the one hand, and the reciprocal relationship between human action and structural transformation on the other. In addition, both rationalities appeared to undertheorize the notion of power and, in doing so, generated different, but equally one-sided, notions of hegemony, ideology, and culture; three concepts that are crucial to developing a radical theory of pedagogy. The importance of the latter issue cannot be overstated. In the accounts of schooling that rely on interpretative rationality, power is defined as the capacity of individuals to generate meanings and achieve outcomes compatible with the intent of such meanings. According to the theoretical canons of reproductive rationality, power is the medium of specific classes and social formations and is embodied in structural arrangements and institutions. Both positions are grossly inadequate. Anthony Giddens sums up the latter point well:

> The first tends to treat domination as a network of decision-making, operating against an unexamined institutional backdrop, the second regards domination as itself an institutional phenomenon, either disregarding power as relating to the active accomplishments of actors, or treating it as in some way determined by institutions.[41]

As I mentioned previously, the nature of the critique that informs the essays in this book is directly related to addressing many (though far from all) of the theoretical shortcomings inherent in the rationalities that dominate educational theory and practice in the United States, not to mention the other industrial countries of the West. The essence of the problematic underlying my own critique is drawn primarily from the tradition of 'Western Marxism', which in the most general sense is based upon a rejection of the economistic model of orthodox Marxism, supports the libertarian dimensions of Marx's early work, and strongly adheres to the notion that as a form of radical theory and practice 'Marxism must be . . . made possible for every generation'.[42] Included in this tradition is the early work of Lukacs, the thought of Gramsci, the Frankfurt School, the writings of Agnes Heller and the Budapest School, and the more recent work of Karol Kosik, Stanley Aronowitz, Anthony Giddens, and other neo-Marxists, theorists and educators.

There are a number of common concerns and issues running through the work of all of these theorists and traditions. What is important about these concerns is that they not only reject positivist technical rationality and its goal of technical control, but demonstrate theoretically, as well, the need for educators to work for the development of an active critical consciousness among teachers and students. That is, to work for modes of reflexivity that allow people to examine critically the taken-for-granted assumptions that shape their discourse, actions and consciousness. Clearly, this does not mean that the world exists simply as we intepret it. Quite the contrary. The value of the nature of Marxian analysis is that it starts from the assumption that men and women are unfree in both objective and subjective terms, and that reality must not only be questioned but that its contradictions must be traced to the source and transformed through praxis.

While it is impossible to mention all of the common themes that unite the diverse traditions in Western Marxism, I can cite briefly those that have strongly influenced my own thinking about what it means to reconceptualize educational radical theory and practice. In general terms, the themes that follow are drawn from attempts to reconcile critical Marxism with certain progressive elements taken from phenomenology, psychoanalysis, and symbolic communication.[43] In more specific terms, these common themes include: (1) a recognition of the importance of the dialectical nature of social reality and the significance of subjectivity as a constituted and constituting part of that reality; (2) a rejection of over-determined, economistic, base-superstructure models of causality as well as their accompanying view that consciousness is simply a reflection of social being;[44] (3) a conception of totality that rejects the dualism of subject and object as well as the firm distinction between macro and micro levels of reality;[45] (4) a notion of liberation defined not only in economic terms, but also in terms that speak to the complexity of humans needs, i.e., psychological, sexual, aesthetic, etc.; (5) a rejection of those tenets of orthodox Marxism in which human behavior is reduced to a reflex of the logic of capital, and Marxism itself is seen simply as a science of predetermined and inevitable laws; (6) a general agreement on the importance of class as a unit of social analysis; (7) the importance of the anthropological dimension and the relevance of everyday life as a theoretical and political sphere of investigation and struggle.

In the following section, the importance of some of these issues for a theory of radical pedagogy is considered by examining specific theorists who have addressed them in a critical and illuminating way. Since I cannot provide a detailed study either of the themes or the theorists who have developed them, I will limit my analysis to some of those neo-Marxist thinkers who have influenced my own thinking regarding the important concepts: ideology, hegemony, and culture.

In the major approaches to the sociology of education and curriculum studies I have mentioned thus far, only the reproductive approach has linked the notions of power and domination to the role that schools play in legitimating the economic and class structure of the industrial societies of the West. But, as politically useful as this approach is, it fails to integrate ideology, hegemony, and culture into a successful theory of reproduction and transformation. Not only does the reproductive approach support a one-dimensional view of domination, it also strips the notion of ideology of whatever possibilities it has of contributing to a dialectical theory of radical pedagogy. For instance, the political economy model ignores the notion of consciousness and ideology altogether and restricts its analysis to the claim that 'the major aspects of educational organization replicate the relationships of dominance and subordination in the economic sphere'.[46] Thus in this perspective the question of the role that schools play as agents of social and cultural reproduction gets absorbed in the political dynamics underlying the hidden curriculum of classroom social relations. From a different perspective, Althusserian models of reproduction provide a broader view of the hegemonic function of schools by viewing them as part of the Ideological State Apparatus. While this position does us the service of linking reproduction to the larger imperatives of the state, it deflates its own possibilities by defining ideology as a form of 'interpellation' in which subjects simply become bearers of imposed roles. Viewed in this way, schools become sites harmoniously linked through a powerfully unified ideology to other institutions that make up the wider society. Lost here is the notion of relative autonomy as well as the possibility of contradictions emerging among schools, the media, the state, the economy and other institutions. Similarly lost from this account is any attempt to provide a systematic analysis of how subjectivity is actually constituted in schools. To ignore such a question represents more than an epistemological error, it represents a theoretical unwillingness to posit schools as sites where ideological struggles are the order of the day. Moreover, it relinquishes the possibility of developing a radical strategy in which oppositional forms of teaching and administration can develop as instances of counter-hegemonic struggles. The result of such a failing is clear in Althusser's response to the question of 'What is taught in schools?'. In Althusser's analysis pedagogical practice is reduced to the inculcation of rules and the implantation of dispositions, coupled with a weak apology for teachers who would dare to burden themselves by attempting to counteract the hegemonic assumptions and practices that are institutionalized by the schools.[47] What we end up with is a notion of ideology that appears to exist without a subject, an empty concept that is as grimly mechanistic as the worst form of orthodox Marxism. Fred Pfeil sums up this critique in the following comment:

> The turning of the mode of production towards ideology without benefit of human enterprise or will, as though gigantic shapes danced far over our heads to music we could not hear, is not wrong because it offends the ears of the liberal humanist. It is wrong because, in its refusal to posit human agency in a past 'conjuncture', it denies human agency to the present as well. Yet the illusion that ideology stands over and against us, a 'formation' *ex nihilo* of a system or 'structure' called capitalism . . . sacrifices the sense of ideology as the thought-production of human beings living in determinate social relations.[48]

It is precisely the notion of ideology as the 'thought-production of human beings' that needs to stand at the center of a Marxist critical theory that can be useful in developing a more radical theory of pedagogy. But in order to recover the critical spirit of ideology, we will have to turn to some of the critical traditions that have informed the concept since Marx first used it in *The German Ideology*.

### Ideology

Though Marx never fully worked out the general implications of his treatment of ideology he made a number of crucial additions to its meaning.[49] For Marx, ideology speaks to both a critique of, and the possibilities inherent in, consciousness. On the one hand, ideology typified forms of consciousness and discourse made false by the social and material conditions in which they emerged. At the same time, ideology was viewed as a system of ideas that distorted reality in order to serve the interest of a dominant class. Furthermore, ideology took on the meaning of a mode of consciousness that falsely construed the representation of history. On the other hand, Marx's view of ideology delineated a form of ideology-critique and a call for political action.[50] That is, 'ideology becomes a mode of penetrating beyond the consciousness of human actors, and of uncovering the "real foundations" of their activity, this being harnessed to the end of social transformation'.[51] What is useful about Marx's underdeveloped notion of ideology is that it calls into question the nature of consciousness and provides a productive starting point for analyzing the historical and contemporary processes whereby existing beliefs and practices exist as legitimations of a given society.

Both the notion of ideology and ideology-critique have been further developed by a number of neo-Marxist thinkers in a way that has application to the sociology of education and curriculum studies. For instance, in *history and class consciousness,* George Lukacs extended Marx's notion of 'commodity fetishism' into the important concept of reification, i.e., the process whereby concrete relations between human beings are made to appear as objectified relations between things.[52] According to Lukacs, reification was both a moment of consciousness and an objective moment in the process of its production. Central to the notion of reification is the critique of both the social relations of production and those forms of everyday consciousness that 'freeze the moment', that accept the factuality of the given world without either questioning its mediations or tracing them back to their determinate sources in the wider society.[53]

Reification as a form of ideology and 'second nature' signifies both the limits and interconnections that exist between consciousness and capitalist society. Its value lies in its analysis of how consciousness becomes 'trapped' within a social reality that objectivizes social relations. Its value for radical pedagogy is implicit in its call for a mode of subjectivity that links mediation with totality in order to break through the false world of appearances and to change the social reality that needs them. Lukacs' theoretical quest for a more profound understanding of the mediations that penetrated the reifying immediacies of capitalist society prefigures a dialectical conception of ideology that strips it of its narrow definition as simply false consciousness.

But ideology is more than the reification of consciousness and social relations, it is also consciousness struggling to constitute itself against the objectified nature of social life. In other words, human beings in the course of their work and everyday lives are never reduced to the objective representations of a reified social order. As Giddens points out:

> . . . there is no circumstance in which the conditions of action can become wholly opaque to agents, since action is constituted via the accountability of practices; actors are always knowledgeable about the structural framework within which their conduct is carried on, because they draw upon that framework in producing their action at the same time as they reconstitute it through that action.[54]

Another important theorist who focusses on the relationship between subjectivity and the logic and forms of capital is Karol Kosik. Kosik uses the term, psuedo-concrete, to refer to a perception of the world in which transformative processes are reduced to fixed objects and objectified social relations appear as natural conditions. For Kosik, the problem of pseudo-concreteness is one of the major problems of the present era, and it finds expression not simply in the workplace but also in the taken-for-granted assumptions of lived experience and discourse that permeate daily life. Like Lukacs, Kosik extends the notion of ideology-critique by restoring subjectivity to its critical position as an active agent in the production of historical conditions and social reality. The premise of ideology-critique is that it not only points, once again, to the active nature of consciousness, but it also focusses on how distorted images and messages become embedded in specific cultural artifacts and social phenomena that often carry messages that must be made subject to criticism.[55] Furthermore, both the notions of reification and pseudo-concreteness point to the problematic relationship that exists between the consciousness of everyday life and those mediations that tie it to a social reality that disclaims those radical possibilities that have been the legacy of history itself. In other words, ideology-critique offers the possibility of restoring historical consciousness as an important dimension of critical thinking, a point that underlies all of the essays in the book.[56] The link between reification and the suppression of historical consciousness is made clear in the following comment by Aronowitz:

> The social amnesia that has penetrated working-class consciousness consists first in the repression of the memories of everyday labor – even as it is in process, but especially after the shift is over. Buying and eating become the wages of alienated labor, the means by which hunger for recognition, satisfying work and play, and decent human relationships are spuriously satiated. Second, consumer goods, especially those associated with estranged leisure, become confused with the self. They are objectified satisfactions. Workers can only perceive meaning in those activities that have been designated as autonomous, even if they are invaded by the instrumentalities of consumer culture. It is the love of things rather than persons that fills the void created by the suppression of the memories of degraded labor.[57]

Unfortunately, the contemporary usage of ideology is one that often abstracts the concept from the critical tradition given to it by Marx, Kosik, Lukacs and others. At the present historical juncture, the term appears to be caught in a paradox that limits its meaning to either a mode of domination or to a mode of critical intervention. That is, on the one hand, the concept of ideology is reduced to false consciousness, the imaginary relations of people to their actual conditions of experience, or to a notion of failed science. On the other hand, ideology is narrowly defined as a system of myth, a program of social reconstruction, or an expression of the totality of an age.[58]

If ideology is to become a useful construct in the service of radical pedagogy, it will have to be rescued from the restrictive meanings that presently dominate its use. While more recent theorists have provided more precise as well as constructive definitions of the concept, they have failed to make a clear distinction between ideology as a form of knowledge and practice and ideology as a form of institutionalized hegemony. Yet it is precisely the distinctiveness, as well as the particularity of the relationship between these two notions of ideology, that need to be clarified. Of course, Herbert Marcuse and Jurgen Habermas, to mention just two examples, have been exceptionally helpful in specifying both the form and content of hegemonic ideology. In pointing to positivist rationality and modes of communication structured in domination as elements of hegemonic ideology, they have extended Marx's critique of political economy into a criticism of the principles of domination that structure the socio-cultural realm itself.[59]

Political education needs a more dialectical notion of ideology; in this case, one that stresses it as a mode of consciousness and practice that is related to specific social formations and movements. In other words ideology, as Richard Johnson points out, refers not to:

> . . . specific institutional sites *but* practices or moments in social processes that have a distinctive character. It involves particular kinds of relations and movements. Social formations and processes may be looked at from this aspect . . . The characteristic feature of the ideological-cultural instance, then, is the production of forms of consciousness-ideas, feelings, desires, moral preferences, forms of subjectivity.[60]

In order to move beyond the false notion that schools are merely sites that impose dominant hegemonic meanings and values upon relatively passive students and teachers, a notion of ideology has to be developed that provides an analysis of *how* schools sustain and produce ideologies as well as *how* individuals and groups in concrete relationships negotiate, resist, or accept them.[61] This means analyzing the way in which domination is concealed at the institutional level. It suggests looking at the way a dominant ideology is inscribed in: (1) the form and content of classroom material; (2) the organization of the school; (3) the daily classroom social relationships; (4) the principles that structure the selection and organization of the curriculum; (5) the attitudes of the school staff; and (6) the discourse and practices of even those who appear to have penetrated its logic. This points to two different but related ideological elements. The first is situated in the relationship of schools to the state and other powerful institutions in the process of social control and class domination. The second exists in the practice and consciousness of individuals and social groups who produce and experience their relationship to the world in structures that are only partly of their making. If we are to understand not only the distinction but the relationship between these two ideological instances, we will have to expand the definition of ideology to include the notion of hegemony.

### Hegemony

Though there exists no fully developed theory of hegemony,[62] the starting point for studying the concept has to begin with the work of Antonio Gramsci.[63] Writing in the wake of economic upheavals, revolutionary struggles, and the rise of fascism in the early decades of the twentieth century in Italy, Gramsci attempted to redefine and redirect the central tenets of Marxist theory. Rejecting the orthodox Marxist faith in objective economic forces and scientific laws, Gramsci turned his attention to the voluntarist side of Marxist theory. He strongly argued that the domination of capital could not be explained by simply pointing to the rule of force and coercion exercised by the capitalist state. Similarly, he argued that revolutionary struggle could not be relegated to a faith in the inevitable breakdown and self destruction of capitalism's inner logic and laws. For Gramsci the historical materialism of orthodox Marxism was blinded by its own wooden metaphors and paralyzed by its economistic straitjacket. Neither political force nor the logic of capitalist development provided the theoretical basis for fully understanding or changing the nature of capitalist society. Gramsci believed that a more suitable approach would have been to take the notion of consciousness more seriously. That is, the assumption that human beings become political actors as they move through and create the 'terrain on which men move, [and] acquire consciousness of their position, struggle'.[64] It is this link between struggle, domination, and liberation, on the one side, and Gramsci's view of the power of consciousness and ideology on the other, that establishes the problematic for understanding his notion of hegemony.

Hegemony as it is used by Gramsci appears to have two meanings.[65] First, it refers to a process within civil society whereby a fundamental class exercises control though its moral and intellectual leadership over allied classes. In this perspective an alliance is formed among ruling groups as a result of the power and 'ability of one class to articulate the interest of other social groups to its own'.[66] Gramsci appears very clear in pointing out that the intellectual and moral leadership exercised by the dominant class does not consist of the imposition of its own ideology upon allied groups. Instead, it represents a pedagogic and politically transformative process whereby the dominant class articulates a hegemonic principle that brings together common elements drawn from the world views and interests of allied groups. The second use of the term takes on a much more dynamic character. Hegemony, as it is used in this case, points to the relationship between the dominant and dominated classes. In this case, hegemony refers to the successful attempt of a dominant class to utilize its control over the resources of state and civil society, particularly through the use of the mass media and the educational system,[67] to establish its view of the world as all inclusive and universal. Through the dual use of force and consent, with consent prevailing, the dominant class uses its political, moral, and intellectual leadership to shape and incorporate the 'taken-for-granted' views, needs, and concerns of subordinate groups. In doing so, the dominant class not only attempts to influence the interests and needs of such groups, it also contains radical opportunities by placing limits on oppositional discourse and practice. As Douglas Kellner observes, 'hegemonic ideologies attempt to define the limits of discourse, by setting the political agenda, by defining the issues and terms of debate, and by excluding oppositional ideas'.[68]

One important feature of hegemonic rule is that it refers to more than the institutionalization and framing of specific modes of discourse; it also includes the messages inscribed in material practices. Put another way, hegemony is rooted in both the meanings and symbols that legitimate dominant interests as well as in the *practices* that structure daily experience. That hegemony functions, for example, through the significations embedded in school texts, films, and 'official' teacher discourse is clear enough. What is less obvious is that it also functions in those practical experiences that need no discourse, the message of which lingers beneath a stuctured silence. Pierre Bourdieu captures this issue with his comment:

> . . . the most successful ideological effects are those which have no need of words, and ask no more than complicitous silence. It follows . . . that any analysis of ideologies, in the narrow sense of 'legitimating discourses', which fails to include an analysis of the corresponding institutional mechanisms is liable to be no more than a contribution to the efficacy of those ideologies.[69]

And in another observation worth quoting at length:

> The whole trick of pedagogic reason lies precisely in the way it extorts the essential while seeming to demand the insignificant: in obtaining the respect for form and forms of respect which constitute the most visible (and at the same time best hidden because most 'natural') manifestation of submission to the established order . . . that is, all the eccentricities and deviations which are the small change of madness.[70]

In schools, as in other institutions, the production of hegemonic ideologies 'hides' behind a number of legitimating forms. Some of the most obvious include: (1) the claim by dominant classes that their interests represent the entire interests of the community; (2) the claim that conflict only occurs outside of the sphere of the political, i.e., economic conflict is viewed as non-political; (3) the presentation of specific forms of consciousness, beliefs, attitudes, values and practices as natural, universal, or even eternal.

To suggest that hegemony is entered into by both the dominated and the dominant classes raises significant questions about the role that the dominated play in contributing to their own oppression and about the nature of hegemony itself. But in order to unravel such questions, the contradictory nature of ideological hegemony must be laid bare. That is, it is important to demonstrate that hegemony in any of its forms or processes does *not* represent a cohesive force. Instead, it is riddled with contradictions and tensions that open up the possibility for counter-hegemonic struggle as well as reinforce the distinction between hegemony and ideology.

The very structure of the ruling class, for instance, makes it almost impossible for a unified hegemonic ideology to prevail over a given society, particularly in the advanced industrial countries of the West. Althusser's Ideological State Apparatus is not dominated by simply one group, as previously mentioned, it is ruled by an alliance of powerful groups who are constantly shifting and changing the form and content of their legitimating interests as historical circumstances change and new forms of resistance emerge.[71] Moreover, as Aronowitz points out, ruling classes do not produce and disseminate ideologies directly; instead, they appropriate the services of intellectuals and other cultural workers who have the creativity and skills to organize and run cultural apparatuses such as schools and the organs of mass media.[72] On the one hand, this limits the control that the dominant classes have over such cultural sectors. On the other hand, it also provides such institutions with the relative autonomy that makes possible the gaps, tensions, and modes of resistance that contain a critique of the hegemonic order.[73] This position takes on added meaning in Gouldner's comment:

> It is precisely because the hegemonic elite is separated from the means of culture, including the production of ideologies, that ideologies developed in capitalist society may often be discomforting to the hegemonic elite, so that they prefer other methods of dominance and integration more fully and routinely accessible to them.[74]

Similarly, in addition to hegemony not being a cohesive force, it is a mode of control that has to be fought for constantly in order to be maintained. In other words, it is not something 'that simply consists of the projection of the ideas of the dominant class into the heads of the subordinate classes'.[75] The terrain on which hegemony moves and functions has constantly to shift ground in order to accommodate the changing nature of historical circumstances and the demands and reflexive actions of human beings. This issue is highlighted in Gramsci's notion of 'contradictory consciousness'. Gramsci meant by the latter that human beings view the world from a perspective that contains both hegemonic forms of thinking and modes of critical insight. In other words, 'contradictory consciousness' represented a form of common sense that was rooted in folklore, but at the same time enriched 'with scientific ideas and philosophical opinions which have entered ordinary life'.[76] In Gramsci's view the consciousness of ordinary people could not be equated with passivity and one-dimensionality. Instead, it had to be seen as a complex combination of thought and practice 'unable to break with the given world and transform it'.[77] Far from being simply the reflex of defeat and passivity, such a consciousness is fragmented and ambivalent. Or to put it another way:

> . . . on an abstract level, the masses manifest a great deal of agreement with the dominant ideology, but this consensus is superficial and coexists with latent instincts of rebellion, which are often expressd in deviant behavior and which compromises, in embryonic form, an alternative Weltanschauung.[78]

This perception of hegemony redefines class rule, and also reveals a relationship between ideology and power, which is viewed not simply as one of imposition but, as Foucault points out, 'a network of relations, constantly in tension, in activity, rather than a privilege one might possess . . . power is exercised rather than possessed'.[79] Power as used here is a form of production, which rather than *constrain* the subject, becomes its constituting feature. Ideology as an element of hegemony points then to one's limited perception of the world and to social practices that mold and shape the structure of dispositions and needs as well. Thus, power represents both a negative and positive moment. As a negative moment, it strips ideology of its critical possibilities and institutionalizes it as a form of hegemony. As a positive moment, it refers to latent as well as manifest modes of critical discourse and practice which constitute the core of ideology.

The duality of power and control represents a crucial concept for viewing sites such as schools as instances of both hegemonic and counter-hegemonic struggles. Gramsci's notion that hegemony represents a pedagogical relationship through which the legitimacy of meaning and practice is struggled over makes it imperative that a theory of radical pedagogy take as its central task an analysis of how both hegemony functions in schools and how various forms of resistance and opposition either challenge or help to sustain it.

Hegemony and ideology represent important concepts in educational theory and practice because they expose the political nature of schooling and point to possibilities for developing alternative modes of pedagogy. However, helpful as these concepts are in the end, they are incomplete because they do not provide the theoretical framework for developing a notion of totality that reveals how a society reproduces and mediates the wide range of conflicting social formations, ideologies, and structures that either give it a specific historical location or expose its underlying determinations. For this we have to turn to the concept of culture.

### Culture

Traditionally, the concept of culture, at least as it has been used in the United States, has contributed little to an understanding of how power functions in a society so as to structure its various socio-economic classes, institutions, and social practices.[80] Stripped of its political dimensions, culture has been reduced to an anthropological or sociological object of study that not only has obscured more than it has revealed, but also, more often than not, has tilted over into an apology for the *status quo*. For example, in the early but influential work of Kroeber and Kluckhorn the 'essential core' of culture consisted 'of traditional ideas and especially their attached values'.[81] After Kroeber and Kluckhorn, theorists such as Talcott Parsons further reduced 'culture' to a form of cultural idealism,[82] or as in the more recent work of Clifford Geertz to the study of a semiotic field.[83]

In all of these examples, the notion of culture is divorced from the important concepts of class, power, and conflict. A more fruitful starting point would politicize the concept of culture by acknowledging that the distinction between power and culture is a false one. At the core of such an acknowledgment rests a redefinition of culture, one in which the concept would be subsumed within the category of society. Rather than viewing culture as either the general expression of society or as existing beyond its significations and material imperatives, culture would be defined in terms of its functional relationship to the dominant social formations and power relations in society.[84] That is, a politicized notion of culture will have to include the dialectical character of the relationship between ideology and the socio-economic system, on the one hand, and on the other hand 'the dialectical character of the relation between critical and apologetic elements within the culture'.[85]

Culture, in this sense, would be defined not simply as lived experiences functioning within the context of historically located structures and social formations, but as 'lived antagonistic relations' situated within a complex of socio-political institutions and social forms that limit as well as enable human action. These 'antagonistic relations' at the heart of any definition of culture suggest that culture is more than an expression of experiences forged within the social and economic spheres of a given society; it is the latter and more. It is a complex realm of antagonistic experiences mediated by power and struggle and rooted in the structural opposition of labor and capital, as one instance, and, in another instance, as the transformative ability of human beings to shape their lives while only being partially constrained by the social, political, and economic determinants that place interventions on their practice.

Culture is the instance of mediation between a society and its institutions such as schools and the experiences of those such as teachers and students who are in them daily. But since culture is informed by the way power is used in a given society, the notion that culture is the 'instance' of a particular social practice that becomes objectified and produces meaning has to be qualified in order to become meaningful. Instead, it is more appropriate to view culture as a number of divergent instances in which power is used unequally to produce different meanings and practices, which in the final analysis reproduces a particular kind of society that functions in the interest of a dominant class. Thus, it is more appropriate to speak of cultures, rather than culture. That is, in a class-specific society one speaks of dominant and secondary cultures, not so as to reduce consciousness and practice to the simple reflex of class as much as to point to the organizing principle in which 'lived antagonistic experiences' emerge. There is no homologous relationship between class and culture, but there are powerful determinations in a class-based society that roughly structure different cultural experiences along class lines. It is the nature of these determinations and the mechanisms by which they function in different social sites such as schools that should be the object of a study of the political notion of culture. Clark, Hall, *et al*, are instructive on these issues:

> . . . though the nature of this struggle over culture can never be reduced to a simple opposition, it is crucial to replace the notion of 'culture' with a more concrete historical concept of 'cultures'; a redefinition which brings out more clearly the fact that cultures always stand in relations of domination – and subordination – to one another, are always, in some sense, in struggle with one another. The singular term, 'culture', can only indicate, in the most general and abstract way, the large cultural configurations at play in a society at any historical moment. We must move at once to the determining relationships of domination and subordination in which these configurations stand; to the processes of incorporation and resistance which define the cultural dialectical between them; and to the institutions which transmit and reproduce 'the culture' (i.e. the dominant culture) in its dominant or 'hegemonic' form.[86]

To rethink the concept of culture is thus to attempt to articulate not only the experiences and practices that are distinctive to a specific group or class, but also to link those experiences in both their transformative and passive relationships to the power exercised by the dominant class and the structural field over which the latter exercise control. Similarly, it is important to stress that underlying the complex of dominant and secondary cultures is a range of historical sediments, values, and attitudes which cannot be reduced to the category of class or to the logic of capital. Issues regarding gender and ethnicity, as well as the dynamics of nature, cannot be framed exclusively within class definitions. Class definitions do not explain adequately the power and workings of gender or ethnicity issues just as the dialectics of nature cannot be reduced to historical laws or class analysis,[87] although, of course, none of the latter can be viewed outside of the societal landscape against which they move. Accordingly, it is against the dynamic image of this historical and contemporary landscape that we see the gaps, tensions, and contradictions that contain, but do not promise, the possibilities for reconstructing schools and the wider society.

The notion that culture represents a 'mediating link between the system of power relations and educational processes and outcomes'[88] suggests an important advance in understanding how schools function as agents of social and cultural reproduction. Unfortunately, it carries with it the tendency towards a certain reductionism. That is, while this view makes problematic the meaning of culture, it often accepts as unproblematic the assumption that schools merely 'transmit' the dominant culture. The hegemonic nature of school culture appears in the latter view to be unified and unchallenged. But hegemonic ideology and practice do not subsume the entirety of school culture. In other words, schools are sites characterized by an unequal interchange between competing class cultures.[89] Thus, it is crucial for educators to analyze and illuminate not simply the lived experiences of a particular class culture, but the *relationship* among the secondary cultures and their articulation with the dominant school culture and each other. Moreover, it is important to move beyond analyses of how hegemony presents itself in the school curricula. This work is important but can lead to a form of 'radical' management theory in which students and teachers appear simply as passive social puppets in the pedagogical process. This is a significant issue that I want to develop a bit further here.

Within the last decade, theorists such as Bourdieu, Bernstein, and Apple have attempted to delineate how the educational field embodies and reproduces those forms of cultural capital deemed legitimate by the dominant society.[90] For instance, Bourdieu has pointed to how the school institutionalizes, in various aspects of the curriculum, modes of knowing, speaking, style, manners, and learning that most closely reflect the culture of the dominant social classes. By appearing to be meritocratic, schools, according to Bourdieu, structure the arbitrary character of curriculum, instruction, and evaluation under the guise of objectivity and fairness. According to Bernstein, the political nature of schooling can be observed in the principles that structure the message systems inherent in the content of school knowledge. Apple, on the other hand, points to the power of a dominant class to influence the production of certain kinds of technical knowledge needed for both the accumulation of capital and the legitimation of the existing power arrangements of the given society.

All of these approaches have been invaluable in making concrete the interconnections between power and culture and how this interconnection assumes a hegemonic function within the schools. But none of these approaches focusses adequately on the dynamic nature of the antagonistic relationships that actually transpire at the day-to-day level of schooling. What we end up with is an illumination of only one side of the hegemonic process. The question of what is actually produced in schools appears to get lost in analyses of how the mechanisms of reproduction actually work. Unless these two issues are brought together more constructively, it will be difficult to discern where radical critiques provide a productive starting point for a reconstructed theory of radical pedagogy.

While it is important to identify the specific content, mechanisms, and principles that underlie hegemonic school practices, it is equally important to situate them within the contradictory lived relations that make up the cultural field of the school itself. This is important for a number of reasons. First, the school with its competing tensions and disjunctions provides a concrete arena for investigating both the strengths and weaknesses of existing hegemonic practices. Second, this approach makes visible how the mediations of language, style, aesthetics and skills function as both transformative and hegemonic tools. Third, it reveals the structural limits imposed by the state and other institutions on the day-to-day practices of teachers and students. Fourth, it provides educators with an oportunity to see how the contradictions of capital get expressed not only in the discourse of teachers and students, but also in the structure of needs and dispositions as they are played out in the classroom. Finally, this approach suggests developing pedagogical practices that use the lived experiences of the students themselves as a starting point for developing classroom experiences in which students discover how they give meaning to the world and how such meaning can be used reflectively to discover its own sources and limits.[91]

In a nutshell, I have argued that certain traditions with a neo-Marxist perspective are essential for further development of the sociology of curriculum and education. I have particularly stressed that the concepts of ideology, culture, and hegemony as reconstructed in this introduction provide the theoretical basis for examining the dialectical relationship between the general relations of society and the field of schooling. Both the distinctiveness as well as the interface among these three concepts provide the tools for moving beyond the existing rationalities and problematics of schooling and unravelling how power, reproduction and resistance structure the complex relations among the state, economic system and the educational field.

As I have mentioned previously, and will highlight throughout the chapters in this book, the link between power and culture cannot be reduced to a simple reflex of the logic of capital. The weak link in such an analysis has been the concept of resistance, particularly as this concept has been developed in radical pedagogy. The concept of resistance is of invaluable importance regarding its theoretical and practical importance for teachers and students, and it is with a general treatment of this issue that I will conclude.

### Resistance and Pedagogy

By taking stock of the forms of resistance in schools, radical educators can begin to raise some important questions essential to developing viable pedagogical strategies. For example, the following questions suggest such a starting point. First, in what way do specific forms of resistance manifest themselves and what is their relationship to determinants in the wider social order? Second, how do these forms of resistance often end up supporting the modes of domination they attack? Put another way, how do the oppositional elements used by students to wrest some power from the authority of the school do the work in bringing about 'the future that others have mapped for them?'[92] In part it is clear that symbolic power if not translated into political power simply ends up reinforcing dominant social relationships. On one level, this is due to the partially realized and often contradictory elements of resistance employed by students (not to mention teachers). For example, Willis shows how 'the lads' in his study of a 'countercultural' group in an urban London high school rightfully celebrated physical labor and masculinity, but they did so at the price of rejecting mental labor. Similarly, their adulation of masculinity was fuelled by a deep-rooted sexism and racism. Thus, while the collective action of these students represents a realistic response to the lived oppression and alienation embedded in the daily routine of the school, it also has built into it 'commonsense' categories that reproduce the division of labor at the source of its genesis. On another level, more psychological than epistemological, the 'objective structures of oppression produce themselves in the internalized dispositions and needs of human actors, i.e., students and teachers alike. As Bourdieu points out, it is in the intersection of competencies and needs 'acquired in the course of a particular history'[93] that the dialectical relations between class structures and practices can be found. This suggests that one element of radical pedagogy will have to focus on classroom social relations that reinforce alternative habits of thought and dispositions. Moreover, 'radical' social relationships should demonstrate in the concrete the existence of alternative needs and ways of breaking away from those that tie people to the existing social order.[94]

For radical educators this means, as Gramsci was well aware, acquiring a critical understanding of the language, modes of experiences, and cultural forms of the students with whom they work. These cultural forms must be historically situated and politically analyzed in connection with wider economic and social determinants. Part of this task has been outlined by Paulo Freire, who rightly emphasizes the need to base pedagogical projects partly on the lived experiences of the students themselves.[95] The task here is to use the spectacle and texts of everyday life as part of the pedagogical process to help students account critically for the nature of those objective and self-formative processes that have made them what they are at the present historical juncture in their lives.

This is not a call for student-centered pedagogy, but for a move beyond the false division over questions of control that have plagued both supporters of the Free School Movement in the United States and many phenomenologically inspired educators in Europe. The endemic paradox between freedom and control cannot be resolved through a paralysis of guilt over one's use of authority in the classroom. Elshtain has correctly addressed this issue by calling for a mode of classroom authority that supports a theory of dialectical persuasion; that is, control informed by the power of reasoned choices operating in the interests of emancipation replaces forms of control in the classroom that are either overtly or covertly manipulative.[96]

All modes of radical pedagogy presuppose a critical education in which students will be given the opportunity to validate their own experiences. These could range from studying their own class-specific histories and interests to an analysis of the popular culture that they use to express and confirm themselves. This should be the basis for a more distanced and critically directed mode of pedagogy, one that provides students with access to the dominant discourse, skills, and academic traditions. Gramsci's position on this issue is illuminated by Aronowitz's claim that:

> . . . the emancipation of those who have been historically excluded from the dominant discourses depends on their ability to grasp the issues presented by the past, many of which are inscribed in the humanistic canon, including scientific theory, history and philosophy . . . This is not to claim that, in the short run, at least, everyone (or no one) needs to be a critical intellectual. On the other hand, a democratic, self-managed society demands the formation of persons whose ties to the subaltern classes is intimate because they originate in those classes, but have succeeded in overcoming the scars imposed by schooling to engage the bourgeois tradition and also create a new one that is of a piece with working-class culture.[97]

Radical educators must seize the positive moment that exists amidst the cracks and disjunctions created by oppositional forces that are only partially realized in the schools. To do so, represents a crucial step in translating political understanding into the kind of political struggle that might contest not only the hegemonic practices of the school, but also could trace their source back to the wider society. The contestation for power in the schools, the very power to think and act in a critical capacity, is only one step in the larger struggle to contest the power concentrated in the capitalist state itself. Radical pedagogy needs an anthropological grounding but one that recognizes the force of structural determinants that do not show up in the most immediate experiences of teachers and students. The ideological and the concrete cannot be reduced to a mere shadow of the institutional workings of capital, but must be seen as starting points by which to analyze their particular relationship to institutions such as schools, family, and work so that these relationships can be viewed critically and transformed when possible.

I have attempted to show that a more critical mode of theory and practice is needed to inform the sociology of education and curriculum studies fields as they presently exist. Moreover, I have suggested that we return to a tradition inspired by the tenets of Western Marxism in order to reconsider the latter's relevance for a radical mode of pedagogy. The need for such an orientation is as critical as it is imperative and demands that we infuse the utopian moment that underlies the possibility for a better future with a moment of praxis that makes the conditions for such a future possible. The conditions for a new mode of pedagogy as well as a more humane society begin when we as educators can reveal how the self-constituting nature of individuals and classes is not something that can be subsumed within the rationality that legitimizes the existing society. For at the heart of praxis is that first moment when the human subject truly believes that he or she can begin to make history. That is the moment that this book attempts to demonstrate and reveal.

## Notes and References

1 See CREMIN, L.A. (1979) 'Curriculum making in the United States' *Harvard Educational Review* Vol. 73, No. 2, December, pp. 207–220; FRANKLIN, B.M. (1974) 'The curriculum field and the problem of social control, 1918–1938: A study in critical theory' unpublished Ph.D. thesis; ANDREWS, B. and HAKKEN, D. (1977) 'Educational technology: A theoretical discussion' *College English* Vol. 39, No. 1, September, pp. 68–109; KLIEBARD, H. (1979) 'The drive for curriculum change in the United States, 1890–1958: I. The ideological roots of curriculum as a field' *Journal of Curriculum Studies* Vol. 2, No. 3, pp. 191–202 and 'II. From local reform to national preoccupation' *Journal of Curriculum Studies* Vol. 2, No. 4, pp. 273–286.

2 FEINBERG, W. (1980) – 'Educational studies and the disciplines of educational understanding' *Educational Studies* Vol. 10, No. 4, Winter, p. 379.

3 LASCH, C. (1977) *Haven in a Heartless World* New York, Basic Books, p. xv.

4 cf. The work of Ulf Lundgren and his colleagues at the Stockholm Institute of Education is invaluable in analyzing the implications of this issue. See LUNDGREN, U.P. and PETTERSON, S. (1979) *Code, Context and Curriculum Processes* Stockholm, Liber.

5 This issue is explored in FREIBERG, J.W. (1979) 'Critical social theory in the American conjecture' in FREIBERG, J.W. (Ed.) *Critical Sociology* London, Halsted Press, pp. 1–21.

6 LASCH, C. (1977) *op. cit.*

7 ARONOWITZ, S. (1973) *False Promises: The Shaping of American Working-Class Consciousness* New York, McGraw Hill.

8 ARONOWITZ, S. (1979) 'The end of political economy' *Social Text* Vol. 1, No. 2, Summer, p. 28.

9 WILSON, H.T. (1977) *The American Ideology: Science, Technology and Organizations as Modes of Rationality in Advanced Industrial Societies* London, Routledge and Kegan Paul, p. 15.

10 ALTHUSSER, L. (1969) *For Marx* London, Penguin, p. 68.

11 *ibid* pp. 253–254.

12 HENDERSON, B. (1980) *A Critique of Film Theory* New York, Dutton, p. 215.

13 cf. JOHNSON, R. (1979) 'Three problematics: Elements of a theory of working-class culture' in CLARKE, J., CRITCHER, C. and JOHNSON, R. (Eds.) *Working-Class Culture: Studies in History and Theory* p. 202. Johnson provides an excellent critique of reducing the problematic to a method that is limited to an analysis of the internal logic of a work.

14 HABERMAS, J. (1971) *Knowledge and Human Interest* Boston, Beacon Press; HABERMAS, J. (1979) *Communication and the Evolution of Society* (trans. Thomas McCarthy) Boston, Beacon Press; APEL, K.O. (1979) *Towards a Transformation of Philosophy* Sussex, England, Harvester Press.

15 APEL, K.O. (1979) 'Types of social science in light of human cognitive interest' in BROWN, S.C. (Ed.) *Philosophical Disputes in the Social Sciences* Sussex, England, Harvester Press, p. 6

16 MARCUSE, H. (1978) 'On science and phemonenology' in ARATO, A. and GEBHARDT, E. (Eds.) *The Essential Frankfurt School Reader* New York, Urizen Books, p. 471.

17 For a good overview of the history of this area see, WEXLER, P. (1976) *The Sociology of Education* Indianapolis, Bobbs–Merrill.

18 APPLE, M. (1979) *Ideology and Curriculum* Boston and London, Routledge and Kegan Paul; PINAR, W.F. (1975) (Ed.) *Curriculum Theorizing* Berkeley, McCutchen.

19 POPKEWITZ, T. (1978) 'Educational research: Values and visions of social order' *Theory and Research in Social Education* Vol. 6, No. 4, December, pp. 20–39; APPLE, M., SIBKOVIAK, M. and LUFLER, H.S. (1974) (Eds.) *Educational Evaluation: Analysis and Responsibility* Berkeley, McCutchen; EISNER, E. (1979) *The Educational Imagination* New York, Macmillan.

20 SMART, B. (1976) *Sociology, Phenomenology and Marxian Analysis* London, Routledge and Kegan Paul, p. 164.

21 WEXLER, P. (1976) *op. cit.* p. 146.

22 BOYD, W. L. (1978) 'The changing politics of curriculum policy making for American schools' *Review of Educational Research* Vol. 48, Fall, pp. 580–581.

23 ARONOWITZ, S. (1980) 'Technocratic rationality and the politics of schooling: The dark side of progressive education' *Social Practice* Spring, pp. 20–21. See also, HOGAN, D. (1979) 'Capitalism, liberals and schooling' *Theory and Society* Vol. 8, No. 3, November, pp. 387–413.

24 The hermeneutic tradition finds its strongest philosophical expression in the works of GADAMER, H.G. (1977) *Philosophical Hermeneutics* (trans. David Linge) Berkeley, University of California Press; SCHUTZ, A. (1967) *The Phenomenology of the Social World* Evanston, Illinois, Northwestern University Press; WINCH, P. (1972) *The Idea of Social Science and Its Relation to Philosophy* London, Routledge and Kegan Paul; and a good collection of writings can be found in DOUGLAS, M. (1973) (Ed.) *Rules and Meanings* London, Penguin.

25 WHITTY, G. (1974) 'Sociology and the problem of radical educational change' in FLUDE, M. and AHIER, J. (Eds.) *Educability, Schools and Ideology* London, Croom Helm, p. 120.

26 See SPRING, J. (1975) *A Primer of Libertarian Education* New York, Free Life Editions; GARTNER, A. (1973) *After Deschooling. What?* New York, Harper and Row; GRAUBARD, A. (1972) *Free the Children: Radical Reform and Free School Movement* New York, Pantheon Books.

27 Representative examples include: CICOUREL, A.V. (1974) *Language Use and School Performance* New York, Academic Press; GARFINKEL, H. (1967) *Studies in Ethnomethodology* New York, Prentice-Hall; MEHAN, H. (1979) *Learning Lessons* Cambridge, Harvard University Press.

28 For decent overviews of this position see: KARABEL, J. and HALSEY, A.H. (1977) (Eds.) *Power and Ideology in Education* New York, Oxford University Press; EGGLESTON, J. (1977) *The Sociology of the School Curriculum* London, Routledge and Kegan Paul.

29 In the United States this type of work is best represented by a number of divergent traditions which include: the Free School Movement of the early 1960s; the Open School Movement and various branches of what has been loosely termed humanistic education. An analysis of these traditions can be found in Chapter Two following.

30 BOWLES, S. and GINTIS, H. (1976) *Schooling in Capitalist America* New York, Basic Books; CARNOY, M. (1975) *Schooling in a Corporate Society* New York, McKay; CARNOY, M. and LEVIN, H.M. (1976) (Eds.) *The Limits of Educational Reform* New York, McKay; BENET, J. and KAPLAN, A. (1980) *Education: Straitjacket or Opportunity?* New Brunswick, Transaction Books.

31 KUHN, A. (1978) 'Ideology, structure and knowledge' *Screen Education* No. 28, Autumn, p. 40.

32 HOLLY, D. (1977) 'Education and the social relations of a capitalist society' in YOUNG, M.F.D. and WHITTY, G. (Eds.) *Society, State and Schooling* Barcombe, England, Falmer Press, p. 178.

33 JOHNSON, R. (1979) 'Histories of culture/theories of ideology: Notes on an impasse' in BARRETT, M., CORRIGAN, P., KUHN, A. and WOLFF, J. (Eds.) *Ideology and Cultural Production* New York, St. Martin's Press, pp. 49–77.

34 ATHUSSER, L. (1969) *op. cit.*

35 JOHNSON, R. (1979) *op. cit.* p. 55.

36 BEST, M.H. and CONNELLY, W.E. (1979) 'Politics and subjects: The limits of structural Marxism' *Socialist Review* Vol. 9, No. 6, Nov./Dec., pp. 88–89.

37 GIDDENS, A. (1979) *Central Problems in Social Theory: Action, Structure and Contradictions in Social Analysis* Berkeley, University of California Press, p. 72.

38 BERNSTEIN, B. (1977) *Class, Codes and Control Vol. 3*. London, Routledge and Kegan Paul. Needless to say, Bernstein approaches this issue in a dialectical fashion rather than in the manner criticized here.

39 MOORE, R. (1978/9) 'The value of reproduction' *Screen Education* No. 29 Winter, p. 49.

40 THOMPSON, E.P. (1978) *The Poverty of Theory and Other Essays* New York, Monthly Review Press, pp. 185–186.

41 GIDDENS, A. (1979) *op. cit.* pp. 88–89.

42 BREWESTER, B. (1966) 'Presentation of Gorz on Satre' *New Left Review* No. 37, May/June, p. 29.

43 SMART, B. (1976) *op. cit.* p. 15.

44 Alvin Gouldner's criticism of this issue is appropriate and worth quoting in full: '. . . those Marxists who, reciting by rote the catechism that "Marxism is the consciousness of the working class", think that this is all that needs saying, conveniently forgetting that Marxism also says "Consciousness is determined by social being". If that is so, how can the proletarian consciousness of Marxism have been generated by the bourgeois social being of its authors'? GOULDNER, A.W. (1980) *The Two Marxisms* New York, Seabury Press, p. 11

45 This is not meant to cover up important distinctions and differences on some of these issues, but to highlight a common concern. For instance, Adorno and Lukacs had conflicting opinions over the issues of totality and reification, but neither of them abandoned the importance or significance of the concepts themselves, particularly as they stood to expose the contradictions of capitalist society and its underlying rationality. See ADORNO, T.W. (1973) *Negative Dialectics* New York, Seabury Press, and LUKACS, G. (1968) *History and Class Consciousness* Cambridge, MIT Press.

46 BOWLES, S. and GINTIS, H. (1976) *op. cit.*, p. 125.

47 ALTHUSSER, L. (1971) 'Ideology and ideological state apparatuses' in *Lenin and Philosophy* New York, Monthly Review Press, especially pp. 155–158.

48 PFEIL, F. (1980) 'Towards a portable Marxist criticism: A critique and suggestion' *College English,* Vol. 41, No. 7, March, p. 758.

49 See especially, MARX, K. *The German Ideology* (New York: International Publishers, 1972 edition). For a discussion of the history of the concept the best book is still LICHTHEIM, G. (1967) *The Concept of Ideology and Other Essays* New York, Random House.

50 This issue is explored in GOULDNER, A. (1976) *The Dialectic of Ideology and Technology: The Origins, Grammar, and Future of Ideology* New York, Seabury Press.

51 GIDDENS, A. (1979) *op. cit.,* pp. 166–167.

52 LUKACS, G. *op. cit.* especially the chapter on 'Reification and the Consciousness of the Proletariat'.

53 For an excellent discussion of Lukacs' early writings and his relationship to Western Marxism see: ARATO, A. and BREINES, P. (1979) *The Young Lukacs and the Origins of Western Marxism* New York, The Seabury Press. A good compilation of Lukacs' work can be found in MESZARON, I. (1972) *Lukacs' Concept of the Dialectic* London, Merlin Press.

54 GIDDENS, A. (1979) *op. cit.,* p. 145.

55 KOSIK, K. (1976) *Dialectics of the Concrete* Boston, D. Reidel Publishing Company.

56 C.f. David Hamilton's work in England is an excellent demonstration of this type of work in the field of education. (forthcoming) HAMILTON, D. 'Educational Research and the Shadow of John Stuart Mill' in SMITH, J. and HAMILTON, D. (Eds.) *The Meritocratic Intellect: Studies in the History of Educational Research* Aberdeen, Aberdeen University Press.

57 ARONOWITZ, S. (1979) *op. cit.,* p. 49.

58 These positions are represented by FEUER, L. (1975) *Ideology and the Ideologists* New York, Harper and Row, who sees ideology as a myth system. Alvin Gouldner (1976) *op. cit.,* who sees it as a form of social reconstructionism; A number of Marxist thinkers who view it as false consciousness; MANNHEIM, K. (1936) *Ideology and Utopia* New York, Harcourt, Brace, and World, who views it as an expression of an age.

59 MARCUSE, H. (1964) *One Dimensional Man* Boston: Beacon Press; HABERMAS, J. (1968) *Towards a Rational Society* Boston, Beacon Press, especially chapter six, pp. 80–122.

60 JOHNSON, R. (1979) *op. cit.,* pp. 231–232.

61 HAMILTON, D. (n.d.) 'Correspondence theories and the promiscuous school: Problems in the analysis of educational change' Unpublished Manuscript, University of Glasgow.

62 Some of the best work being done in the area can be found in WILLIAMS, R. (1977) *Marxism and Literature* New York, Oxford University Press. Also see the various publications coming out of the Centre for Contemporary Cultural Studies at the University of Birmingham, Birmingham, England.

63 GRAMSCI, A. (1971) *Selections from the Prison Notebooks,* (edited and translated by Quinten Hoare and Geoffrey Smith) New York, International Publishers.

64 *ibid.* p. 377.

65 *ibid.* pp. 12, 52, 17–182.

66 MOUFFE, C. (1979) 'Hegemony and Ideology in Gramsci' in MOUFFE, C. (Ed.) *Gramsci and Marxist Theory* Boston and London, Routledge and Kegan Paul, pp. 182–183.

67 GITLIN, T. (1979) 'News as ideology and contested area: Toward a theory of hegemony, crisis and opposition' *Socialist Review* Vol. 9, No. 6, November–December, pp. 11–54

68 KELLNER, D. (1978) *op. cit.,* p. 52.

69 BOURDIEU, P. (1977) *Outline of Theory and Practice* Cambridge, London, Cambridge University Press, pp. 188–189.

70 *ibid.,* pp. 94–96.

71 KELLNER, D. (1978) *op. cit.,* pp. 58–60.

72 ARONOWITZ, S. (1973) *op. cit.,* p. 119.

73 ENZENBERGER, H.M. (1974) *The Consciousness Industry* New York, Seabury Press.

74 GOULDNER, A. (1976) *op. cit.,* pp. 230–231.

75 NIELD, K. and SEED, J. (1979) 'The theoretical poverty or the poverty of theory: British Marxist historiography and the Althusserians' *Economy and Society* Vol. 8, No. 4, November, p. 408.

76 GRAMSCI, A. (1971) *op. cit.,* p. 326, Note 5.

77 VAJDA, M. (1973) 'Antonio Gramsci: Prison Notebooks Review', *Telos* No. 15, Spring, p. 151.

78 FEMIA, J.V. (1979) 'The Gramsci phenomenon: Some reflections' *Political Studies* Vol. 27, No. 3, September, p. 481.

79 FOUCAULT, M. (1977) *Discipline and Punish: The Birth of the Prison* New York: Pantheon, pp. 26–27.

80 Of course, a much more critical tradition has emerged in England. For instance, see the work of THOMPSON, E.P. (1963) *The Making of the English Working Class* London, and WILLIAMS, R. (1958) *Culture and Society, 1780-1950* London.

81 KROEBER, A. and KLUCKHORN, C. (1952) *Culture: A Critical Review of Concepts and of Social Systems* Cambridge, Harvard University Press, p. 181.

82 KROEBER, A. and PARSONS, T. (1958) 'The concept of culture and of social systems' *American Sociological Review* No. 23, pp. 582–583.

83 GEERTZ, C. (1972) 'Deep play: Notes on the Balinese cockfight' *Daedalus,* Vol. 101, No. 1, pp. 1–37.

84 See WILLIAMS, R. (1977) *op. cit.;* BARRETT, M. *et. al,* (1979) *op. cit.;* CLARKE, J. *et. al.,* (1979) *op. cit.*

85 DREITZEL, H.P. (1977) 'On the political meaning of culture' in BIRNBAUM, N. *Beyond the Crisis* (Ed.) Norman Birnbaum New York, Oxford University Press, pp. 83–129.

86 CLARKE, J., HALL, S., JEFFERSON, T. and ROBERTS, B. (1976) 'Subcultures, cultures, and class' in HALL, S. and JEFFERSON, T. (Eds.) *Resistance Through Rituals,* London, Hutchinson Press, pp. 12–13.

87 I am indebted to a conversation with Stanley Aronowitz for this insight.

88 BREDO, E. and FEINBERG, W. (1974) provide an excellent critique of the one-sided nature of this position in 'Meaning, power and pedagogy', *Journal of Curriculum Studies,* Vol. 11, No. 4, p. 316.

89 WILLIS, P. (1978) *Learning to Labour: How Working-Class Kids Get Working-Class Jobs* Westmead, England: Saxon House.

90 BORDIEU, J. and PASSERON, J.-P. (1977) *Reproduction in Education, Society, and Culture* London, Sage; BERNSTEIN, B. (1977) *op. cit.;* APPLE, M. (1979) *op. cit.*

91 Maxine Greene's work represents the most intelligent and passionate attempt at both demonstrating and analyzing the importance of this issue. Her most recent work includes: (1978) *Landscapes of Learning* New York, Teachers College Press.

92 WILLIS, P. (1976) 'The class significance of school counter-culture', in HAMMERSLEY, M. and WOODS, P. (Eds.) *The Process of Schooling,* London, Routledge and Kegan Paul, p. 198.

93 BOURDIEU, P. (1977) *op. cit.,* p. 81.

94 HELLER, A. (1974) *Theory of Needs in Marx* London, Allison and Busby.

95 FREIRE, P. (1973) *Pedagogy of the Oppressed* New York, Seabury Press.

96 ELSHTAIN, J.B. (1976) 'The social relations of the classroom' *Telos* No. 27, Spring, pp. 107–108.

97 ARONOWITZ, S. (1980) *op. cit.,* pp. 25–26.

# 1    *Schooling and the Culture of Positivism:*
##     *Notes on the Death of History\**

> There is no neutral material of history. History is not a spectacle for us because it is our own living, our own violence and our own beliefs.[1]

One of the more fundamental questions raised by educators in recent years focuses on how public school classroom teachers might develop an orientation to curriculum development and implementation which acknowledges the important underlying ethical and normative dimensions that structure classroom decisions and experiences. The absence of such an orientation has been well noted.[2] For example, in different ways both phenomenological and neo-Marxist perspectives on educational thought and practice have pointed to the atheoretical, ahistorical, and unproblematic view of pedagogy that presently characterizes curriculum development particularly in the social sciences.

Some phenomenological critics have charged that teaching practices are often rooted in 'common sense' assumptions that go relatively unchallenged by both teachers and students and serve to mask the social construction of different forms of knowledge. In this view the focus of criticism is on the classroom teacher who appears insensitive to the complex transmission of socially based definitions and expectations that function to reproduce and legitimize the dominant culture at the level of classroom instruction.[3] Teachers and other educational workers, in this case, often ignore questions concerning how they perceive their classrooms, how students make sense of what they are presented, and how knowledge is mediated between teachers (themselves) and students.

On the other hand, some neo-Marxist critics have attempted to explain how the politics of the dominant society are linked to the political character of the classroom social encounter. In this perspective the focus shifts from an exclusive concern with how teachers and students construct knowledge to the ways in which the social order is legitimated and reproduced through the production and distribution of 'acceptable' knowledge and classroom social processes.[4] Thus, neo-Marxist educators are not simply concerned with how teachers and students view knowledge; they are also concerned with the mechanisms of social control and how

---

\*   This chapter first appeared in *Educational Theory* (1979) Vol. 29, No. 4. Copyright © 1980 by the Board of Trustees of the University of Illinois.

these mechanisms function to legitimate the beliefs and values underlying wider societal institutional arrangements.

Both views have led to a greater appreciation of the hermeneutic and political nature of public school pedagogy. Unfortunately, neither view has provided a thorough understanding of how the wider 'culture of positivism', with its limited focus on objectivity, efficiency, and technique, is both embedded and reproduced in the form and content of public school curricula. While it is true that some phenomenologists have focussed on the relationship between the social construction of classroom knowledge and the major tenets of positivism, they have generally ignored the forms and social practices involved in its transmission. On the other hand, while neo-Marxist critiques have emphasized the ideological underpinnings of classroom social practices, they have done so at the cost of providing an in-depth analysis of how specific forms of knowledge are produced, distributed, and legitimated in schools.[5]

While it is clear that the hermeneutic and political interests expressed by both groups must be used in a complementary fashion to analyze the interlocking beliefs and mechanisms that mediate between the wider culture of positivism and public school pedagogy, the conceptual foundation and distinct focus for such an analysis need to be further developed. This paper attempts to contribute to that development by examining the culture of positivism and its relationship to classroom teaching through the lens of a recently focussed social and educational problem, the alleged 'loss of interest in history' among American students and the larger public. This issue provides a unique vehicle for such an analysis, because it presents a common denominator through which the connection between schools and the larger society might be clarified.

Within the last decade a developing chorus of voices has admitted to the public's growing sense of the 'irrelevance' of history. Some social critics have decried the trend while others have supported it. For instance, the historian, David Donald believes that the 'death of history' is related to the end of the 'age of abundance'. History, in Donald's view, can no longer provide an insightful perspective for the future. Voicing the despair of a dying age, Donald resigns himself to a universe that appears unmanageable, a socio-political universe that has nothing to learn from history. Thus, he writes:

> The 'lessons' taught by the American past are today not merely irrelevant but dangerous . . . Perhaps my most useful function would be to disenthrall [students] from the spell of history, to help them see the irrelevance of the past, . . . [to] remind them to what a limited extent humans control their own destiny.[6]

Other critics, less pessimistic and more thoughtful, view the 'death of history' as a crisis in historical consciousness itself, a crisis in the ability of the American people to remember those 'lessons' of the past that illuminate the developmental preconditions of individual liberty and social freedom. These critics view the 'crisis' in historical consciousness as a deplorable social phenomenon that buttresses the existing spiritual crisis of the seventies and points to a visionless and politically reactionary future. In their analyses the 'irrelevance of history' argument contains conservative implications, implications which obscure the political nature of the problem: the notion that history has not become irrelevant, but rather that historical consciousness is being suppressed. To put it another way, history has been stripped of its critical and transcendent content and can no longer provide society with the historical insights necessary for the development of a collective critical consciousness. In this view the critical sense is inextricably rooted in the historical sense. In other words, modes of reasoning and interpretation develop a sharp critical sense to the degree that they pay attention to the flow of history. When lacking a sense of historical development, criticism is often blinded by the rule of social necessity which parades under the banner of alleged 'natural laws'. The assault on historical sensibility is no small matter. Marcuse claims that one consequence is a form of false consciousness, 'the repression of society in the formation of concepts . . . a confinement of experience, a restriction of meaning'.[7] In one sense, then, the call to ignore history represents an assault on thinking itself.

While it is true that both radicals and conservatives have often drawn upon history to sustain their respective points of view, this should not obscure the potentially subversive nature of history. Nor should it obscure the changing historical forces that sometimes rely upon 'history' to legitimate existing power structures. Historical consciousness is acceptable to the prevailing dominant interest when it can be used to buttress existing social order. It becomes dangerous when its truth content highlights contradictions in the given society. As one philosopher writes, 'Remembrance of the past might give rise to dangerous insights, and the established society seems to be apprehensive of the subversive content of memory'.[8]

The suppression of history has been accurately labelled by Russell Jacoby as a form of 'social amnesia'. 'Social amnesia is a society's repression of its own past . . . memory driven out of mind by the social and economic dynamic of this society'.[9] Jacoby's analysis is important because it situates the crisis in history in a specific socio-historical context. If Jacoby is right, and I think he is, then the 'crisis' in historical consciousness, at least its underlying ideological dimensions, can be explained in historical and political terms. This perspective can be put into sharper focus if we begin with an explanation of the changing nature of the mechanisms of social control over the last sixty years in the United States. To do this, we will have to turn briefly to the work of the late Italian theorist, Antonio Gramsci.

Gramsci was deeply concerned about what he saw as the changing modes of domination in the advanced industrial societies of the West. He claimed that with the rise of modern science and technology, social control was exercised less through the use of physical force (army, police, etc.) than through the distribution of an elaborate system of norms and imperatives. The latter were used to lend institutional authority a degree of unity and certainty and provide it with an apparent universality and legitimation. Gramsci called this form of control 'ideological hegemony', a form of control which not only manipulated consciousness but also saturated and constituted the daily experiences that shaped one's behavior.[10] Hence, ideological hegemony referred to those systems of practices, meanings, and values which provided legitimacy to the dominant society's institutional arrangements and interests.

Gramsci's analysis is crucial to understanding how cultural hegemony is used by ruling elites to reproduce their economic and political power. It helps us to focus on the myths and social processes that characterize a specific form of ideological hegemony, particularly as it is distributed through different agencies of socialization such as schools, families, trade unions, work places and other ideological state apparatuses.[11] Thus, the concept of cultural hegemony provides a theoretical foundation for examining the dialectical relationship between economic production and social and cultural reproduction.[12] At the core of this perspective is the recognition that advanced industrial societies such as the United States inequitously distribute not only economic goods and services but also certain forms of cultural capital, i.e., 'that system of meanings, abilities, language forms, and tastes that are directly and indirectly defined by dominant groups as socially legitimate'.[13] This should not suggest that primary agencies of socialization in the United States simply mirror the dominant mode of economic production and function to process passive human beings into future occupational roles. This over-determined view of socialization and human nature is both vulgar and mystifying. What is suggested is that the assumptions, beliefs, and social processes which occur in the primary agencies of socialization neither 'mirror' wider societal interests nor are they autonomous from them. In other words, the correspondences and contradictions that mediate between institutions like schools and the larger society exist in dialectical tension with each other and vary under specific historical conditions.[14]

It is within the parameters of the historically changing dialectical relationship between power and ideology that the social basis for the existing crisis in historical consciousness can be located. Moreover, it is also within this relationship that the role schooling plays in reproducing this crisis can be examined. Underlying the suppression of historical consciousness in the social sphere and the loss of interest in history in the sphere of schooling in the United States at the present time are the rise of science and technology and the subsequent growth of the culture of positivism. It is this historical development that will be briefly traced and analyzed before the role that public school pedagogy plays in reproducing the crisis in historical consciousness is examined.

With the development of science and new technology in the United States in the early part of the twentieth century, both the pattern of culture and the existing concept of progress changed considerably. Both of these changes set the foundation for the suppression of historical consciousness. As popular culture became more standardized in its attempt to reproduce not only goods but also the needs to consume those goods, 'industrialized' culture reached into new forms of communication to spread its message. Realms of popular culture, formerly limited to dance and dime store novels, were now expanded by almost all of the media of artistic expression.[15] The consolidation of culture by new technologies of mass communication, coupled with newly found social science disciplines such as social psychology and sociology, ushered in powerful, new modes of administration in the public sphere.[16]

Twentieth century capitalism gave rise to mass advertising and its attendant gospel of unending consumerism. All spheres of social existence were now informed, though far from entirely controlled, by the newly charged rationality of advanced industrial capitalism. Mass marketing, for example, drastically changed the realms of work and leisure and, as Stuart Ewen has pointed out, set the stage for the contestation and control over daily life:

> During the 1920s the stage was set by which the expanding diversity of corporate organization might do cultural battle with a population which was in need of, and demanding, social change. The stage was in the theatre of daily life, and it was within the intimacies of that reality – productive, cultural, social, psychological – that a corporate pièce-de-théâtre was being scripted.[17]

While industrialized culture was radically transforming daily life, scientific management was altering traditional patterns of work. For instance, the integration of skill and imagination that had once characterized craft production gave way to a fragmented work process in which conception was separated from both the execution and experience of work. One result was a fragmented work process that reduced labor to a series of preordained and lifeless gestures.[18]

Accompanying changes in the workplace and the realm of leisure was a form of technocratic legitimation based on a positivist view of science and technology. This form of rationality defined itself through the alleged unalterable and productive effects of the developing forces of technology and science were having on the foundations of twentieth century progress. Whereas progress in the United States in the eighteenth and nineteenth centuries was linked to the development of moral self-improvement and self-discipline in the interest of building a better society, progress in the twentieth century was stripped of its concern with ameliorating the human condition and became applicable only to the realm of material and technical growth.[19] What was once considered humanly possible, a question involving values and human ends, was now reduced to the issue of what was technically possible. The application of scientific methodology to new forms of technology apeared as a social force generated by its own laws, laws governed by a rationality that appeared to exist above and beyond human control.[20]

Inherent in this notion of progress and its underlying technocratic rationality is the source of logic that denies the importance of historical consciousness. Moreover, this form of rationality serves to buttress the *status quo* by undermining the dialectic of human potential and will. As a mode of legitimation, this form of rationality has become the prevailing cultural hegemony. As the prevailing consciousness, it celebrates the continued enlargement of the comforts of life and the productivity of labor through increasing submission of the public to laws that govern the technical mastery of both human beings and nature. The price for increased productivity is the continued refinement and administration of not simply the forces of production but the constitutive nature of consciousness itself. For example, in spite of its own claims, positivist rationality contains a philosophy of history that 'robs' history of its critical possibilities. Thomas McCarthy writes that this philosophy of history 'is based on the questionable thesis that human beings control their destinies to the degree to which social techniques are applied, and that human destiny is capable of being rationally guided to the extent of cybernetic control and the application of these techniques'.[21] If critical consciousness, in part, represents an ability to think about the process as well as the genesis of various stages of reflection, then this notion of history contains few possibilities for its development as a critical and emancipatory force.

This form of rationality now represents an integral part of the social and political system of the United States and, as noted previously, can be defined as the culture of positivism. If we are to understand its role in suppressing historical consciousness, the culture of positivism must be viewed through its wider function as a dominant ideology, powerfully communicated through various social agencies. The term 'positivism' has gone through so many changes since it was first used by Saint-Simon and Comte that it is virtually impossible to narrow its meaning to a specific school of thought or a well-defined perspective. Thus, any discussion of positivism will be necessarily broad and devoid of clear-cut boundaries. However, we can speak of the culture of positivism as the legacy of positivistic thought, a legacy which includes those convictions, attitudes, techniques, and concepts that still exercise a powerful and pervasive influence on modern thought.[22]

'Culture of positivism', in this context, is used to make a distinction between a specific philosophic movement and a *form* of cultural hegemony. The distinction is important because it shifts the focus of debate about the tenets of positivism from the terrain of philosophy to the field of ideology. For our purposes it will be useful to indicate some of the main elements of 'positivism'. This will be followed by a short analysis of how the culture of positivism undermines any viable notion of critical historical consciousness.

The major assumptions that underlie the culture of positivism are drawn from the logic and method of inquiry associated with the natural sciences.[23] Based upon the logic of scientific methodology with its interest in explanation, prediction, and technical control, the principle of rationality in the natural sciences was seen as vastly superior to the hermeneutic principles underlying the speculative social sciences. Modes of rationality that relied upon or supported interpretative procedures rated little scientific status from those defending the assumptions and methods of the natural sciences. For instance, Theodore Abel echoed a sentiment about hermeneutic understanding that still retains its original force among many supporters of the culture of positivism:

> Primarily the operation of Verstehen (understanding human behavior) does two things: It relieves us of a sense of apprehension in connection with behavior that is unfamiliar or unexpected and it is a source of

'hunches', which help us in the formulation of hypotheses. The operation of Verstehen does not, however, add to our store of knowledge, because it consists of the application of knowledge already validated by personal experience; nor does it serve as a means of verification. The probability of a connection can be ascertained only by means of objective, experimental, and statistical tests.[24]

Given the positivist emphasis on technical control and coordination, it is not surprising that the role of theory in this perspective functions as a foundation to boost scientific methodology. At the heart of this perspective is the assumption that theory plays a vital role in manipulating certain variables to either bring about a certain state of affairs or to prevent its occurrence.[25] The basis for deciding what state of affairs is to be brought about, or the interests such state of affairs might serve, are not questions that are given much consideration. Thus, theory, as viewed here, becomes circumscribed within certain 'methodological prohibitions'.[26] It was August Comte who laid the foundaion for the subordination of theory to the refinment of means when he insisted that theory must be 'founded in the nature of things and the laws that govern them, not in the imaginary powers that the human mind attributes to itself, erroneously believing itself to be a free agent and the center of the universe'.[27] What is missing from Comte's perspective can be seen when it is instructively compared to the classical Greek notion of theory. In classical thought, theory was seen as a way men could free themselves from dogma and opinions in order to provide an orientation for ethical action.[28] In other words, theory was viewed as an extension of ethics and was linked to the search for truth and justice. The prevailing positivist consciousness has forgotten the function that theory once served. Under the prevailing dominant ideology, theory has been stripped of its concern with ends and ethics, and appears 'unable to free itself from the ends set and given to science by the pre-given empirical reality'.[29] The existing perspective on theory provides the background for knowledge is value free.

Since theory functions in the interest of technical progress in the culture of positivism, the meaning of knowledge is limited to the realm of technical interests. In brief, the foundation for knowledge is drawn from two sources: 'the empirical or natural sciences, and the formal disciplines such as logic and mathematics'.[30] In this scheme knowledge consists of a realm of 'objective facts' to be collected and arranged so they can be marshalled in the interest of empirical verification. Knowledge is relevant to the degree that it can be viewed '. . . as description and explanation of objectified data, conceived – *a priori* – as cases of instances of possible laws'.[31] Thus, knowledge becomes identified with scientific methodology and its orientation towards self-subsistent facts whose law-like connections can be grasped descriptively. Questions concerning the social construction of knowledge and the constitutive interests behind the selection, organization, and evaluation of 'brute facts' are buried under the assumption that knowledge is objective and value free. Information or 'data' taken from the subjective world of intuition, insight, philosophy and nonscientific theoretical frameworks is not acknowledged as being relevant. Values, then, appear as the nemises of 'facts', and are viewed at best, as interesting, and at worst, as irrational and subjective emotional responses.[32]

The central assumption by which the culture of positivism rationalizes its position on theory and knowledge is the notion of objectivity, the separation of values from knowledge and methodological inquiry alike. Not only are 'facts' looked upon as objective, but the researcher himself is seen as engaging in value-free inquiry, far removed from the untidy world of beliefs and values. Thus, it appears that values, judgments, and normative-based inquiry are dismissed because they do not admit of either truth or falsity. It seems that empirical verification exacts a heavy price from those concerned about 'the nature of truth'.[33]

The severance of knowledge and research from value claims may appear to be admirable to some, but it hides more than it uncovers. Of course, this is not to suggest that challenging the value-neutrality claims of the culture of positivism is tantamount to supporting the use of bias, prejudice, and superstition in scientific inquiry. Instead, what is espoused is that the very notion of objectivity is based on the use of normative criteria established by communities of scholars and intellectual workers in any given field. The point is that intellectual inquiry and research free from values and norms is impossible to achieve. To separate values from facts, social inquiry from ethical considerations is pointless. As Howard Zinn points out, it is like trying to draw a map that illustrates every detail on a chosen piece of terrain.[34] But this is not just a simple matter of intellectual error; it is an ethical failing as well. The notion that theory, facts, and inquiry can be objectively determined and used falls prey to a set of values that are both conservative and mystifying in their political orientation.

While it is impossible to provide a fully detailed critique of the assumptions that underlie the culture of positivism, it is appropriate to focus on how these assumptions undermine the development of a critical historical consciousness and further serve to diminish public communication and political action. Consequently, it is important to look briefly at how these assumptions function as part of the dominant ideology. Functioning both as an ideology and a productive force in the interest of a ruling elite, the culture of positivism cannot be viewed as simply a set of beliefs, smoothly functioning so as to rationalize the existing society. It is more than that. The point here is that the culture of positivism is not just a set of ideas, disseminated by the culture industry; it is also a material force, a set of material practices that are embedded in the routines and experiences of our daily lives.[35] In a sense, the daily rhythm of our lives is structured, in part, by the technical imperatives of a society that objectifies all it touches. This is not meant to suggest that there are no contradictions and challenges to the system. They exist, but all too often the contradictions result in challenges that lack a clear-cut political focus. Put another way, challenges to the system often function as a cathartic force rather than as a legitimate form of protest; not infrequently, they end up serving to maintain the very conditions and consciousness that spurred them in the first place. Within such a posture, there is little room for the development of an active, critical historical consciousness.

The present crisis in historical consciousness is linked to the American public's deepening commitment to an ever-expanding network of administrative systems and social control technologies. One consequence of this has been the removal of political decisions from public discourse by reducing these decisions to technical problems answerable to technical solutions. Underlying this crisis are the major assumptions of the culture of positivism, assumptions which abrogate the need for a viable theory of ideology, ethics, and political action.

Silent about its own ideology, the culture of positivism provides no conceptual insight into how oppression might mask itself in the language and lived experiences of daily life. 'Imagining itself valuable only to the extent that it escapes history',[36] this form of rationality prevents us from using historical consciousness as a vehicle to unmask existing forms of domination as they reproduce themselves through the 'facts' and common-sense assumptions that structure our view and experience of the world. The flight from history is, in reality, the suppression of history. As Horkheimer writes, 'Again and again in history, ideas have cast off swaddling clothes and struck out against social systems that bore them'.[37] The logic of positivist thought suppresses the critical function of historical consciousness. For underlying all the major assumptions of the culture of positivism is a common theme: the denial of human action grounded in historical insight and committed to emancipation in all spheres of human activity. What is offered as a replacement 'is a form of social engineering analogous to the applied physical sciences'.[38] It is this very denial which represents the essence of the prevailing hegemonic ideology.

Instead of defining itself as an historically produced perspective, the culture of positivism asserts its superiority through its alleged suprahistorical and supra-cultural posture. Theory and method are held to be historically neutral. By maintaining a heavy silence about its own guiding interest in technical control, it falls prey to what Husserl once called the fallacy of objectivism.[39] Unable to reflect on its own presuppositions, or to provide a model for critical reflection in general, it ends up uncritically supporting the status quo and rejecting history as a medium for political action.

As the fundamental false consciousness of our time, the positivist mode of rationality operates so as to undermine the value of history and the importance of historical consciousness in other significant ways. First, it fosters an undialectical and one-dimensional view of the world; second, it denies the world of politics and lacks a vision of the future; third, it denies the possibility that human beings can constitute their own reality and alter and change that reality in the face of domination.[40]

Wrapped in the logic of fragmentation and specialization, positivist rationality divorces the 'fact' from its social and historical context and ends up glorifying scientific methodology at the expense of a more rational mode of thinking. Under these conditions the interdependence of knowledge, imagination, will, and creativity are lost in a reduction of all phenomena to the rule of the empirical formulation.

Rather than comprehending the world holistically as a network of interconnections, the American people are taught to approach problems as if they existed in isolation, detached from the social and political forces that give them meaning. The central failing of this mode of thinking is that it creates a form of tunnel vision in which only a small segment of social reality is open to examination. More important, it leaves unquestioned those economic, political, and social structures that shape our daily lives. Divorced from history, these structures appear to have acquired their present character naturally, rather than having been constructed by historically specific interests.

It seems clear that the mode of reasoning embedded in the culture of positivism cannot reflect upon meaning and value, or, for that matter, upon anything that cannot be verified in the empirical tradition. Since there is no room for human vision in this perspective, historial consciousness is stripped of its critical function and progress is limited to terms acceptable to the *status quo*. Yet, as Horkheimer points out, it is the contradiction between the existent society and the utopian promise of a better life that spurs an interest in both history and historical progress.[41] The suppression of mankind's longing for justice and a better world are the motive forces that usurp the meaningfulness of history and an historical consciousness. These forces are an inherent part of the logic of positivist rationality.

The culture of positivism rejects the future by celebrating the present. By substituting what is for what should be, it represses 'ethics' as a category of life and reproduces the notion that society has a life of its own, independent of the will of human beings. The neutralization of ethics effectively underscores the value of historical consciousness as well as public discourse on important political issues. Instead, we are left with a mode of reasoning that makes it exceptionally difficult for human beings to struggle against the limitations of an oppressive society.[42]

Finally, inherent in this perspective is a passive model of man. The positivist view of knowledge, 'facts', and ethics has neither use nor room for an historical reality in which man is able to constitute his own meanings, order his own experience or struggle against the forces that prevent him from doing so. Meaning, like 'time and memory', becomes objectified in this tradition and is eliminated as a radical construct by being made to exist independently of human experience and intention. In a society that flattens contradictions and eliminates evaluative and intellectual conflict, the concept of historical consciousness appears as a disturbing irrationality. Marcuse puts it well:

> Recognition and relation to the past as present counteracts the functionalization of thought by and in the established reality. It militates against the closing of the universe of discourse and behavior; it renders possible the development of concepts which de-stabilize and transcend the closed universe by comprehending it as historical universe. Confronted with the given society as object of its reflection, critical thought becomes historical consciousness; as such it is essentially judgment.[43]

I have argued so far that the loss of interest in history in the public sphere can only be viewed within the context of existing socio-political arrangements; and that what has been described as a marginal problem by some social critics, in essence, represents a fundamental problem in which the dominant culture actively functions to suppress the development of a critical historical consciousness among the populace.[44] This is not meant to imply a conscious conspiracy on the part of an 'invisible' ruling elite. The very existence, interests, and consciousness of the dominant class are deeply integrated into a belief system that legitimizes its rule. This suggests that existing institutional arrangements reproduce themselves, in part, through a form of cultural hegemony, a positivist world view, that becomes a form of self delusion, and in addition, leaves little room for an oppositional historical consciousness to develop in the soiety at large. In other words, the suppression of historical consciousness works itself out in the field of ideology. In part this is due to an underlying 'self-perpetuating' logic that shapes the mechanisms and boundaries of the culture of positivism. This logic is situated in a structure of dominance and exists to meet the most fundamental needs of the existing power relations and their corresponding social formations.[45] It appears to be a logic that is believed by the oppressed and oppressors alike, those who benefit from it as well as those who do not.

I now want to examine how the culture of positivism has influenced the process of schooling, particularly in relation to the way educators have defined the history 'crisis' and its relationship to educational theory and practice at the classroom level. I will begin by analyzing how the nature of the loss of interest has been defined by leading members of the educational establishment.

Unlike critics such as Lasch and Marcuse, American educators have defined the 'loss of interest' in history as an academic rather than political problem. For instance, the Organization of American Historians published findings indicating that history was in a crisis, and that the situation was 'nationwide, affecting both secondary schools and higher education in every part of the country'.[46] According to the OAH report, the value of history is being impugned by the growing assumption on the part of many educators that history is not a very practical subject. What is meant by practical appears problematic. For example, the Arizona Basic Goals Commission urged teachers to make history more practical by placing a stress on '. . . positive rather than negative aspects of the American past, eschew conflict as a theme, inculcate pride in the accomplishments of the nation and show the influence of rational, creative, and spiritual forces in shaping the nation's growth'.[47]

For other educators, making history practical has meant reversing the growing divisions and specializations in history course offerings at all levels of education. This group would put back into the curriculum the broad-based history courses that were offered in the 1950s. In this perspective, the loss of interest in history among students has resulted from the fragmented perspective provided by specialized offerings in other disciplines. Warren L. Hickman sums this position up well when he writes:

The utility of history is perspective, and that is in direct opposition to specialization at the undergraduate level. History's position in the curriculum, and its audience, have been eroded steadily as specialization, fragmentation, and proliferation of its offerings have increased.[48]

Both of these responses view the loss of interest in history as a purely academic problem. Severed from the socio-economic context in which they operate, schools, in both of these views, appear to exist above and beyond the imperatives of power and ideology. Given this perspective, the erosion of interest in history is seen in isolation from the rest of society and the 'problem' is dealt with in technical rather than political terms, i.e., history can be rescued by restructuring courses in one way or another. These positions, in fact represent part of the very problem they define. The loss of interest in history in schools is due less to the changes in course structure and offerings, though these have some effect, than to the growing effect of the culture of positivism on the process of schooling itself, and in this case, particularly the social studies field. It is to this issue that we will now turn.

Classroom pedagogy in varying degrees is inextricably related to a number of social and political factors. Some of the more important include: the dominant societal rationality and its effect on curriculum thought and practice; the system of attitudes and values that govern how classroom teachers select, organize and evaluate knowledge and classroom social relationships; and, finally, the way students perceive their classroom experiences and how they act on those perceptions. By focussing on these limited, but nonetheless, important areas we can flesh out the relationships between power, ideology, and social studies pedagogy.

As I have pointed out, within the United States the social sciences have been modelled largely against the prevailing assumptions and methods of the natural sciences.[49] In spite of recent attacks on this mainstream perspective, the idea of social science conceived after the model of the natural sciences exerts a strong influence on contemporary educational thought and practice. Historically, the curriculum field, in general, has increasingly endeavored to become a science. That is, it has sought to develop a rationality based on objectivity, consistency, 'hard data', and replicability. As Walter Feinberg writes, 'the social scientists and policy makers who laboured in the field of education in this century were born under the star of Darwin, and . . . this influence was to have a profound impact upon the direction of educational theory'.[50]

Moreover, in the seventies, as financial aid to education has decreased and radical critics have dwindled in number, the positivist orientation to schooling appears to be stronger than ever. Calls for accountability in education, coupled with the back-to-basics and systems management approaches to education have strengthened rather than weakened the traditional positivist paradigm in the curriculum field. As William Pinar and others have pointed out, the field is presently dominated by traditionalists and conceptual-empiricists, and while both groups view curriculum in different ways, neither group steps outside of the positivist or technocratic world view.[51]

These two groups must be viewed in something other than merely descriptive, categorical terms. Both the assumptions they hold and the modes of inquiry they pursue are based upon a world view that shapes their respective educational perspectives. Moreover, these world views precede and channel their work and influence the development of public school curricula.[52] This suggests that, whether adherents to these positions realize it or not, their theoretical frameworks are inherently valuative and political; thus, they share a relationship to the wiser social order. Thomas Popkewitz captures the essence of this when he writes:

> . . . educational theory is a form of political affirmation. The selection and organization of pedagogical activities give emphasis to certain people, events and things. Educational theory is potent because its language has prescriptive qualities. A theory 'guides' individuals to reconsider their personal world in light of more abstract concepts, generalizations and principles. These more abstract categories are not neutral. They give emphasis to certain institutional relationships as good, reasonable and legitimate. Visions of society, interests to be favored and courses of action to be followed are sustained in history.[53]

One way of looking at the political and valuative nature of educational thought and practice is through what Thomas Kuhn has called a 'paradigm'. A paradigm refers to the shared images, assumptions, and practices that characterize a community of scholars in a given field. In any specific field one can find different paradigms; thus, it is reasonable to conclude that any field of study is usually marked by competing intellectual and normative perspectives. As Kuhn has written, 'a paradigm governs, in the first instance, not a subject matter but a group of practitioners'.[54]

The concept of paradigm is important not merely because it guides practitioners in their work, it also illustrates that paradigms are related to the nexus of social and political values in the larger society. That is, the genesis, development, and effects of a given paradigm have to be measured against wider social and cultural commitments. In a simple sense, a paradigm might be viewed as in opposition or in support of the dominant ideology, but it cannot be judged independently of it. Educational workers in public education are not only born into a specific historical context, they embody its history in varying ways both as a state of consciousness and a sedimented experience, as a felt reality. To what degree they critically mediate that history and its attendant ideology is another issue. Thus, educational practitioners can be viewed as not only products of history but as producers of history as well. And it is this dynamic process of socialization that links them and the schools in which they work to the larger society.[55] Finally it is important to stress that acknowledging the social and cultural basis of the character of different modes of pedagogy is important but incomplete. This approach must be supplemented by analyzing the assumptions embedded in a given educational paradigm against larger social and political interests. Questions which arise out of this type of analysis might take the following form: What interest do these assumptions serve? What are their latent consequences? What are the material and intellectual forces that sustain these assumptions and their corresponding paradigm?

Both the traditionalists and conceptual-empiricists in the curriculum field share the basic assumptions of the culture of positivism. Furthermore, these assumptions shape their view of social science knowledge, classroom pedagogy, as well as classroom evaluation and research. In brief, both groups support a form of positivist rationality in which it is assumed that: (1) The natural sciences provide the 'deductive-nomological' model of explanation for the concepts and techniques proper for social science; (2) Social science ought to aim at the discovery of lawlike propositions about human behavior which are empirically testable; (3) Social science modes of inquiry can and ought to be objective; (4) The relationship between theory and practice in the social science domain is primarily a technical one, i.e., social science knowlede can be used to predict how a course of action can best be realized; (5) Social science procedures of verification and falsification must rely upon scientific techniques and 'hard data', which lead to results that are value free and intersubjectively applicable.[56]

At the core of this social science paradigm is a preoccupation with the instrumental use of knowledge. That is, knowledge is prized for its control value, its use in mastering all dimensions of the classroom environment. In this perspective, technical rationality eschews notions of meaning that cannot be quantified and objectified. This becomes clear when we examine the relationship between theory and practice in the culture of positivism as it affects the curriculum field in general. For instance, traditionalists in the curriculum field like Robert Zais, Glen Nass, and John McNeil, whose influence on public school pedagogy is no small matter, view theory as secondary to meeting the existing needs and demands of social practioners. In this case, theoretical formulations used in the shaping of curriculum development, design, and evaluation are guided by assumptions that bend to the dictates or exigencies of administrators and teachers in the 'real' world of public school education. In this perspective, the 'iron link' between knowledge and practical needs dissolves theory into utility.[57]

While the traditionalists may be viewed as atheoretical, the conceptual-empiricists acknowledge the importance of theory in curriculum work, but limit its meaning and importance by subordinating it to technical interests. The conceptual-empiricists have developed an approach to curriculum which 'celebrates' rigorous and systematic research. Theory is used to generate and accumulate 'hard data' and knowledge. Theory, in this sense, is linked to forms of explanation that are subject only to the criteria of empirical verification or refutation. Theory, as used in this paradigm, capitalizes upon one type of experience. As Habermas writes, 'only the controlled observation of physical behavior, which is set up in an isolated field under reproducible conditions by subjects interchangeable at will, seems to permit intersubjectively valid judgments of perceptions'.[58]

Central to this form of rationality in the curriculum field is the notion of objectivity and neutrality. Guided by the search for reliability, consistency, and quantitative predictions, positivist educational practice excludes the role of values, feelings, and subjectively defined meanings in its paradigm. Normative criteria are dismissed either as forms of bias or are seen as subjective data that contribute little to the goals of schooling. Criticism of this sort is often couched in calls for more precise methods of pedagogy. W. James Popham, a leading spokesman for systems analysis methods, illustrates this position when he writes:

> I believe that those who discourage educators from precisely explicating their educational objectives are often permitting, if not promoting, the same kind of unclear thinking that has led to the generally abysmal quality of education in this country.[59]

More guarded critics such as George Beauchamp acknowledge that normative-based curriculum theories have their place in the field but, true to the spirit of his own view, he reminds us that 'we [need to] grow up in the use of conventional modes of research in curriculum before we can hope to have the ingenuity to develop new ones'.[60] In both Popham's and Beauchamp's arguments, the underlying notion of the superiority of efficiency and control as educational goals are accepted as given and then pointed to as a rationale for curriculum models that enshrine them as guiding principles. The circularity of the argument can best be gauged by the nature of the ideology that it thinly camouflages.

Missing from this form of educational rationality is the dialectical interplay among knowledge, power and ideology. The sources of this failing can be traced to the confusion between objectivity and objectivism, a confusion which, once defined, lays bare the conservative ideological underpinnings of the positivist educational paradigm. If objectivity in classroom teaching refers to the attempt to be scrupulously careful about minimizing biases, false beliefs, and discriminating behavior in rationalizing and developing pedagogical thought and practice, then this a laudable notion that should govern our work. On the other hand, objectivism refers to an orientation that is atemporal and ahistorical in nature. In this orientation 'fact' becomes the foundation for all forms of knowledge, and values and intentionality lose their political potency by being abstracted from the notion of meaning. When objectivism replaces objectivity, the result, as Bernstein points out, 'is not an innocent mistaken epistemological doctrine'.[61] It becomes a potent form of ideology that smothers the tug of conscience and blinds its adherents to the ideological nature of their own frame of reference.

Objectivism is the cornerstone of the culture of positivism in public education. Adulating 'facts' and empirically based discourse, positivist rationality provides no basis for acknowledging its own historically contingent character. As such, it represents not only an assault on critical thinking, it also grounds itself in the politics of 'what is'. As Gouldner points out, 'it is the tacit affirmation that "what is", the *status quo,* is basically sound'.[62] Assuming that problems are basically technocratic in nature, it elevates methodology to the status of a truth and sets aside questions about moral purposes as matters of individual opinion. Buried beneath this 'end of ideology' thesis is a form of positivist pedagogy that tacitly supports deeply conservative views about human nature, society, knowledge, and social action.

Objectivism suggests more than a false expression of neutrality. In essence, it tacitly represents a denial of ethical values. Its commitment to rigorous techniques, mathematical expression and lawlike regularities supports not only *one* form of scientific inquiry but social formations that are inherently repressive and elitist as well. Its elimination of 'ideology' works in the service of the ideology of social engineers. By denying the relevance of certain norms in guiding and shaping how we ought to live with each other, it tacitly supports principles of hierarchy and control. Built into its objective quest for certainty is not simply the elimination of intellectual and valuative conflict, but the suppression of free will, intentionality, and collective struggle. Clearly, such interests can move beyond the culture of positivism only to the degree that they are able to make a distinction between emancipatory political practice and technological administrative control.

Unfortunately, 'methodology madness' is rampant in public school pedagogy and has resulted in a form of curricula design and implementation that *substitutes* technological control for democratic processes and goals. For instance, Fenwick W. English, a former superintendent of schools and curriculum designer, provides a model for curriculum design in which technique and schooling become synonymous. Echoing the principles of the scientific management movement of the 1920s, English states that there are three primary developments in curriculum design. These are worth quoting in full:

> The first is to establish the mission of the school system in terms that are assessable and replicable. The second is to effectively and efficiently configure the resources of the system to accomplish the mission. The third is to use feedback obtained to make adjustments in order to keep the mission within agreed-upon costs.[63]

In perspectives such as this, unfortunately pervasive in the curriculum field, manipulation takes the place of learning, and any attempt at intersubjective understanding is substituted for a science of educational technology in which 'choices exist only when they make the systems more rational, efficient, and controllable'.[64] In a critical sense, the Achilles heel of the culture of positivism in public school pedagogy is its refusal to acknowledge its own ideology as well as the relationship between knowledge and social control. The claim to objectivism and certainty are themselves ideological and can be most clearly revealed in the prevailing view of school knowledge and classroom social relationships.

The way knowledge is viewed and used in public school classrooms, particularly at the elementary through secondary levels, rests on a number of assumptions that reveal its positivist ideological underpinnings. In other words, the way classroom teachers view knowledge, the way knowledge is mediated through specific classroom methodologies, and the way students are taught to view knowledge, structure classroom experiences in a way that is consistent with the principles of positivism.

In this view, knowledge is objective, 'bounded and "out there"'.[65] Classroom knowledge is often treated as an external body of information, the production of which appears to be independent of human beings. From this perspective, objective knowledge is viewed as independent of time and place; it becomes universalized, ahistorical knowledge. Moreover, it is expressed in a language that is basically technical and allegedly value free. This language is instrumental and defines knowledge in terms that are empirically verifiable and suited to finding the best possible means for goals that go unquestioned.[66] Knowledge, then, becomes not only countable and measureable, it also becomes impersonal. Teaching in this pedagogical paradigm is usually discipline-based and treats subject matter in a compartmentalized and atomized fashion.[67]

Another important point concerning knowledge in this view is that it takes on the appearance of being context free. That is, knowledge is divorced from the political and cultural traditions that give it meaning. And in this sense, it can be viewed as technical knowledge, the knowledge of instrumentality.[68] Stanley Aronowitz points out that this form of empiricist reasoning is one in which 'reality is dissolved into objecthood',[69] and results in students being so overwhelmed by the world of 'facts' that they have 'enormous difficulty making the jump to concepts which controvert appearances'.[70]

By resigning itself to the registering of 'facts', the positivist view of knowledge not only represents a false mode of reasoning that undermines reflective thinking, it does this and more. It is also a form of legitimation that obscures the relationship between 'valued' knowledge and the constellation of economic, political, and social interests that such knowledge supports. This is clearly revealed in a number of important studies that have analyzed how knowledge is presented in elementary and secondary social studies textbooks.[71]

For example, Jean Anyon found in her analysis of the content of elementary social studies textbooks that the 'knowledge which "counts" as social studies knowledge will tend to be that knowledge which provides formal justification for, and legitimation of, prevailing institutional arrangements, and forms of conduct and beliefs'.[72] In addition to pointing out that social studies textbooks provide a systematic exposure to selected aspects of the dominant culture, she found that material in the texts about dominant institutional arrangements was presented in a way that eschewed social conflict, social injustice, and institutional violence. Instead, social harmony and social consensus were the pivotal concepts that described American society. Quoting Fox and Hess, she points out that in a study of fifty-eight elementary social studies textbooks used in eight states, the United States political system was described in one-dimensional consensual terms. 'People in the textbooks are pictured as easily getting together, discussing their differences and rationally arriving at decisions . . . [Moreover], everyone accepts the decisions'.[73] These textbooks present a problematic assumption as an unquestioned truth: conflict and dissent among different social groups is presented as inherently bad. Not only is American society abstracted from the dictates of class and power in the consensus view of history, but students are viewed as value receiving and value transmitting persons.[74] There is no room in consensus history for intellectual, moral, and political conflict. Such a view would have to treat people as *value creating* agents. While it is true that some of the newer elementary and secondary texts discuss controversial issues more often, 'social conflict' is still avoided.[75]

Popkewitz has argued cogently that many of the social studies curriculum projects that came out of the discipline-based curriculum movements of the sixties did more to impede critical inquiry tan to promote it. Based on fundamentally flawed assumptions about theory, values, knowledge, and instructional techniques in social studies curricular design and implementation, these projects 'ignored the multiplicity of perspectives found in any one discipline'.[76] With the social nature of conflict and skepticism removed from these projects, ideas appear as inert and ahistorical, reified categories whose underlying ideology is only matched by the tunnel vision they produce.

Human intentionality and problem solving in these texts are either ignored or stripped of any viable, critical edge. For instance, in one set of texts pioneered under the inquiry method, comparative analysis exercises are undercut by the use of socially constructed biases built into definitional terms that distort the subjects to be compared. In analyzing the political systems of the United States and the Soviet Union, the United States is labelled as a 'democratic system' and the Soviet Union as a 'totalitarian state'.[77] Needless to say, the uncriticized and simplistic dichotomy revealed in categories such as these represent nothing other than an updated version of the vulgar 'democracy' versus 'communism' dichotomy that characterized so much of the old social studies of the 1950s and early 1960s. While the labels have changed, the underlying typifications have not. What is new is not necessarily better. The 'alleged' innovative discipline-centered social studies curriculum of the last fifteen years has based its reputation on its claim to promote critical inquiry. Instead, this approach appears to have created 'new forms of mystification which make the social world seem mechanistic and predeterministic'.[78]

A more critical view of knowledge would define it as a social construction linked to human intentionality and behavior. But if this view of knowledge is to be translated into a meaningful pedagogical principle, the concept of knowledge as a social construct will have to be linked to the notion of power. On one level this means that classroom knowledge can be used in the interest of either emancipation or domination. It can be critically used and analyzed in order to break through mystifications and modes of false reasoning.[79] Or it can be used unrefletively to legitimize specific socio-political interests by appearing to be value free and beyond criticism. If the interface between knowledge, power, and ideology is to be understood, knowledge will have to be defined not only as a set of meanings generated by human actors, but also as a communicative act embedded in specific forms of social relationships. The principles that govern the selection, organization, and control of classroom knowledge have important consequences for the type of classroom encounter in which such knowledge will be distributed.

The point is that the notion of 'objectified' knowledge as it operates in the classroom obscures the interplay of meaning and intentionality as the foundation for all forms of knowledge. Absent from this perspective is a critical awareness of the varying theoretical perspectives, assumptions, and methodologies which underlie the construction and distribution of knowledge.[80] Unfortunately, the notion of 'objectified' knowledge represents more than a conceptual problem; it also plays a decisive role in shaping classroom experiences. Thus, one is apt to find classroom situations in which 'objective' information is 'impartially' relayed to 'able' students willing to 'learn' it. Within this pedagogical framework, what is deemed 'legitimate' public school knowledge is often matched by models of socialization that reproduce authoritarian modes of communication. Regardless of how a pedagogy is defined, whether in traditional or progressive terms, if it fails to encourage self-reflection and communicative interaction, it ends up providing students with the illusion rather than the substance of choice; moreover, it ends up promoting manipulation and denying critical reflection.[81] Alternative forms of pedagogy, such as those developed by Paulo Freire, not only emphasize the interpretive dimensions of knowing, they also highlight the insight that any progressive notion of learning must be accompanied by pedagogical relationships marked by dialogue, questioning, and communication.[82] This view of knowledge stresses structuring classroom encounters that *synthesize and demonstrate* the relationship between meaning, critical thinking, and democratized classroom encounters.

The role that teachers play in the schooling process is not a mechanistic one. To the degree that they are aware of the hidden assumptions that underlie the nature of the knowledge they use and the pedagogical practices they implement, classroom teaches will be able to minimize the worst dimensions of the culture of positivism. More specifically, under certain circumstances teachers can work to strip away the unexamined reality that hides behind the objectivism and fetishism of 'facts' in positivist pedagogy. In doing so, the fixed essences, the invariant structures, and the commonsense knowledge that provide the foundation for much of existing public school pedagogy can be shown for what they are: social constructs that serve to mystify rather than illuminate reality.

But at the present time, it appears that the vast majority of public school teachers have yet to step beyond the taken-for-granted assumptions that shape their view of pedagogy and structure their educational experiences. Mass culture, teacher training institutions, and the power of the state all play a powerful role in pressuring teachers to give unquestioning support to the basic assumptions of the wider dominant culture. Maxine Greene captures part of this when she writes:

> It is not that teachers consciously mystify or deliberately concoct the positive images that deflect critical thought. It is not even that they themselves are necessarily sanguine about the health of the society. Often submerged in the bureaucracies for which they work, they simply accede to what is taken-for-granted. Identifying themselves as spokespersons for or representatives of the system in its local manifestations, they avoid interrogation and critique. They transmit, often tacitly, benign or neutral versions of the social reality. They may, deliberately or not, adopt these to accommodate to what they perceive to be the class origins or the capacities of their students, but, whether they are moving those young people towards assembly lines or administrative offices, they are likely to present the world around as given, probably unchangeable and predefined.[83]

For many students, the categories that shape their learning experience and mediate their relationship between the school and the larger society have little to do with the value of critical thinking and social commitment. In this case, the objectification of knowledge is paralleled by the objectification of the students themselves. There is little in the positivist pedagogical model that encourages students to generate their own meanings, to capitalize on their own cultural capital, or to participate in evaluating their own classroom experiences. The principles of order, control, and certainty in positivist pedagogy appear inherently opposed to such an approach.

In the objectified forms of communication that characterize positivist public school pedagogy, it is difficult for students to perceive the socially constructed basis of classroom knowledge. The arbitrary division between objective and subjective knowledge tends to remain undetected by students and teachers alike. the results are not inconsequential. Thus, though the routines and practices of classroom teachers and the perceptions and behavior of their students are sedimented in varying layers of meaning, questions concerning how these layers of meaning are mediated and in whose interest they function are given little attention in the learning and research paradigms that dominate public school pedagogy at the present time. The behavioral and management approaches to such pedagogy, particularly at the level of middle and secondary education, reduce learning to a set of practices that neither define nor respond critically to the basic normative categories that shape day-to-day classroom methods and evaluation procedures. As C.A. Bowers writes, '. . . the classroom can become a precarious place indeed, particularly when neither the teacher nor student is fully aware of the hidden cultural messages being communicated and reinforced'.[84]

The objectification of meaning results in the objectification of thought itself, a posture that the culture of positivism reproduces and celebrates in both the wider society and in public schools. In the public schools prevailing research procedures in the curriculum field capitalize upon as well as reproduce the most basic assumptions of the positivist paradigm. For instance, methodological elegance in educational research appears to rate higher esteem than its purpose or truth value. The consequences are not lost on schools. As one critic points out:

> Educational research has social and political ramifications which are as important as the tests of reliability. First, people tacitly accept institutional asumptions, some of which are defined by school professionals themselves. Achievement, intelligence and 'use of time' are accepted as useful variables for stating problems about schools and these categories provide the basis for research. Inquiry enables researchers to see how school categories relate, but it does not test assumptions or implications underlying the school categories. For example, there is no question about the nature of the tasks at which children spend their time. Research conclusions are conceived within parameters provided by school administrators. Second, researchers accept social myths as moral prescriptions. Social class, social occupation (engineer of machinist) or divorce are

accepted as information which should be used in decision making. These assumptions maintain a moral quality and criteria which may justify social inequality. Third, the research orientation tacitly directs people to consider school failure as caused by those who happen to come to its classes. Social and educational assumptions are unscrutinized.[85]

It does not seem unreasonable to conclude at this point that critical thinking as a mode of reasoning appears to be in eclipse in both the wider society and the sphere of public school education. Aronowitz has written that critical thought has lost its contemplative character and 'has been debased to the level of technical intelligence, subordinate to meeting operational problems'.[86] What does this have to do with the suppression of historical consciousness? This becomes more clear when we analyze the relationship between critical thinking, historical consciousness, and the notion of emancipation.

If we think of emancipation as praxis, as both an understanding as well as a form of action designed to overthrow structures of domination, we can begin to illuminate the interplay between historical consciousness, critical thinking, and emancipatory behavior. At the level of understanding, critical thinking represents the ability to step beyond commonsense assumptions and to be able to evaluate them in terms of their genesis, development, and purpose. In short, critical thinking cannot be viewed simply as a form of progressive reasoning; it must be seen as a fundamental, political act. In this perspective, critical thinking becomes a mode of reasoning that, as Merleau-Ponty points out, represents the realization that 'I am able', meaning that one can use individual capacities and collective possibilities 'to go beyond the created structures in order to create others'.[87] Critical thinking as a political act means that human beings must emerge from their own 'submersion and acquire the ability to intervene in reality as it is unveiled'.[88] Not only does this indicate that they must act with others to intervene in the shaping of history, it also means that they must 'escape' from their own history, i.e., that which society has made of them. As Sartre writes, 'you become what you are in the context of what others have made of you'.[89] This is a crucial point which links praxis and historical consciousness. For we must turn to history in order to understand the traditions that have shaped our individual biographies and intersubjective relationships with other human beings. This critical attentiveness to one's own history represents an important element in examining the socially constructed sources underlying one's formative processs. To become aware of the processes of historical self-formation indicates an important beginning in breaking through the taken-for-granted assumptions that legitimize existing institutional arrangements.[90] Therefore, critical thinking demands a form of hermeneutic understanding that is historically grounded. Similarly, it must be stressed that the capacity for a historically grounded critique is inseparable from those conditions that foster collective communication and critical dialogue. In this case, such conditions take as a starting point the need to delegitimize the culture of positivism and the socio-economic structure it supports.

Schools play a crucial, though far from mechanistic, role in reproducing the culture of positivism. While schools function so as to mediate the social, political, and economic tensions of the wider society, they do so in a complex and contradictory fashion. This is an essential point. Schools operate in accordance, either implicitly or explicitly, with their established roles in society. But they do so in terms not entirely determined by the larger society. Diverse institutional restraints, different school cultures, varied regional and community forces, different social formations and a host of other factors lend varying degrees of autonomy and complexity to the school setting. All of these factors must be analyzed and taken into account if the mechanisms of domination and social control in day to day school life are to be understood.[91]

Moreover, the assumptions and methods that characterize schooling are themselves representations of the historical process. But the mechanisms of social control that characterize school life are not simply the factual manifestations of the culture of positivism. They also represent a historical condition that has functioned to transform human needs as well as buttress dominant social and political institutions. Put another way, the prevailing mode of technocratic rationality that permeates both the schools and the larger society has not just been tacked on to existing social order. It has developed historically over the last century and with particular intensity in the last fifty years; consequently, it deeply saturates our collective experiences, practices, and routines. Thus, to overcome the culture of positivism means that social studies educators will have to do more than exchange one set of principles of social organization for another. They will have to construct alternative social formations and world views that affect both the consciousness as well as the deep vital structure of needs in their students.[92]

Unfortunately, classroom teachers and curriculum developers, in general, have been unaware of the historical nature of their own fields. This is not meant to suggest that they should be blamed for either the present failings in public education or the suppression of historical consciousness and critical thinking in the schools. It simply means that the pervasiveness of the culture of positivism and its attendant commonsense assumptions exert a powerful mode of influence on the process of schooling. Moreover, this analysis does not suggest that there is little that teachers can do to change the nature of schooling and the present structure of society. Teachers at all levels of schooling represent a potentially powerful force for social change. But one thing should be clear, the present crisis in history, in essence, is not an academic problem but a political problem. It is a problem that speaks to a form of technological domination that goes far beyond the schools and permeates every sphere of our social existence. There is a lesson to be learned here. What classroom teachers can and must do is work in their respective roles to develop pedagogical theories and methods that link self-reflection and understanding with a commitment to change the nature of the larger society. There are a number of strategies that teachers at all levels of schooling can use in their classrooms. In general terms, they can question the commonsense assumptions that shape their own lives as well as those assumptions that influence and legitimize existing forms of public school classroom knowledge, teaching styles, and evaluation. In adopting such a critical stance while concomitantly reconstructing new educational theories and practices, classroom teachers can help to raise the political consciousness of themselves, their fellow teachers and their students.[93]

In more specific terms, social studies teachers can treat as problematic those socially constructed assumptions that underlie the concerns of curriculum, classroom social relationships, and classroom evaluation. They can make these issues problematic by raising fundamental questions such as: (1) What counts as social studies knowledge? (2) How is this knowledge produced and legitimized? (3) Whose interests does this knowledge serve? (4) Who has access to this knowledge? (5) How is this knowledge distributed and reproduced in the classroom? (6) What kinds of classroom social relationships serve to parallel and reproduce the social relations of production in the wider society? (7) How do the prevailing methods of evaluation serve to legitimize existing forms of knowledge? (8) What are the contradictions that exist between the ideology embodied in existing forms of social studies knowledge and the objective social reality?

Similarly, questions such as these, which focus on the production, distribution, and evaluation of classroom knowledge and social relationships, should be related to the principles and practices that characterize institutional arrangements in the larger society. Moreover, these questions should be analyzed before social studies teachers structure their classroom experiences. In other works, these are important subsequent questions that should provide the foundation for educational theory and practice. It is important to recognize that these questions can become an important force in helping teachers identify, understand, and generate those pivotal social processes needed to encourage students to become active participants in the search for knowledge and meaning, a search designed to foster rather than suppress critical thinking and social action.

While it is true that such action will not in and of itself change the nature of existing society, it will set the foundation for producing generations of students who might. As indicated, an important step in that direction can begin by linking the process of classroom pedagogy to wider structural processes. To do so will enable educators to develop a better understanding of the political nature of schooling and the role they might play in shaping it. The relationship between the wider culture of positivism and the process of schooling is, in essence, a relationship between ideology and social control. The dynamic at work in this relationship is complex and diverse. To begin to understand that dynamic is to understand that history is not dead, it is waiting to be seized. Marcuse has stated elegantly what it means to 'remember history':

> All reification is forgetting . . . Forgetting past suffering and past joy alienates life under a repressive reality principle. In contrast, remembrance is frustrated: joy is overshadowed by pain. Inexorably so? The horizon of history is still open. If the remembrance of things past would become a motive power in the struggle for changing the world, the struggle would be waged for a revolution hitherto suppressed in the previous historical revolutions.[94]

## Notes and References

1 O'NEIL, J. (1978 'Merleau-Ponty's criticism of Marxist scientism' *Canadian Journal of Political and Social Theory* Vol. 2, No. 1, Winter, p. 45.
2 APPLE, M. (1971) 'The hidden curriculum and the nature of conflict' *Interchange* Vol. 2, No. 4, pp. 22–70; BOWERS, C.A. (1976) 'Curriculum and our technocracy culture: The problem of reform' *Teachers College Record* Vol. 78, No. 1, September, pp. 53–67; POPKEWITZ, T.S. (1977) 'The latent values of the discipline-centred curriculum' *Theory and Research in Social Education* Vol. 1, April, pp. 41–61; GIROUX, H.A. (1979) 'Toward a new sociology of curriculum' *Educational Leadership;* GIROUX, H.A. and PENNA, A.N. (1979) 'Social education in the classroom: The dynamics of the hidden curriculum' *Theory and Research in Education* Vol. 2, No. 1, Spring, pp. 21–42.
3 YOUNG, M.F.D. (1976) (Ed.) *Knowledge and Control* London, Collier Macmillan.
4 BOWLES, A. and GINTIS, H. (1976) *Schooling in Capitalist America* New York, Basic Books; BOURDIEU, P. and PASSERON, J.-P. (1977) *Reproduction in Education, Society and Culture* London, Sage.
5 SHARP, R. (1978) 'The sociology of the curriculum: A Marxist critique of the work of Basil Bernstein, Pierre Bourdieu and Michael Young' unpublished m/s; SARUP, M. (1978) *Marxism and Education* London, Routledge and Kegan Paul.
6 David Donald quoted in LASCH, C. (1978) *The Culture of Narcissism* New York, W.W. Norton, p. xiv.
7 MARCUSE, H. (1964) *One Dimensional Man* Boston, Beacon Press, p. 208.
8 *ibid.* p. 98.
9 JACOBY, R. (1975) *Social Amnesia* Boston, Beacon Press, p. 4.
10 GRAMSCI, A. (1971) *Selections From Prison Notebooks* (trans. Hoare and Smith) New York, International Publishers.
11 ALTHUSSER, L. (1971) *Lenin and Philosophy* New York, Monthly Review Press, pp. 127–186.
12 APPLE, M. (1978) 'The new sociology of education: Analysing cultural and economic reproduction' *Harvard Educational Review* Vol. 48, No. 4, November, pp. 495–503; BERNSTEIN, B. (1977) *Class, Codes and Control Vol. 3* London and Boston, Routledge and Kegan Paul.
13 APPLE, M. (1978) *op. cit.* p. 496.
14 WILLIS, P. (1977) *Learning to Labour* Westmead, England, Saxon House.
15 ADORNO, T.W. (1967) *Prisms* London, Nevill Spearman.
16 ENZENBERGER, H.M. (1974) *The Consciousness Industry* New York, Seabury Press; SCHROYER, T. (1973) *The Critique of Domination* Boston, Beacon Press; NOBLE, D. (1978) *America by Design* New York, Knopf; LASCH, C. (1978) *Haven in a Heartless World* New York, Basic Books.
17 EWEN, S. (1976) *Captains of Consciousness* New York, McGraw Hill, p. 202.
18 BRAVERMAN, H. (1974) *Labour and Monopoly Capital* New York, Monthly Review Press; EWEN, S. (1976) *op. cit.* p. 195.
19 MARCUSE, M. (1965) 'Remarks on a redefinition of culture' *Daedalus* Winter, pp. 190–207.
20 MCCARTHY, T. (1978) *The Critical Theory of Jurgen Habermas* Cambridge, Mass., MIT Press, p. 37.
21 *ibid* p.11.
22 MARKOVIC, M. (1974) *From Affluence to Praxis* Ann Arbor, University of Michigan Press; BERNSTEIN, R. (1976) *The Restructuring of Social and Political Theory* Philadelphia, University of Pennsylvania Press.
23 DALLMAYR, F.R. and MCCARTHY, T. (1977) (Eds.) *Understanding and Social Inquiry* Notre Dame, University of Notre Dame Press, p. 285.
24 ABEL, T. 'The operation called Verstehen' *The American Journal of Sociology* Vol. 54, pp. 211–218.
25 FAY, B. (1975) *Social Theory and Political Practice* London, George Allen and Unwin, p. 39.
26 HABERMAS, J. (1971) *Knowledge and Human Interest* Boston, Beacon Press, p. 304.
27 LENZER, G. (1975) *August Comte and Positivism* New York, Harper and Row, p. xxxix.
28 ARENDT, H. (1958) *The Human Condition* Chicago, University of Chicago Press.
29 MARCUSE, H. (1978) 'On science and phenomenology' in ARATO, A. and GEBHART, E. (Eds.) *The Essential Frankfurt Reader* New York, Urizen Books, pp. 466–476.
30 BERNSTEIN, R. (1976) *op. cit.* p. 5.
31 APEL, K.O. (1977) 'The a priori of communication and the foundation of the humanities' in

DALLMAYR, F.R. and MCCARTHY, T. (Eds.) *Understanding and Social Inquiry* Notre Dame, University of Notre Dame Press, p. 293.

32 HABERMAS, J. (1970) *Toward a Rational Society* (trans. Jeremy Shapiro) Boston, Beacon Press, pp. 81–122.

33 MISHLER, E.G. (1979) 'Meaning in context: Is there any other kind?' *Harvard Educational Review* Vol. 49, No. 1, February, pp. 1–19.

34 ZINN, H. (1970) *The Politics of History* Boston, Beacon Press, pp. 10–11.

35 WILLIAMS, R. (1977) *Marxism and Literature* New York, Oxford University Press.

36 GOULDNER, A.W. (1976) *The Dialectic of Ideology and Technology* New York, Seabury Press, p. 50.

37 HORKHEIMER, M. (1974) *Eclipse of Reason* New York, Seabury Press, p. 178.

38 FAY, B. (1975) *op. cit.* p. 27.

39 HUSSERL, E. (1966) *Phenomenology and the Crisis of Philosophy* New York, Harper.

40 SCHROYER, T. (1973) *op. cit.* p. 213.

41 HORKHEIMER, M. (1974) *op. cit.* p. 73.

42 HABERMAS, J. (1970) *op. cit.* p. 113.

43 MARCUSE, H. (1964) *op. cit.* p. 99.

44 *ibid;* JACOBY, R. (1975) *op. cit.*

45 POULANTZAS, N. (1973) *Political Power and Social Classes* (trans. Timothy O'Hagan) London, New Left Books.

46 KIRKENDALL, R.S. (1975) 'The status of history in the schools' *The Journal of American History* September, pp. 557–558.

47 *ibid.* p. 465

48 HICKMAN, W.L. (1977) 'The erosion of history' *Social Education* Vol. 43, No. 1, January, p. 22.

49 BERNSTEIN, R. (1976) *op. cit.;* MISHLER, E.G. (1979) *op. cit.*

50 PATTON, M.Q. (1975) *Alternative Evaluation Research Design* North Dakota Study Group Evaluation Monograph, Grand Forks, University of North Dakota Press, p. 41.

51 PINAR, W. (1978) 'The reconceptualization of curriculum studies' *Journal of Curriculum Studies* Vol. 10, No. 3, July–September, pp. 205–214.

52 MCDONALD, J. (1975) 'Curriculum and human interests' in PINAR, W.F. (Ed.) *Curriculum Theorizing* Berkeley, McCutchen, p. 289.

53 POPKEWITZ, T.S. (1978) 'Educational research: Values and visions of a social order' *Theory and Research in Social Education* Vol. 4, No. 4, December, p. 28.

54 KUHN, T.S. (1970) *The Structure of Scientific Revolutions* Chicago, University of Chicago Press, p. 80.

55 SCHUTZ, A. and LUCKMANN, T. (1973) *The Structure of the Life-World* Evanston, Illinois, Northwestern University Press.

56 MARCUSE, H. (1964) *op. cit.* p. 172; SCHROYER, T. (1970) 'Toward a critical theory of advanced industrial society' in DREITZEL, H.P, (Ed.) *Recent Sociology No. 2* New York, Macmillan, pp. 210–234.

57 PINAR, W.F. (1978) 'Notes on the curriculum field 1978' *Educational Researcher* September, pp. 5–12.

58 ADORNO, T.W., ALBERT, H., DAHRENDORF, R., HABERMAS, J., PILOT, H. and POPPER, K.R. (1976) *The Positivist Dispute in German Sociology* New York, Harper and Row, p. 135.

59 POPHAM, W.J. (1970) 'Probing the validity of arguments against behavioral goals' in KIBLER, R.J. (Ed.) *Behavioral Objectives and Instruction* Boston, Allyn and Bacon, p. 116.

60 BAUCHAMP, G. (1978) 'A hard look at curriculum' *Educational Leadership* p. 409.

61 BERNSTEIN, R. (1976) *op. cit.* p. 112.

62 GOULDNER, A.W. (1976) *op. cit.*

63 ENGLISH, F.W. (1979) 'Management practice as a key to curriculum leadership' *Educational Leadership* March, pp. 408–409.

64 POPKEWITZ, T.S. (1978) *op. cit.* p. 32.

65 WOODS, P. (1979) *The Divided School* London and Boston, Routledge and Kegan Paul, p. 137.

66 FRIEDMAN, J. (1978) 'The epistemology of social practice: A critique of objective knowledge' Theory and Society Vol. 6, No. 1, July, pp. 75–92.

67 An interesting lament on this subject can be found in HARRISON, F.R. (1978) 'The humanistic lesson of Solzhenitzen and proposition 13' *Chronicle of Higher Education* July 24, p. 32.

68 APPLE, M.W. (1979) 'The production of knowledge and the production of deviance' Speech given at Sociology of Knowledge Conference in Birmingham, England, January 2–4.

69 ARONOWITZ, S. (1973) *False Promises* New York, McGraw-Hill, p. 270.

70 *ibid.* p. 270.
71 FOX, T.E. and HESS, R.D. (1972) 'An analysis of social conflict in social studies textbooks' Final Report, Project No. 1–1–116, United States Department of Health, Education and Welfare; POPKEWITZ, T.S. (1977) *op. cit.;* ANYON, J. (1978) 'Elementary social studies textbooks and legitimating knowledge' *Theory and Research in Social Education* Vol. 6, No. 3, pp. 40–55.
72 ANYON, J. (1978) *op. cit.* p. 40.
73 *ibid.* p. 43.
74 GOULDNER, A.W. (1970) *The Coming Crisis in Western Sociology* New York, Basic Books, p. 193.
75 ANYON, J. (1978) *op. cit.* p. 44.
76 POPKEWITZ, T.S. (1978) *op. cit.* p. 44.
77 FENTON, E. (1967) (Ed.) *Holt Social Studies Curriculum* New York, Holt, Rinehart and Winston.
78 POPKEWITZ, T.S. (1977) *op. cit.* p. 58.
79 GREENE, M. (1978) *Landscapes of Learning* New York, Teachers College Oress.
80 PATTON, M.Q. (1975) *op. cit.* p. 22.
81 SHARP, R. and GREEN, A. (1975) *Education and Social Control* London, Routledge and Kegan Paul.
82 FREIRE, P. (1973) *Pedagogy of the Oppressed* New York, Seabury Press.
83 GREENE, M. (1978) *op. cit.* p. 56.
84 BOWERS, C.A. (1976) *op. cit.*
85 POPKEWITZ, T.S. (1978) *op. cit.* pp. 27–28. See also KARABEL, J. and HALSEY, A.H. (1977) (Eds.) 'Educational research: A review and an interpretation' in *Power and Ideology* New York, Oxford University Press, pp. 1–88; LUNDGREN, U.P. and PETTERSSON, S. (1979) (Eds.) *Code, Context and Curriculum Processes* Stockholm, Stockholm Institute of Education, pp. 5–29.
86 ARONOWITZ, S. (1973) *op. cit.* p. 278.
87 MERLEAU-PONTY, M. (1967) *The Structure of Behavior* Boston, Beacon Press, p. 175.
88 FREIRE, P. (1973) *op. cit.* pp. 100–101; GIROUX, H.A. (1980) 'Beyond the limits of radical educational reform' *Journal of Curriculum Theorizing* Vol. 2, No. 1, pp. 20–46.
89 SATRE, J.-P. (1977) *Satre by Himself* (trans. Michael Seaver) New York, Urizen Books, p. 54.
90 GIROUX, H.A. and PENNA, A.N. (1970) 'Social education in the classroom' *Theory and Research in Social Education* 7, Spring, pp. 21–42.
91 WILLIS, P. (1977) *op. cit.;* WILLIAMS, R. (1977) *op. cit.* Other penetrating critiques of the correspondence theory as a truncated view of 'manipulation' theory can be found in LICHTMAN, R. (1975) 'Marx's theory of ideology' *Socialist Revoluton* 23, April, pp. 45–76. See also BEN-HORIN, D. (1977) 'Television' *Socialist Review* 35, September–October, pp. 7–35.
92 HELLER, A. (1974) *Theory of Need in Marx* London, Allen and Busby.
93 GIROUX, H.A. (1978) 'Writing and critical thinking in the social studies' *Curriculum Inquiry* Vol. 8, No. 4, pp. 219–310; BATES, R.J. (1978) 'The new sociology of education: Directions for theory and research' *New Zealand Journal of Educational Studies* Vol. 13, No. 1, May, pp. 3–22.
94 MARCUSE, H. (1978) The *Aesthetic Dimension* Boston, Beacon Press, p. 73.

# 2 Beyond the Limits of Radical Educational Reform: Toward a Critical Theory of Education*

Within the last two decades there has developed an impressive array of ideas and activities aimed at redefining and reexamining the meaning of radical educational reform.[1] Out of this has come a renewed interest in the development and application of Marxism, critical theory, phenomenology, critical sociology, and the sociology of knowledge to the area of radical educational change. Yet in spite of this, the American left often appears baffled over the question of what constitutes radical educational theory and practice. Beneath the plethora of pedagogical approaches, that range from deschooling to alternative schools, one searches in vain for a comprehensive critical theory of education which bridges the gap between educational theory on the one hand and social and political theory on the other. One also searches in vain for a systematic theoretical approach to a radical analysis of the day-by-day socio-political texture of classroom structure and interaction, i.e., how specific forms of knowledge and meaning penetrate, develop, and are transmitted within the context of the classroom experience.

While this chapter cannot examine the many radical educational movements of the last two decades, it is useful to analyze the major tendencies that have dominated them. From this an attempt will be made to formulate a critique of these tendencies and to move tentatively toward a critical theory of radical pedagogy. In addition, this paper suggests some general approaches which might be useful in implementing radical educational reform.

Amidst the theoretical shambles characteristic of the educational left, two major positions stand out: these can be loosely represented, on the one hand, by the content-focussed radicals and, on the other, by the strategy-based radicals. These representations are, of course, ideal-typical and should not be seen as exhibiting rigid boundries. It is clear that many educators fall between these ideal-types; but this should not obscure the fact that few radical educators have provided a theoretical perspective that equally acknowledges and integrates both positions. The content-focussed radicals define radical pedagogy by their insistence on the

* This chapter is a revised version of an article which first appeared in *The Journal of Curriculum Theorizing* Vol. 2, No. 1 (Winter 1980) pp. 20–46. Copyright © 1980 JCT.

use of a Marxist-based perspective to provide a demystifying analysis for students of the dominant ideology reproduced in varied forms in the prevailing system of schooling.[2] On the other side, there are the strategy-based radical education. This group defines radical pedagogy as the development of 'healthy', non-alienating classroom social relationships.[3] In this case, specific classroom social encounters are designed to help students break through the engineered boredom and oppression characteristic of late capitalist relations of production and its everyday life. Although both groups have made significant gains in furthering radical educational reform, each ends up with a limited pedagogical model, one which fails to integrate theory and process, content and methodology. Moreover, beyond their differences, both groups share perspectives which not only reveal theoretical gaps, but each also provides theoretical building blocks for a more integrated form of radical pedagogy. As such, both positions warrant further examination.

The theoretical cornerstone of the content-focussed radical position lies in its stress on the relationship between the economic and political structures of capitalism and the ideological superstructures, of which schools occupy a paramount position. According to this group, schools deepen social and economic domination by functioning *as agents of legitimation.* Consequently schools help to mediate the contradictions between the ruling-class and the oppressed by fostering a collective consciousness reared on 'myths' and steeped in the 'virtues' of passivity, docility, and unquestioning obedience. While this view in general suffers from an overdetermined and oversocialized perception of the way schools function, it raises fundamental questions about how institutionally selected and sanctioned knowledge is used to confer cultural legitimacy on dominant belief and value systems. Michael F.D. Young writes clearly about the focus of this position:

> . . . to tackle the dialectical relationship between access to power and the opportunity to legitimize certain dominant categories and processes by which the availability of such categories to some groups enables them to assert power and control over others.[4]

Translated into classroom pedagogical practice, this view of knowledge undermines the positivist teaching practices which presently characterize contemporary American education, particularly in elementary and secondary education.[5] The idea of categorically imposed meanings lays bare the ideological underpinnings of the positivist elevation of value-free classroom methodology to the status of an unquestioned truth. Moreover, content-focussed radicals have also helped students to move beyond the anti-theoretical, fragmented, skills-oriented modes of pedagogy so deeply entrenched in American schools.[6] Consequently, a small but significant number of radical teachers have helped their students to recognize the ideological basis of the division of knowledge characteristic of most school curricula and to view knowledge as more than a 'neutral picturing of fact'.[7] Through their efforts, these radicals have helped to expose the prevailing belief that traditional pedagogy represents a better mode of learning; instead, they have exposed its functional underside: a sustained, institutionalized attack on the radical dimensions of critical thinking.

The strategy-based position springs from a long tradition of thought including such diverse notables as Rousseau, Wilhelm Reich, A.S. Neil, Carl Rogers, and Erich Fromm.[8] Steeped in what can be generally termed a radical humanism, this group acknowledges the oppressive power and control exercised by schools, but they differ from the content-focussed radicals in their assessment of the nature of such control. For the strategy-based radicals the essence of schooling lies in its reproduction of traditional, hierarchical, social relationships. In general these relationships replicate top-to-down models of authority and sanction social conformity rather than student initiative and imagination. The strategy-based radicals believe that the process of schooling inculcates in students a form of domination that is deeply felt, lived, and experienced as part of one's own history and self-formation. The nature of this domination is not to be found by pointing to social, political, and cultural ideas that are merely imposed on students. According to the strategy-based position, conventional ideology may be significant as a mode of mystification, but the essence of social control in the schools is to be found in the reproduction of reified social relationship, in the confinement and restriction of individual and social experiences. The theoretical cornerstone of this group's position is that industrial society is lodged not only in men's minds but in their personalities and character structures as well.[9] Implicit in this view is a perception of domination and control which involves unconscious as well as conscious dimensions of the personality. The strategy-based position thus shows, even if loosely, that domination is a multi-varied phenomenon, much more complex than the content-focussed radicals have claimed. Moreover, by indicating that the shaping of the personality and character structures of students is not limited simply to the manipulation of knowledge, these radicals also have called into question the political and normative underpinnings of traditional classroom pedagogical styles.[10] It is in the latter area that the strategy-based radicals have made their most significant contributions.

Reacting against orthodox pedagogical methods, strategy-based radicals have focussed their energies on developing classroom social relations which would free students from ideological manipulation and internalized control. The radical core of this perspective lies in its presupposition that as students experience a qualitative change in their classroom encounters, they will be in a better position to redeem their own subjectivity, their psychic autonomy. Ronald and Beatrice Gross capture this sentiment in their claim that 'in social relations radical means libertarian: an affirmation of the autonomy of the individual against the demands of the system'.[11]

In so far as the strategy-based radicals have illuminated the complexities of domination, introduced more humanistic teaching methodologies, and revealed the need for a child-centered psychology which supports a more complex mode of knowing and personal growth, they have partly supported their program for a radical pedagogy. Taken as a whole, however, strategy-based approaches to radical pedagogy appear to have ended up as a palliative for reformers whose interests are more closely aligned with Rousseau than Marx.[12] While this group attempts to restructure and reshape the social relations of students along lines conducive to democratic socialist values, they, in fact, end up by divorcing the social relations of the classroom from the kind of theoretically informed action that could link classroom social relations to a viable political perspective. By down-playing the role of content and the need for an overt political framework by which students can examine and come to an understanding of the ideological assumptions embedded in specific forms of classroom social relations, the strategy-based group, in effect, depoliticizes the function of methodology and ends up reproducing in their pedagogy a limited subjectivist notion of freedom.[13] As a result, the political significance of the social relations of the classroom are not explored relationally by establishing their meaning within the context of corresponding socio-political forces in the larger society. Under such circumstances, 'personal warmth, trust, and community' become solipsistic categories that deny the intersubjective realms of morality and history. Self-indulgence becomes synonymous with liberation, and the privatized morality of the classroom becomes an affective antidote for the moral complexities and political problems that characterize the society at large. In brief, the systematic, boring socialization of the traditional classroom gives way to a 'radical' socialization which – while parading under the banner of self-actualization, warmth, and personal autonomy – may appear more palatable, but, in the final analysis, may be no less 'oppressive'.

The strategy-based radicals are caught in a curious but fatal paradox. On the one hand, they acknowledge the power of the dominant social order to manipulate students into docile, obedient members of the society. But, on the other hand, they do little to help them to move beyond a cheery spontaneity, the substance of which is anchored in the manipulative behavior it is alleged to overcome. Lost to sight in this perspective is a distinction between spontaneity and freedom. Radical praxis, as Herbert Marcuse argues, is based on more than simply the expression of unfettered spontaneity: 'spontaneity can advance the movement of liberation only as mediated spontaneity, that is, resulting from the transformation of consciousness'.[14] Furthermore, social relationships that encourage letting-go and feeling good without mediating these actions through a critical conceptual framework end up reproducing a subjectivity riddled through and through with a 'happy but no less mystifying false consciousness. Under such conditions, the social forces that perpetuate reified social relations are driven from sight by a program of 'feel more and think less'.[15] Instead of promoting radical praxis, strategy-based radicals in many cases, unwittingly end up humanizing the very social and political forces they initially attempt to eliminate. As Russell Jacoby argues:

> . . . the insistence of finding humanity everywhere by underestimating the objective and social foundations of inhumanity perpetuates the latter – it humanizes inhumanity.[16]

Many content-focussed radicals have rightly criticized the strategy-based approach for assuming that pedagogical techniques in themselves 'represent a critique of capitalist domination and ideology'.[17] But rather than acknowledge the liberatory possibilities that classroom social relations have in fostering a critical political consciousness, the content-based radicals dismiss the importance of social relations and posit as an alternative a reductionist undialectical pedagogical model. Consequently, for this group the social relations of education are insignificant compared to the 'content' of a given course.

> Assume a 'traditional' teacher-scholar who gives (more or less) formal lectures with provision for discussion. The teacher stands in the front. The students sit lined up in rows. This teacher requires tests and written essays and even grades them with the criteria for what he considers coherent, rigorous, intellectual work set forth as clearly as possible well in advance. If one were to pose the question as to whether or not the creation of critical consciousness could emerge within this traditional 'form' the answer must, of course, be 'yes' . . . The determination of the critical thrust of a course must be posed and answered with reference to content, not form.[18]

Content in this case, however, is abstracted from the classroom social encounter. As a result, the distinction between oppressive and radical classroom relationships is blurred and a pedagogical model is developed which fails to recognize the covert 'messages' inherent in the pedagogical styles usd to transmit information. Thus the content-focussed radicals bypass an important ideological dimension of the learning experience, a learning experience they claim to redeem!

Yet it is precisely because of this mechanical relationship between content and process that American radical educational theory is at an impasse. Ignoring the 'political content' embodied in classroom arrangements leaves radicals open to an unexamined contradiction between the radical nature of their theoretical analysis and their use of top-to-bottom models of socialization. At stake here is whether radical pedagogy represents more than simply providing the 'correct' analysis for students. It is also a matter of developing a compatible radical educational style The content-focussed radicals have ignored that learning demands not only the critical comprehension of a given social reality but also a hermeneutic examination of the social context in which learning takes place. Paulo Freire states the position well. 'In thinking about practice, we learn to think correctly'.[19] Divorcing content from process not only suggests a rather crude pedagogical simplification, it also helps to reproduce a social division of labor that prevents radical praxis.

At first glance, it appears that both the content-focussed and strategy-based radicals exist on different pedagogical planets. Both groups appear wedded to uncompromising theoretical views that prevent them from moving beyond the bifurcation of content and process. Locked into their respective positions, their theoretical differences appear to be matched only by the strengths of their theoretical shortcomings. On further examination, both groups share commonalities that reveal not only the incompleteness of their respective pedagogical approaches, but also suggest limits that can serve as starting points for a genuinely radical critical theory of pedagogy.

One of the most serious limitations shared by both groups centers around their implicit denial of the student as subject. Both groups underestimate subjectivity in their respective pedagogical approaches. The strategy-based radicals succumb to a vision of human liberation in which 'healthy' vibes and feeling good slide into a subtle form of manipulation. Beneath the smiles and warmth lies a rather reductionist behaviorism that substitutes the crude external calculus of limited pain and maximum pleasure for social responsibility and critical thinking. As such, self-realization ends up as a sophisticated form of self-indulgence. Pleasure-oriented classroom encounters are reduced to the role of a medicinal bath in which the notion of the student as subject in the learning process is denied rather than affirmed. Joy and 'happiness' become engineered antidotes for the repression and false consciousness which the strategy-based radicals unknowingly perpetuate.

The content-focussed radicals deny the subject less through the manipulation of feelings than through their refusal to acknowledge the legitimacy of classroom social relations, the very relations which provide the foundation for students to engage in critical thought as a form of meaningful social discourse. This failure on the part of the content-focussed radicals rests with their indiscriminate use of pedagogical methods which, as Freire argues 'cease to be identified with the power men have to think, to imagine, to risk themselves in creation, and rather comes to mean carrying out orders from above precisely and punctually'.[20]

In addition to the denial of subjectivity, both groups share a limited theory of knowledge. The content-focussed radicals view knowledge in the narrow epistemological sense as being theoretical, abstract, and verbal. The importance of the social process that gives shape to the epistemological dimensions of 'knowing' are not stressed. The strategy-based group, on the other hand, ignores the critical epistemological dimensions of knowledge and stresses social relationships that give meaning to the *act* of knowing. Both groups fail to emphasize the complementary of the emancipatory content and the liberating classroom structure and end up unaware of the ideological interest served by their different pedagogical approaches. Paul Ricoeur writes well of the need to attend to both emancipatory subject matter and communication in the search for radical praxis:

> It seems to me that only the conjunction between the critique of ideologies, animated by our interests in emancipation, and the reinterpretation of the heritages of the past, animated by our interest in communication, may yet give a concrete content to this effort. A simple critique of distortions is just the reverse side and the other half of an effort to regenerate communicative action in its full capacity.[21]

In the most radical sense, knowledge should be viewed as a shared process, a mediation between teachers and students, a creative political exchange that forges commonalities and the kind of critical reflection that allows all to be seen as both teachers and learners. Under such circumstances, knowledge is not treated simply as problematic, *it becomes* the vehicle for teachers and students *to discuss* its problematic grounding and meaning. Knowledge in this instance becomes situated in ideological and political choices; in other words, knowledge becomes de-reified in terms of both its content and the social context in which it is mediated.

Content-focussed radicals have not moved beyond their static notion of knowledge as a set of radical ideas to be transmitted to students. Yet, if the notion of the student as subject is not to be denied, what is needed is a definition of knowledge which recognizes it not only as a body of conceptual thought, but also as a process which demands radical educational relationships. If radicals of both groups are going to take seriously the Marxian view of the relationship between form and content, they will have to develop a conception of knowledge in which radical theoretical and conceptual thought is paralleled by similarly radical social relationships. In the final analysis, both groups can only move beyond their one-sided notion of knowledge if they begin to look more critically at the relationship between radical 'knowledge' and 'the roles that the act of knowing demands of its subjects-creator, recreator, reinventor'.[22]

Another perspective shared by both radical groups is the correspondence theory. With minor variations, radicals define this theory as something of a one-to-one correspondence among the cultures of the workplace, the family, and the school, with the workplace exercising a determinate and formative role on the latter two socializing agencies. According to this view, the family and the schools play a major role in inculcating in the populace those values and dispositions conducive to the continual reproduction of the dominant relations of production. Leaning heavily on the correspondence principle in their own analysis of schooling, Samuel Bowles and Herbert Gintis highlight its workings:

> The educational system helps integrate youth into the economic system, we believe, through a structural correspondence between its social relations and those of production. The structure of social relations in education not only inures the student to the discipline of the workplace, but develops the types of personal demeanor, modes of self-presentation, self-image, and social class identifications which are the crucial ingredients of job adequacy.[23]

Embedded in the correspondence principle is the particularly important insight that the school cannot be analyzed as an institution removed from the socio-economic institutions in which it is situated, particularly the 'institutions and proceses of work'.[24] While the correspondence principle is of critical importance in understanding the nature and role of legitimating institutions such as schools, many radicals stretch the principle to the point of caricature and end up with an oversocialized model of schooling. The result is a mechanistic analysis that encloses itself in the dead-end of one-dimensionality; thus litle room is left for radicals to explore the contradictions inherent in the schooling process or to analyze the tensions, rejection of values, and the deep disjunctions experienced by many students. Schools may legitimate the social relations of production and existing forms of consciousness but they do so in a complex and often contradictory fashion and setting.[25] As Paul Willis has pointed out, schools do not simply 'process' students by imposing an ideology on them. 'Social agents are not passive bearers of ideology, but active appropriators who reproduce existing structures only through struggle, contestation, and partial penetration of these structures'.[26] Karabel and Halsey raise questions about the correspondence principle that echo a number of similar criticisms by both radical and liberal critics:

There is a tidiness about the family-school-work triumverate that in the neo-Marxist view serves to transmit inequality from generation to generation, the process seems to work so smoothly and is based upon such an imposing system of domination that one must wonder how it is that educational change ever takes place.[27]

Many of the attacks against the radical use of the correspondence theory have been well focussed.[28] For instance, with few exceptions radicals of both schools have ignored the work of revisionist historians who have documented the conflict-ridden story of the development and fight for control of American education.[29] Moreover, they have also failed to do justice to the conflicts and contradictions that have characterized the very process of schooling itself. Instead, one is treated to flattened out and conflict-free accounts of the schooling process which not only suffer from a great simplemindedness, but also fall back upon a mystifying Marxism that reduces culture to a mere reflex of the material base. One example will suffice:

> The school serves to transmit the social and eonomic structure from generation (to generation) through pupil selection, defining culture and rules, and teaching certain cognitive skills. Children become a form of natural resource to be molded by the schools and fed into the industrial machine. The school becomes an instrument of social, economic, and political control. It is an institution which consciously plans to turn people into something. In this situation, the educational system tends to become functionally reduced to its role in generating labor for the economy, and the developments of the individual becomes more or less *fully tailored* [italics mine] to the needs of 'economic rationality'. Instead of discovering and developing the natural aptitudes of children, the schools 'discover' the aptitudes which are essential to the needs of the capitalist system.[30]

Lost from this type of trivializing perspective are the contradictions and tensions among and within each of the individual school-family-work agencies. For instance, as Michael Apple points out, the school curriculum attempts to convince working-class students that the world of labor is filled with jobs offering opportunities for mobility, material and personal gratification, and opportunities for a better future. But working-class students know better. 'They have already experienced the world of work from their parents, their acquaintances, and in their own part-time jobs. This experience clearly contradicts the messages of the school which are viewed cynically'.[31] The principle of contradiction is an essential one since it provides a focus for political action. Furthermore, it raises fundamental questions about the quasi-autonomy of schools, the family, and other primary institutions of mass culture.[32] These questions are instrumental in assessing accurately the relationship between social reproduction and cultural reproduction.

The concepts of social and cultural reproduction need to be clarified at this point, particularly since the definitions provided by some of the radical educational theorists to be analyzed are at odds with those associated with the structural-functional view characteristic of mainstream social science.[33] In the functionalist usage, cultural reproduction refers to the 'transmission', via the schools and other agencies of socialization, of cultural norms and values which are seen as the necessary and unproblematic functional requirements of the larger society. In this view, social reproduction, the ongoing maintenance and reproduction of existing socio-economic and political arrangements, is the regenerative process characteristic of a social order marked by consensus and social harmony. The principle of contradiction, particularly as it applies to the intra and extra classroom levels, has little relevance in this approach.[34]

Social and cultural reproduction are viewed in distinctly different terms in some of the more recent work by radical educational theorists. In this perspective, both concepts are defined in highly political and ideological terms and are linked to the relationships between power and control. For instance, Pierre Bourdieu views social reproduction as the reproduction of power relations between classes.[35] Rejecting apolitical and atheoretical notions of social reproduction, he views the latter as the reproduction of the hierarchical distribution of class and power relations all of which buttress the existing capitalist mode of production and its concomitant social division of labor power. Similarly, cultural reproduction, from this perspective represents the transmission of the culture of the dominant class. In more specific terms, the cultural hegemony, or dominant form of cultural capital, consists of those attitudes, dispositions, tastes, linguistic competencies, and systems of meaning that the ruling-class deems as being legitimate. This specific form of cultural capital is institutionalized in schools and is passed off as natural, unchanging, and even eternal. As a mechanism of social control, dominant cultural capital posits itself in both the form and process of the educational experience. Thus it structures not only the selection and distribution of knowledge, it also structures, legitimates, and saturates the day-by-day experience of the classroom encounter. In essence, cultural reproduction as used here is a vehicle of social reproduction. But unlike functionalist theories of reproduction, the more recent radical perspective recognizes that there are serious disjunctions and tensions inherent in the relationship between social and cultural reproduction. As Willis points out, capitalist cultural hegemony is characterized by an element of uncertainty, and 'always carries with it the possibility of producing alternative outcomes'.[36] What is significant is that these contradictions and tensions have recently been highlighted by a number of educational theorists, and it is their work which suggests a rationale for studying both the form and process of the classroom encounter and its dialectical interconnections with larger social and economic forces.[37]

A new direction for radical educational praxis is implicit in the work of a growing number of educational theorists who have helped to strip the correspondence principle of its reactionary trappings while preserving its radical core. Both theoretically and empirically they have attempted to show how the organization, distribution, and evaluation of selected aspects of the culture function as reproductive mechanisms within schools. Moreover, by examining knowledge stratification and its relationship to social stratification, they have begun to illuminate the often subtle political connections between economic power and ideological control.[38] By exploring the differences among and between classes in the role of cultural reproduction, Bourdieu and Bernstein, in particular, have made an impressive case indicting schools as agencies which legitimize the principles of social control inherent in the institutions of late capitalist societies. More specifically, by looking at the latent specialized meanings inherent in the school's three message systems: curriculum, pedagogy, and evaluation, they bring into focus class-based contradictions centering around both the nature of classroom social relationships as well as the organization and transmission of linguistic and cultural competencies.[39] By focussing on the selection, organization, and distribution of knowledge as well as the various pedagogical styles used in the transmission process, they have provided a conceptual schema that enlarges our understanding of the hidden curriculum and the mechanisms of domination as they operate at the everyday level of schooling. This represents a significant theoretical leap beyond traditional functionalist and radical analyses of the hidden curriculum. Unfortunately, neither Bernstein nor Bourdieu have developed a Marxist conceptual framework suitable for a viable form of radical educational praxis. In specific terms, neither theorist has developed an adequate theory of ideology and concept of hegemony to explain adequately the dialectical relationship between the ideological principles that structure the classroom encounter and the power relationships that characterize the larger society.[40] Nevertheless, both theorists should be read as an important force and contribution to the study of the connection between knowledge, schooling, and the reproduction of the social relations of production.

While many radicals have used the term 'hidden curriculum' to categorize the unstated but effective distribution of norm, values, and attitudes to students in classrooms, few have provided more than a one-sided analysis of this important phenomenon.[41] And yet the notion of the hidden curriculum represents one of the most important conceptual tools by which radicals can explore the dialectical relationships and tensions that accompany the process of reproduction at the level of day-to-day classroom interactions. The paramount issue to be explored below is that radical educational reform will continue to be stalled until radicals begin to reexamine and redefine the meaning of the hidden curriculum. Because it is only on the basis of such an analysis that a new conception of radical educational theory and action can be developed.

To make sense of the hidden curriculum means that schools have to be analyzed as agents of legitimation, organized to produce and reproduce the dominant categories, values, and social relationships necessary for the maintenance of the larger society.[42] This should not suggest that schools simply mirror the interests and wishes of a conspiratorial ruling-class. Nor should it be denied that schools have immense power to manipulate the consciousness and actions of students, and function to pass on selected aspects of the dominant culture. The process of legitimation is clearly much more complex than most radical educators have suggested.[43]

The process of legitimation should be viewed in terms of what may be called the special ambiguity of schools. This special ambiguity stems, on the one hand, from the representation of schooling as '. . . a vital human need – common to all societies and all people in some form, and as basic as subsistence or shelter'.[44] On the other hand, schools are a fundamental part of the power structure, ideologically and structurally committed to the socio-economic forces that nourish them. It is in this nexus of vital needs and power that the special ambiguity of schooling takes on its meaning. Also embedded in this nexus is the key to the socio-political structure of schooling, the hidden curriculum.

The notion of the hidden curriculum is not new. Both liberal and radical educators have helped to identify some of its structural properties as well as many of the norms and values which it reproduces. While these analyses and critiques have illuminated the tacit socializing function of the schools, they have failed to integrate the complex and dynamic interconnections between the hidden ideological underpinnings of classroom knowledge and the hidden messages and values underlying clasroom social relationships.[45] Consequently, liberals and radicals have provided an incisive but limited definition of the hidden curriculum and schooling. In general, they have limited their definitions to those 'non-academic' norms and attitudes that are systematically and effectively taught to students but are not openly stated in a school's or teacher's statement of objectives.[46] Central to this perspective is the assumption that what students learn from the formal curriculum is much less important than what they learn from the structure of classroom relationships. Bowles and Gintis state this position as clearly as anyone else: 'The heart of the (educational) process is to be found not in the content of the educational encounter – or the process of information transfer – but in the form: the social relations of the educational encounter'.[47] While many liberals and radicals agree that schools do more than teach cognitive tasks, they part company over the political nature and ideological function of the hidden curriculum.

Liberals such as Talcott Parsons and Robert Dreeben view the function of the hidden curriculum as a necessary one. For them, the hidden curriculum offers students the opportunity to learn vital social norms and skills more fully than they could within the family structure. Dreeben, for instance, points positively to the learning by students of such norms as independence, universalism, achievement, and specificity.[48] Missing from his analysis is any clear-cut examination of the relationship between the normative underpinnings of the hidden curriculum and a capitalist ethos fuelled by the necessity to legitimate and reproduce its class-based interests. In general terms, the liberal analysis abstracts the normative basis of the hidden curriculum from its ideological context and appears mute over the question of why certain sets of values are considered legitimate while others are not. Wrapped in the guise of 'objectivity', the liberal position appears to suffer from what Nietzsche once termed 'the dogma of the immaculate perception'.[49]

While there is a certain amount of agreement among liberals over the meaning and importance of the hidden curriculum, radicals are divided over the definitional nature of the concept. On the one hand, there are the strategy-based radicals who limit the concept of the hidden curriculum to the social relations of the classroom; on the other hand, there are the content-focussed radicals who deny the radical implications of classroom social encounters and therefore ignore this dimension of the hidden curriculum. More importantly, this group does not adequately understand how the hidden curriculum operates in the formal curriculum, though they would not deny that the hidden curriculum plays a strong role in reproducing ideologies in the formal curriculum. Until recently, the only radical analysis of the hidden curriculum has been made by the strategy-based group.

For the strategy-based radicals, schooling entails a hidden curriculum representing an oppressive cultural hegemony, the purpose of which is to reproduce the streamlined personalities necessary for the alienated realms of work and leisure. But cultural hegemony as it is used here does not refer to the various forms of false consciousness that are drummed into students' heads via the formal curriculum. Instead, cultural hegemony refers to material practices embedded in the roles and routines through which students give expression and meaning to their classroom experiences. In other words, hegemony here is produced not simply through the diffusion of ideas but in the everyday routines and rituals of the classroom social encounter and its corresponding reward and punishment system. In this view, schools function through the hidden curriculum to manipulate the student's 'psychic space', those aspects of character structure which contain the possibilities for emancipatory behavior and action. The whittling away of this 'private space' is matched only by the school's efforts to create student personalities which offer little resistance to the alienated worlds of work and consumerism. Bowles and Gintis speak to this issue by pointing to specific personality characteristics fostered in schools which allegedly prepare students for 'acceptable' job performance in hierarchically and bureaucratically organized workplaces. The corporate sanctioned personality traits include: punctuality, proper level of subordination, intellectual over-affective modes of response, respect for external rewards, and orderly work habits. While schools tend to label these as desirable personal qualities, radicals view them as modes of social conformity strongly correlated to a student's chances for academic and future economic success.[50]

The strategy-based radicals do not believe that schools provide all students with the same socializing experiences. In fact, the nature of a student's socializing experience is determined largely by their socio-economic background. In other words, the socializing experience of the hidden curriculum itself is class-based. The substance of hegemonic ideology remains the same, but the form varies depending upon the types of students and the specific socio-historical conditions of a given period. Thus we can say that in conditioning youth for the realities of the workplace '. . . the schools serve to prepare workers to fill the work hierarchy by differentiating both the amounts of and types of schooling experience they receive'.[51] For example, schools which serve minorities of class and color are characterized by rigid rules and order. Students in these schools are often expected to conform to clearly arranged patterns of hierarchical authority. Conformity, powerlessness, and impersonalization are the governing characteristics of the student's school experience. Classroom social relations for these students are typified by what Basil Bernstein has called a visible pedagogy. This type of pedagogy refers to teacher-student relationships marked by a high degree of certainty, control, and student powerlessness. The nature of this type of pedagogy is exhibited by an explicit set of criteria for student evaluation, an explicit sequencing of time and rules, and an explicit hierarchy of authority. [52] The socialization process, however, appears quite different for most middle and upper-class students. These students not only receive higher levels of cognitive input, they also operate within a classroom experience where flexibility and interpersonal relations (soft socialization), replace overt rule conformity. Under these conditions, external control is replaced by internalized behavior. [53]

The radical critique of the hidden curriculum has persuasively discredited the technocratic notion of a neutral and value-free system of schooling. Yet while such a critique has helped to clarify the connection between knowledge and human interest, it has failed to provide a more encompassing and detailed analysis of the intricate links between ideology and the workings of the formal curriculum. Radicals, in general, in the United States have been too little interested in the actual structure, complexity and interrelationship between classroom knowledge and classroom social relations to provide a convincing account of how the latter manifest themselves in ideological terms. Moreover, the existing analyses of the hidden curriculum have been dominated by a one-sided concern with the *forms* of schooling, while more in-depth analyses of the nature and function of curriculum knowledge have been ignored. In brief, radical educators have failed to develop what Michael Apple calls the sociology of school knowledge. [54]

The first step in developing a radical sociology of school knowledge, one which extends the notion of the hidden curriculum to the formal curriculum, must begin with the recognition that classroom knowledge is shaped by hidden structures of meaning steeped in a complex interplay of ideology and power. Put another way, each of the three message systems of the school: curriculum, pedagogy, and evaluation prefigures a selection, organization, and distribution of meanings based on ideological considerations. The focus in this case is one step removed from a simple acknowledgement of the ideological nature of the form and content of knowledge. The question to be analyzed is not so much *what* is considered legitimate knowledge as much as *how* is it that some knowledge is labeled legitimate and some is not. What is the source of legitimation? Or put another way, what is the relationship between school knowledge and the distribution of power and privileges in the larger society?

In pedagogical terms this means that radical educators will have to help students recognize what might be called the 'hidden curriculum' of classroom knowledge. This can be done by clearly showing them how the taken-for-granted meanings which govern classroom knowledge in many instances represent a constellation of imposed meanings selected from specific social and economic ideologies and interests. [55] Learning can only become politically significant for the student and teacher when they are able to understand how meaning emerges, how constitutive ideologies structure their learning processes. The *first* step towards such an understanding has been suggested by some advocates of radical pluralism who stress giving students the opportunity to examine knowledge from a variety of theoretical perspectives. For instance, Maxine Greene writes:

> Significant learning can only take place when the individual consciously looks from a variety of vantage points upon his own lived world, and when he achieves what Alfred Schutz calls a 'reciprocity of perspectives' upon his own reality. When he recognizes that he himself has blended those perspectives and permitted his perceptions to confirm one another, he knows that he himself has constituted meanings and brought whatever order there is into his own world. [56]

Of course, it must be quickly realized that one must move beyond radical pluralism by refusing to give equal weight to all theoretical perspectives. To tolerate each one equally is simply another way of banalizing the truth through the prism of a substanceless methodology. Radical pluralism is a necessary but incomplete step towards acknowledging the social construction of reality. If the relationship between ideology and school knowledge is to be fully comprehended, the relations between dominant and subordinate ideologies must be clarified. A more critical exploration would investigate the links between power and the various categories of knowledge by analyzing the specific socio-economic contexts and interests which allow certain types of knowledge to become legitimized. Utilizing this approach, students are given the opportunity to focus on the pre-eminent questions of why reality takes on a particular meaning, or for that matter is ignored, in both the schools and the society in general.

The importance of the hidden curriculum of knowledge can be further illuminated by analyzing *both* the style and content of bourgeois hegemony. While radicals have spent some time in criticizing the content of the dominant ideology, they have often failed to spend a reasonable amount of intellectual effort analyzing bourgeois styles of thought. And yet, as Sherry Gorelick argues, 'these styles of thought are far more subtle than facts, but they powerfully shape the selection and omission of facts, the interpretation of facts, and the shaping of facts into a theoretical structure. A picture of the world'. [57]

Bourgeois styles of thought are linked to a number of powerful and misleading assumptions which radicals have left relatively unexamined. Two of the more important assumptions center around questions relating to what might be called the form and content of Anglo–American philosophy. The first assumption raises questions about the nature of traditional Anglo–American methodology. This methodology, particularly in the social sciences, is characterized by a fragmented, anti-theoretical, and undialectical approach to the construction and analysis of socio-political reality. Therefore, within this perspective knowledge is not only artificially compartmentalized and divided, it also lacks any type of socio-historical grounding. Thus, questions are raised and problems generated which usually appear to be unconnected, or at best, only connected marginally to the fundamental structure of society. Drawing upon an amalgam of philosophical strains such as logical positivism, pragmatism, 'tough-minded' empiricism, and some shades of liberlism, Anglo–American philosophy has given rise to a slew of methodological approaches in the social sciences all of which share one flaw: they are 'wedded' to the individual fact or item 'at the expense of the network of relationships in which that item may be embedded . . . and encourage submission to what is by preventing its followers from making connections, and in particular from drawing the otherwise unavoidable conclusions on the political level'.[58] Knowledge, in this case, becomes reified because the methodological stance which it 'celebrates' undermines the variable and historically changing nature of knowledge by presenting it as a natural and necessary fact, unrelated to the social conditions that give it meaning.

A second assumption centers around the failure of radical educators to analyze sufficiently what might be called the hidden meanings embedded in the *cultural* styles of bourgeois thought. This is not to suggest that radical educators have overlooked classroom messages which transmit specific ideological content. They have overlooked the selective messages inherent in differing sets of linguistic and cultural competencies. What many radical educators have failed to do is to link the concept of knowledge to what Pierre Bourdieu has termed cultural capital. As previously mentioned, cultural capital suggests more than the content-based issues and 'facts' which are used to reproduce the existing relations of domination. Cultural capital refers to the socially determined tastes, certain kinds of prior knowledge, language forms, abilities, and modes of knowing that are unevenly distributed throughout society.[59]

Bourdieu's important contribution rests with his insight that schools have institutionalized forms of cultural capital which help to reproduce the social relations outside it. And that any understanding of how class and economic interests penetrate the form and substance of classroom pedagogy will be incomplete unless one comprehends the dynamic and function of cultural capital in the schools. For instance, though Nell Keddie does not highlight adequately the need for teachers to understand the socio-political interests that govern the distribution of knowledge, she has shown how classroom knowledge and meaning are not the result of negotiation between students and teachers in cases where they are *alleged* to be; instead the knowledge used represented the imposition of 'acceptable' symbolic meanings and norms mediated, albeit unknowingly, though the classroom teacher.[60] By accepting the legitimacy of institutionalized definitions of cultural capital, radical educators run the risk of unknowingly structuring classroom experiences with students according to how well the latter imitate middle-class linguistic and cultural styles. The point here is that even though teachers may argue against tracking and other pedagogical mechanisms of social control, they continue to relate to students differently as a result of the specific cultural capital which characterizes students from working-class and minority cultural backgrounds. Hence, students who do not relate to the style, taste, language, and competencies of the middle-class are viewed and treated in a discriminatory fashion. Whether they are viewed as 'deprived' or 'distressed' or in need of 'therapy', students emerge from this type of pedagogy learning more about the various forms of social control than they do about the possibilities and mechanics of human liberation.[61]

For radical pedagogy to become meaningful, radical educators will have to begin by recognizing and understanding the cultural capital of the students they will be working with. It is crucial that students learn to understand and move comfortably within their own culturally determined subjectivity. Students must learn to recreate and politically analyze the world in terms of their own cultural capital and not only in terms based on the teacher's cultural capital. The categories that students use to give meaning to the world must be taken seriously, and *then* checked for their truth and validity. Any other approach points to an objectification of the student's subjectivity. One of Paulo Freire's students has put it well. 'The democratization of culture has to start from what we are and what we do as a people, not from what some people think and want for us'.[62] What the notion of cultural capital suggests is that any progressive pedagogy is steeped in a dual dialectic. On the one hand, knowledge is historically grounded and contextualized; while on the other, knowledge has to be linked to the existential situation of the learner. One without the other suggests a pedagogy that is incomplete. The interpenetration of the historical and existential dimensions of knowledge and knowing results in a pedagogy that helps both students and teachers to think at '. . . deeper and deeper levels, about how human beings live in their world. It means taking the daily routine itself as an object of analysis, trying to penetrate its meaning'.[63] The critical message here is that once students learn to view their daily experiences as problematic, using their own cultural capital, they can then move beyond the personal sphere and attempt the leap to more abstract theoretical conceptualizations and cultural codifications.

In short, my main purpose thus far has been to show that radical eduational theory faces a number of difficult tasks in the search for redefinition and renewal. Trapped by assumptions which have largely shaped either a content-focused or strategy-based approach to radical pedagogy, radical educational theory has been unable to confront either holistically or dialectically the normative and political realities of the educational process. Existing radical pedagogy has been plagued by a limiting correspondence theory, a truncated notion of the hidden curriculum, and an objectification of the student as learner, and, finally, a myopic vision of what constitutes radical classroom practice.

In general terms, the construction of a radical educational theory will have to begin by developing a broader and more organized view of schooling and its place within the entire social, political, economic, and ideological superstructure. Schooling must be studied, on the one hand, as part of a critical theory of society which is logically prior to and inclusive of a radical theory of education. On the other hand, schooling must be seen not only as part of a 'global' dimension of oppression, but must also be studied in its own right. What this means is that schooling must be viewed in non-mechanistic terms as a superstructural agency that has both relative and dependent features which characterize its relationship to the dominant mode of production. Moreover, it follows that proponents of a genuinely radical educational theory will have to spend more time in understanding how the many variables at work in the classroom encounter, reproduce and contradict the prevailing ideologies and social relationships in the larger society. As such, the entirety of the educational process will have to be analyzed for its normative and ideological meanings. Curriculum, teaching methods, forms of evaluation, textbooks, school organization, and the organization of teachers will have to be seen as components of the educational process, shaped by the latter's dialectical role as a representation of a vital human need and as a class-based instrument of the established power structure. Such an analysis demands that we begin the difficult task of laying the groundwork for a substantive critical theory of education. The following section represents a modest step in that direction.


This section of the paper deals with a critical theory of education. But it is intended to do no more than raise some questions and suggestions for the construction of such a theory. Some of these will be elaborated in following chapters. Moreover, more time and analysis will be spent on developing concrete, radical classroom practices than on analyzing the overall relationships of the system of schooling to the larger socio-economic order. But while educational practices need to be analyzed critically one cannot even begin a cursory examination without illuminating those theories which inform and sustain such practice.

With few exceptions, radical educational theory appears to suffer from either an explicit or implicit dose of unwarranted pessimism. For instance, on one side, there are those radicals who in the Ivan Illich tradition argue that changing schools will do little to alter the oppressive nature of the society in which they are embedded. On the other side, there are radicals who believe that working in schools serves a viable radical purpose, but when one examines their theoretical baggage there is little to reveal how such work can be justified. Thus one position favors abandoning radical activity in the schools altogether, while the other provides little reason, in spite of its supportive political rhetoric, for not doing so. Neither view, in the final analysis, constitutes a viable theoretical stance for a radical reform movement in the schools. More specifically, neither approach has analyzed sufficiently the tensions and contradictions that exist in schools or the ways in which teachers and students can effectively challenge the hegemonic function of schooling and organize to change the fundamental structure of the larger society.

Any radical educational theory must start with the recognition that radical educational reform in and by itself will do little to change the fundamental structure of society. This does not suggest that radical pedagogical reform is a liability or a waste of time. It simply means that such reform has to recognize its limits while capitalizing upon its strengths in the struggle for radical social and political reconstruction. When viewed from this perspective radical educational reform represents an important force for radical change. The most that can be expected of such reform is that it will contribute to changing the consciousness and drives the teachers and students who *could* then work to change society. The truth of radical pedagogy lies in its power to negate the power of those who define what is legitimate and real. The parameters of a radical educational theory designed to provide educators with such a 'truth' must be shaped by an analysis that not only challenges the predominant notions of sanctioned educational culture but also the political and social hierarchies to which they are linked. Such a theory must highlight the contradictions that exist in the formal and hidden curricula of schooling; it must also provide the foundation for developing strategies designed to help teachers overcome those contradictions. Some of the components in such a theory might take the following form.

As has been pointed out one important component of radical educational theory centers around the necessity of situating the politics of schooling within the politics of the wider community. But this means looking at schools not only with reference to their existing connections with other agencies in the fields of production and cultural reproduction, it also means tracing historically the ever-changing pattern of connections. For it is only through a historical examination of the dialectical linkages between the educational system and other systems of economic and cultural production that we will be able to understand both the development of different modes of domination and the complex relationship between schooling and ruling-class interests.[64] The reality of educational systems at both the broad policy level as well as the level of daily classroom interaction is more dynamic and complex than exaggerated versions of the correspondence principle suggest. By historically grounding the fight for control of schooling among competing political and socio-economic forces and their accompanying educational theories, radical educational theory provides the framework for a viable strategy for radical educational reform. The strength of this framework lies in its usefulness in illuminating not only the contradictions that exist in the system of schooling but also the political interests which it legitimates and the ideologies which it perpetuates.[65]

Educational practice embodies specific values, purposes, and meanings. But all too often the various dimensions of the schooling process are viewed by teachers and students as apolitical and ahistorical in nature; and, in the final analysis, schooling itself is perceived as an instrumental process governed by technical problems and answerable to 'common-sense' solutions. This perspective flattens reality and effectively removes the dynamics of schooling from the realm of ethical and political debate. Educators, in this case, tend to view themselves as impartial facilitators who operate in a value-free and ideologically uncontaminated classroom setting. A viable radical educational theory will have to provide the theoretical framework by which teachers and students can come to understand that the 'common-sense' world of pedagogy is an ideological smokescreen that dissolves theory into practice. Or to put it another way, it divorces methodology from ideology by advocating the use of pedagogical 'practice without, or with a minimum theoretical content'.[66] The normative interests behind educational practice must be illuminated and questioned through the use of a critical theoretical perspective, one that employs the terminology of social criticism to question the source, meaning, and rationality behind all forms of pedagogical practice. Radical educators must provide a central place in their pedagogy for helping other teachers and students transcend the limitations of social and pedagogical theories which ignore both the historical development as well as the relationship between the legitimation of certain forms of knowledge and the distribution of power. It is on this basis that radical educators can begin to unveil the hidden structures and over-looked contradictions that underlie so much of the prevailing thinking about schooling.

Another component of radical educational theory would center around a dialectical concept of knowledge, one which is linked to a progressive pedagogy of critical thinking. Knowledge would be seen as a historical and social construct 'created by past and present generations, inlaid with strata of meaning which we learn to reactivate and interpret in original ways, finding new sense in the old, and old sense in the new'.[67] Moreover, as a social construct, knowledge would also be defined through the social mediations and social roles which provide the context for its production and distribution. The latter point is important in defining a radical dialectical conception of knowledge because it moves beyond the rather conservative phenomenological recognition that knowledge is simply a social construct. Knowledge must also be viewed as the basis for social action. The limitations of the phenomenological perspective have been aptly summarized by Richard Lichtman:

> But the view is inadequate as it stands. It is overly subjective . . . and lacks an awareness of historical concreteness, is naive in its account of mutual typification and ultimately abandons the sense of human beings in struggle with an alien reality which they both master and to which they are subordinate. It is a view which tends to dissolve the concept of ideology or false consciousness and leaves us, often against its will, without defense against the present inhuman reality.[68]

A dialectical notion of knowledge represents a transition from a contemplative analysis of constructed meanings to the transformation of socio-economic structures which narrowly define and legitimize such meanings. The means for such a transition rests, in part, with the development of a pedagogy of critical thinking, a pedagogy which helps students link knowledge to power and human interest. A radical pedagogy of critical thinking would help students reflect on the hermeneutic meaning beneath falsified appearances; it would also help them to recognize and act upon those social processes and forces which *prevent* them from creating their own meanings.

The first task in constructing a radical pedagogy of critical thinking would focus on giving students the conceptual tools by which they could free themselves from what might be termed the tyranny of imposed meanings. The ideological bedrock of the latter rests with its pseudo-objectivism and anti-theoretical definition of facts. Wrapped in the language of 'common-sense', facts become the epistemological fodder of false-consciousness. Within this empiricist model, the *a priori* values and beliefs which determine the facts are situated in a curious silence. Thus reality becomes no more than that which is codified in the language and logic of facts – established and enforced by those who *benefit* from such facts! As such an important task of radical pedagogy would be to help students analyze 'facts' as more than descriptive, self-contained data. The absolutizing of facts, of course, represents more than an epistemological failing, it also represents the normative core of a theoretical framework, the essence of which is the abdication of reflection and the capitulation of reason before the status-quo.[69] Given this premise, it is crucial that students understand that knowledge is not an objective, inert phenomenon which gives *rise* to theory. In other words, theory does not merge after the collection of facts. Theories about intelligence, ability, motivation, learning, and interest '. . . do not demonstrate how they arise from the "facts" that they are supposed to explain, but take for granted what they are supposed to explain'.[70] Therefore, it must be demonstrated that theory constitutes both the selection as well as the meaning of facts. In the final analysis, theory would be viewed as crucial to almost every stage of thinking. Not only because it helps us to order and select data, but because it also provides the conceptual tools by which to question the 'data' itself. Students must be taught to recognize that theory and facts, the subjective and objective dimensions of learning, are an inseparable part of what we define as knowledge. Then the first step will be made to help them assess both their own theoretical framework as well as to move beyond the 'factuality of the observed world' to that stage of thought where they can '. . . make inferences, offer arguments, and develop explanations of social events which may counter those that are considered authoritative'.[71]

The critical use of theory for the student is thus steeped in a need to recognize the difference not only between appearance and reality, but between the world as it is and the world as *he or she thinks* it should be. Thus, theory becomes more than a structural device for selecting and defining facts; it also becomes the medium for social action, the medium for understanding and changing reality by acknowledging its emancipatory possibilities and working to make those possibilities a reality. Consequently, theory within this context becomes an axiomatic construct, the purposefulness of which is shaped by the nature of its emancipatory vision, a vision that is always transcendent, but never complete.

Underlying a dialectical notion of knowledge is the recognition that viewing one issue or problem at a time leads to a form of tunnel vision. What is important here is that students learn to view the world in its complexity and then to use a frame of reference or world view which can provide some explanatory power in shaping their own lives in a liberating fashion. It is at this point that a radical theory of knowledge and a pedagogy of critical thinking moves beyond the limiting content-focussed and strategy-based pedagogical frameworks discussed earlier. For in addition to the emphasis on theory, the normative basis of knowledge, and the historical and dialectical dimensions of knowing, radical educational theory must concern itself with classroom social relations, particularly with what has been defined as the hidden curriculum underlying classroom social encounters.

A critical task of radical educational theory is to identify and move beyond those classroom structures and processes which maintain an oppressive hidden curriculum. As we have seen, the hidden curriculum of schooling operates at two levels of classroom experience. On one level, specific ideological assumptions and norms are embodied in the cultural capital and modes of reasoning institutionalized by schools and used by teachers in the formal curriculum. On another level, students also learn roles, feelings, norms, attitudes, and social expectations from the social context, interpersonal relations, and organizational structures of the classroom. By pressing for a classroom environment in which the influence of the hidden curriculum can be understood and thus minimized, radical educators can help students develop the capacity and determination to struggle collectively to control their own lives and to 'regulate their social interactions with a sense of equality, reciprocity, and communality'.[72] Here lies the key to helping students bridge the gap between theory and practice at the level of their classroom experiences. This would take the form of developing classroom social relationships in which students would be able to analyze the context of their schooling experience and thus be able to intervene in it in order to alter and overcome its reactionary features – the degree to which such change could take place would of course depend on more than the subjective insight of the students, a great deal would depend on the very real material and power restraints embedded in the school and larger community. The essential lesson here is that any viable radical educational theory has got to point to the development of classroom interactions in which the pedagogical practices used are no less radical than the messages transmitted through th specified content of the course. In brief, the content of classroom instruction must be paralleled by a pedagogical style which is consistent with a radical political vision.[73] Some of the guidelines for such an approach can only be discussed briefly.

In general terms, radical classroom relationships must be developed with the aim of overcoming those alienating divisions of labor which help to reproduce the relations of domination and powerlessness in the classroom.[74] Both students and teachers must learn to operate out of a context of shared respect and trust. Put another way, power in the classroom must be both democratized and humanized. It is only on the basis of this theoretical premise that a foundation can be built for developing more specific classroom practices.

Power operates in the classroom in both visible and not so visible ways. On the visible level, hierarchical relations of power manifest themselves in top-to-bottom methods of communication, rigid time-schedules, rigid prescriptions about classroom behavior, and inflexible modes of evaluation. All of these practices make one thing clear: the student is viewed as a spectator rather than a choice-making participant. As such, democratized relationships are replaced by authoritarian encounters in which communiques are substituted for communication, lectures are consistently substituted for discussions, obedience is substituted for creativity, and formulas are substituted for critical thinking.

On a less visible level, power operates in the classroom through the form of social encounters in which knowledge is divorced from the student's own level of experience and knowing. Regardless of how provoking and insightful such knowledge might be, it is curiously disconnected from the student's own day-to-day reality. It is a form of knowledge that is objectified, removed from the concrete issues which touch students' lives; moreover, it usually is also removed fom the language and systems of meanings used by students to understand and negotiate their own life experiences. The message here for students is more implicit but no less powerful; they are being told that their cultural center of gravity, their mode of generating meaning in the world, does not matter. Instead, they are told that what they bring to the class is less important than what they are given.

The democratization and humanization of power in the classroom should not suggest that radical educators retreat from positions of authority. What is suggested is that we should abandon authority roles that deny the subjectivity and power students have to create and generate their own meanings and visions. Power and knowledge are intimately related in the classroom. And students must be given the opportunity to understand the political truth of the relationship. Radical educators will have to use their authority in a progressive way to build classroom social relationships which will provide the basis for helping students to understand and analyze the meaning of authority and knowledge in socio-political terms. For instance, students must learn the distinction between authority which dictates meaning and authority which fosters a critical search for meaning. This points to the understanding that knowledge must become an instrument of both the teacher and learner. Knowledge must be seen as problematic, as a mediating force between teachers and students, subject to dialogue and analysis. Under such circumstances, radical educators must recognize the limits of both their own as well as their students' own knowledge and then use these limits as a foundation for continued exploration and growth.

The correlation between power and subordinacy in the clasroom finds its most blatant expression in the grading process. Grades are used, in many cases, as 'soft-cops' to promote social conformity and to enforce institutional sanctions. Grades become, in this case, the ultimate discipline instruments by which teachers impose their desired values, behavior patterns, and beliefs upon students.[75] Sometimes this is done consciously, sometimes it is not; the pattern has become so institutionalized that it seems to have transcended the need for analysis and criticism. One answer to this problem is dialogical grading. Dialogical grading represents an extension of Paulo Freire's emphasis on the role of dialogue among students and teachers over the criteria, function, and consequences of the grading system.[76] At the outset, such dialogue will have to address itself to eliminating the most arbitrary aspects of the evaluation process. Criteria for evaluation must not only be negotiated (depending to a great degree on the grade level one is working with), they must also be clear, with little or no room for arbitrary judgments, i.e., grading attitude! The most important issue here is that students learn how to play a meaningful role in the grading process, one that gives them the opportunity to understand the ideological assumptions behind the choices that determine the process of grading itself.

Developing a consciousness that is nurtured in a shared struggle to democratize classroom social relationships is imperative for students if they are to overcome the passivity that accompanies the hierarchical division characteristic of most classrooms. We must make it clear to ourselves and others that such a consciousness is not going to appear spontaneously in students by simply eliminating oppressive classroom constraints and controls. The democratizing of classroom social relationships is often approached by radicals through libertarian conceptions of freedom which underplay the importance for critical conceptual mediations and overplay the personal rather than collective struggle against authority. The former ignores the notion of false consciousness and results in unfettered spontaneity while the latter fosters excessively privatized notions of freedom. Both do little to help students critically reexamine the assumptions they bring to the classroom about authority or to develop and capitalize upon new assumptions that would allow them to engage in a shared struggle to minimize the use of arbitrary authority and power in the classroom.[77]

Any radical pedagogy must also strive to make concrete links between schools and society by taking students outside of the classroom. The reality of the classroom represents an ensemble of social relationships and norms whose meaning and social value can best be seen only if students are given the chance to look at these roles from outside the school itself.[78] Radical educators must link up with progressive workers from other sectors of the economy so that students and workers can discuss mutually the socio-political realities that underlie their respective places in the larger society. Through this type of contact with other sectors of the labor force, students may be able to understand that communication and dialogue are not merely pedagogical devices for classroom use, but also represent valid political tools to be used in the struggle for a better society.[79] Classroom insights, if they are to become meaningful, must develop in a context in which they can be explored as social truths. And this can happen only if classroom relations, grounded in the here and now of mutual respect and critical analysis among teachers and students, are extended to broder socio-political contexts which include a wider cross-section of humanity. There is another important message in this approach. Students must be able to see through the false and mystifying notion that work is inherently alienating and boring, and that working with one's hands is accorded limited status because it is considered to be practical labor. Implicit in this message is a rationale for a division of labor, one that separates craft and discipline from imagination and extolls a false view of creativity by disconnecting it from two of its most essential components: the disciplined skill and craftmanship that constitute the practical realm. The practical and the creative are part of the same world, and any pedagogical position which does not recognize this 'dignifies the division'.[80] In addition, this perspective promotes a false elitism in students and obscures the distinction between alienating and non-alienating labor, the latter being represented, in part, by the union of craft and imagination, the practical and the aesthetic.

In conclusion, the moment of truth for a radical theory of schooling rests, on the one hand, with its ability to help students move critically within their own subjectivity and to break with the 'common-sense' assumptions that tie them to the dominant structures of power and control. On the other hand, the viability of such a theory also depends on its success in fostering the subjective preconditions necessary for a movement of liberation aimed at restructuring and reshaping the basic structure of society. As we have seen, existing perspectives on radical educational theory lack the proper analytical depth or direction for developing a radical sociology of knowledge, one that illuminates and extends existing notions of the hidden curriculum and provides a theoretical perspective on the interrelationship between schooling and ideology, knowledge and social control. A radical educational theory which links content and process, curriculum and pedagogical styles, with their corresponding forces in the larger society provides the theoretical basis for social action mediated by critical analysis. Within this context, radical educators can broaden their base of political struggle and build alliances around an organizing principle which is clearly democratic-socialist in nature.[81] It is from the vantage point of such alliances that radical educators can define the meaning of education in terms which indict not only the existing system of education, but also the fundamental structures of a society that reproduces the worst features of itself through the experience of schooling.

The search for building new possibilities for human relations within both the schools and society will not be an easy one. Many of the suggestions outlined in this chapter represent a direction rather than a detailed blueprint for action. But in the final analysis we can be sure of one thing. Such a search will have to be steeped in a self-conscious attempt by radical educators to unite content and process at all levels of thought and action. The message here should be clear for all of us. The radical core of any pedagogy will be found not in its insistence on a doctrinal truth as much as in its ability to provide the theoretical and structural conditions necessary to help students search for and act upon the truth.

## Notes and References

1 Some of the more representative collections of radical educational writings include: GROSS, R. and GROSS, B. (1969) (Eds.) *Radical School Reform* New York, Simon and Schuster; SHIELDS, J.J. and GREER, C. (1974) (Eds.) *Foundations of Education: Dissenting Views* New York, John Wiley; SPRING, J. (1975) *A Primer of Libertarian Education* New York, Free Life Editions; GARTNER, A. (1973) *After Deschooling, What?* New York, Harper and Row; GRAUBARD, A. (1972) *Free the Children: Radical Reform and the Free School Movement* New York, Pantheon Books.
   Some of the more current anthologies on what might be loosely called a neo-Marxist perspective include: KARABEL, J. and HALSEY, A.H. (1977) (Eds.) *Power and Ideology in Education* New York, Oxford University Press; PINAR, W. (1975) (Ed.) *Curriculum Theorizing: The Reconceptualists* Berkeley, McCutchen; and NORTON, T.M. and OLLMAN, B. (1978) (Eds.) *Studies in Socialist Pedagogy* New York, Monthly Review Press.
2 Examples of this form of pedagogy can be found in MEEROPOL, M. (1975) 'A radical teaching a straight principles of economics course' *The Review of Radical Political Economics* Vol. 6, No. 4, Winter, pp. 2–9; OLLMAN, B. (1976) 'On teaching Marxism' *The Insurgent Sociologist* Summer, pp. 39–46; see also FAY, M. and STUCKEY, B. (1978) 'Who was Marx? What is Socialism? An experiment in Socialist Pedagogy' *Radical Teacher* No. 9, September, pp. 9–14. A radical justification for this can be found in HAROLD, B. (1978) 'Beyond student-centered teaching' in NORTON, M.N. and OLLMAN, B. (Eds.) *Studies in Socialist Pedagogy* New York, Monthly Review Press, pp. 314–334.
   Also ELSHTAIN, J.B. (1976) 'The social relations of the classroom: A moral and political perspective' *Telos* No. 27, Spring, pp. 97–110; ENTWHISTLE, H. (1979) *Antonio Gramsci: Conservative Schooling for Radical Politics* Boston, Routledge and Kegan Paul.
3 Examples can be found in WEBER, S.M. and SOMERS, B.J. (1973) 'Humanistic education at the college level: A new strategy and some techniques' unpublished m/s; RAPPAPORT, B. (1978) 'Toward a Marxist theory and practice of teaching' in NORTON, T.M. and OLLMAN, B. (Eds.) *Studies in Socialist Pedagogy* New York, Monthly Review Press, pp. 275–290.
4 YOUNG, M.F.D. (1976) 'Knowledge and control' in *Knowledge and Control* London, Collier–Macmillan, p. 8.

5 MCDONALD, J.B. (1971) 'Curriculum theory' in *Journal of Educational Research* Vol. 64, No. 5, January, pp. 196–200; also PINAR, W.F. (1978) 'The reconceptualization of curriculum studies' *Journal of Curriculum Studies* Vol. 10, No. 7, July–September, pp. 205–214.

6 APPLE, M.W. (1973) 'The adequacy of systems management procedures in education and alternatives' in YEE, A. (Ed.) *Perspectives in Systems Management Approaches in Education* Englewood Cliffs, Educational Technology Publications, pp. 3–31; ARONOWITZ, S. (1977) 'Mass culture and the eclipse of reason: The implications for pedagogy' *College English* Vol. 38, No. 8, April, pp. 768–774.

7 SCHROYER, T. (1970) 'Toward a critical theory for advanced industrial society' in DREITZEL, H.P. (Ed.) *Recent Sociology No. 2* London, Collier-Macmillan, p. 211.

8 NEILL, A.S. (1960) *Summerhill* New York, Hart; GRAUBARD, A. (1972) *op. cit.;* KOHL, H. (1969) *The Open Classroom* New York, Random House; GOWER, R. and SCOTT, M. (1977) *Five Dimensions of Curriculum Design* Dubuque, Iowa, Kendell Hunt, pp. 89–134; SPRING, J. (1975) *op. cit.*

9 HORKHEIMER, M. and ADORNO, T.W. (1972) *Dialectic of Enlightenment* New York, Herder and Herder, p. 127.

10 SPRING, J. (1975) *op.cit.*, pp. 33–34.

11 GROSS, R. and GROSS, B. (1969) *op. cit.*, p. 14.

12 HOARE, Q. (1977) 'Education: Programmes and people' in HOYLES, M. (Ed.) *The Politics of Literacy* London, Writers and Readers Publishing Cooperative, pp. 42–44; ELSHTAIN, J.B. (1976) *op. cit., passim.*

13 It has been pointed out that many radical educators foster subjective and individualist notions of freedom and autonomy which are at odds with the development of collectivist values that encompass social consciousness, social responsibility, and group solidarity. CAGEN, E. (1978) 'Individualism, collectivism, and radical educational reform' *Harvard Educational Review* Vol. 48, No. 2, May, pp. 227–228; KOZOL, J. (1972) *Free Schools* Boston, Houghton Mifflin.

14 MARCUSE, H. (1978) *The Aesthetic Dimension* Boston, Beacon Press, p. 52.

15 JACOBY, R. (1975) *Social Amnesia* Boston, Beacon Press, p. 64.

16 *ibid.* p. 68.

17 ELSHTAIN, J.B. (1976) *op. cit.*, p. 102.

18 *ibid.* p. 103; HAROLD, B. (1978) *op. cit.*, pp. 314–334.

19 FREIRE, P. (1978) *Pedagogy in Process* New York, Seabury Press, p. 102.

20 FREIRE, P. (1970) *Cultural Action for Freedom* Cambridge, Mass., p. 50.

21 RICOEUR, P. (1974) 'Ethics and culture' in *Political and Social Essays* Athens, Ohio, Ohio University Press, p. 267.

22 FREIRE, P. (1978) *op. cit.*, p. 12.

23 BOWLES, S. and GINTIS, H. (1976) *Schooling in Capitalist America* New York, Basic Books, p. 131.

24 CARTER, M.A. (1976) 'Contradictions and correspondence' in CARNOY, M. and LEVIN, H.M. (Eds.) *The Limits of Educational Reform* New York, David McKay, p. 58.

25 While Bowles and Gintis rely heavily on the correspondence principle, they are in no way guilty of the mechanistic usage of which many critics accuse them. See GORELICK, S. (1977) 'Schooling problems in capitalist America' *Monthly Review* October, pp. 20–36; also BOWLES, S. and GINTIS, H. (1978) 'Reply to Sherry Gorelick' *Monthly Review* November, pp. 59–64.

26 WILLIS, P. (1977) *Learning to Labour* Lexington, D.C., Heath, p. 175.

27 KARABEL, J. and HALSEY, A.H. (1977) *op. cit.*, p. 40–41.

28 Some of the better critiques include: BERNSTEIN, B. (1977) *Class, Codes and Control Vol. 3* London, Routledge and Kegan Paul, pp. 174–200; LABREQUE, R. (1978) 'The correspondence theory' *Educational Theory* Vol. 28, No. 3, Summer, pp. 194–213.

29 What is suggested here is that radical educators have failed to match these accounts with historical accounts of the struggle and contradictions that have characterized the day-to-day process of schooling itself. In both the past and the present students of various classes have refused to accept the 'process' and 'imposition' of schooling. Unfortunately, the vulgarity that characterizes overly-determined versions of the correspondence theory seem to get their weight from historians who distort the very richness and complexity of a revisionist history. See RAVITCH, D. (1978) *The Revisionists Revised: A Critique of the Radical Attack on the Schools* New York, Basic Books. See also the reply by KATZ, M. (1978) 'An apology for American educational history' *Harvard Educational Review* Vol. 49, No. 2, pp. 256–266.

30 ROSEMBLUM, S. (1977) 'Education against freedom' *Social Praxis* No. 3, June, p. 246.

31 APPLE, M. (in press) 'What correspondence theories of the hidden curriculum miss' in *The Review of Education*.

32  APPLE, M. (1975) 'Common sense categories and curriculum thought' in MCDONALD, J.B. and ZARET, E. (Eds.) *Schools in Search of Meaning* Washington, D.C., Association for Supervision and Curriculum Development, pp. 116–148; BOURDIEU, P. (1977) *Outline of a Theory of Practice* London, Cambridge Univesity Press; BOURDIEU, P. and PASSERON, J.-P. (1977) *Reproduction in Education, Society and Culture* London, Sage.
33  KARABEL, J. and HALSEY, A.H. (1977) *op. cit.*, p. 3.
34  SHARP, R. and GREEN, A. (1975) *Education and Social Control* Boston, Routledge and Kegan Paul, p. 6.
35  BOURDIEU, P. and PASSERON, J.-P. (1977) *op. cit.*, p. 11.
36  WILLIS, P. (1977) *op. cit.*, p. 172.
37  APPLE, M. (1978) 'The new sociology of education: Analyzing cultural and economic reproduction' *Harvard Educational Review* Vol. 48, No. 4, November, pp. 495–503.
38  More recent publications include APPLE, M. (1979) *Ideology and Curriculum* Boston, Routledge and Kegan Paul; GRACE, G. (1978) *Teachers, Ideology and Control* Boston, Routledge and Kegan Paul; SARUP, M. (1978) *Marxism and Education* Boston, Routledge and Kegan Paul.
39  BERNSTEIN, B. (1977) *op. cit.;* BOURDIEU, P. (1977) *op. cit.;* YOUNG, M.F.D. (1976) *op. cit.*
40  SHARP, R. 'The sociology of the curriculum: A Marxist critique of the work of Basil Bernstein, Pierre Bourdieu and Michael Young' unpublished m/s.
41  OVERLY, N. (1970) (Ed.) *The Unstudied Curriculum* Washington, D.C., Association for Supervision and Curriculum Development.
42  BOURDIEU, P. and PASSERON, J.-P. (1977) *op. cit.*
43  An excellent analysis can be found in WILLIAMS, R. (1973) 'Base and superstructure in Marxist cultural theory' *New Left Review* 82, November/December, pp. 3–16; see also DREITZEL, H.P. (1977) 'On the political meaning of culture' in BIRNBAUM, N. (Ed.) *Beyond the Crisis* New York, Oxford University Press, pp. 83–129.
44  HOARE, Q. (1977) *op. cit.*, p. 35.
45  A representative sampling can be found in SILBERMAN, M.L. (1970) (Ed.) *The Experience of Schooling* New York, Holt, Rinehart and Winston.
46  VALLANCE, E. (1973/4) 'Hiding the hidden curriculum: An interpretation of the language of justification in nineteenth-century educational reform' *Curriculum Theory Network* No. 4, p. 6.
47  BOWLES, S. and GINTIS, H. (1976) *op. cit.*, p. 265.
48  DREEBEN, R. (1968) *On What is Learned in School* Reading, Addison-Wellsley, pp. 20–22; PARSONS, T. (1968) 'The school class as a social system' in *Socialization in Schools* Cambridge, Harvard Educational Review, pp. 69–90.
49  For a more comprehensive theory on the social control of 'private space', see MARCUSE, H. (1964) *One Dimensional Man* Boston, Beacon Press; TOURAINE, A. (1977) *The Self-Production of Society* (trans. Derek Coltman) Chicago, University of Chicago Press.
50  BOWLES, S. and GINTIS, H. (1976) *op. cit.*, pp. 298–302.
51  KARABEL, J. (1977) 'Community colleges and social stratification' in KARABEL, J. and HALSEY, A.H. *op. cit.*, pp. 232–254.
52  BERNSTEIN, B. (1977) 'Class and pedagogies: Visible and invisible' in BERNSTEIN, B. *op. cit.*, pp. 116–156.
53  ANYON, J. (1980) 'Social class and the hidden curriculum of work' *Journal of Education* Vol. 162, No. 1, Winter, pp. 67–92.
54  APPLE, M.W. (1976) 'Curriculum as ideological selection' *Comparative Educational Review* XX, pp. 209–215. Of course, this position has been developed extensively in England.
55  KEDDIE, N. (1976) 'Classroom knowledge' in YOUNG, M.F.D. *op. cit.*, pp. 133–160. Also JENCKS, C. (1977) (Ed.) *Rationality, Education and the Social Organization Knowledge* London, Routledge and Kegan Paul.
56  GREEN, M. (1974) 'Cognition, consciousnes and curriculum' in PINAR, W.F. (Ed.) *Heightened Consciousness, Cultural Revoluton and Curriculum Theory* Berkeley, Calif., McCutchen Publishing, p. 273.
57  GORELICK, S. (1977) *op. cit.*, p. 21.
58  JAMESON, F. (1971) *Marxism and Form: Twentieth Century Dialectical Theories of Literature* New Jersey, Princeton University Press, p. x.
59  BOURDIEU, P. and PASSERON, J.-P. (1977) *op. cit.*, *passim.*
60  KEDDIE, N. (1976) *op. cit.*
61  ELSHTAIN, J.B. (1976) *op. cit.*
62  SKILBECK, M. (1976) 'Ideologies and values' in SKILBECK, M. and HARRIS, A. (Eds.) *Culture, Ideology and Society* London, the Open University Press, pp. 17–18.

63 FREIRE, P. (1978) *op. cit.*, p. 134
64 TOURAINE, A. (1977) *op. cit.*, pp. 1–175; BOURDIEU, P. (1977) *op. cit.*
65 The distinction between legitimation and ideology does not represent or suggest in any way the rejection of ideology as a form of legitimation. It simply acknowledges ideology as one form of legitimation, a point often overlooked by many radical educators. For instance, Pierre Bourdieu points to the hidden structures of domination which have ideological consequences but do not 'overtly speak' in an ideological language: 'The most successful ideological effects are those which have no need of words, and ask no more than complicitous silence'. BOURDIEU, P. (1977) *op. cit.*, p. 188.
66 VAZQUEZ, A.S. (1977) *The Philosophy of Praxis* London, Merlin Press, p. 170.
67 HOWARD, R. (1977) *The Marxian Legacy* New York, Urizen Boks, p. 5.
68 LICHTMAN, R. (1971) 'Social reality and consciousness' in COLFAX, J.D. and ROACH, J.C. (Eds.) *Radical Sociology* New York, Basic Books, p. 161.
69 MARCUSE, H. (1960) *Reason and Revolution* Boston, Beacon Books.
70 SARUP, M. (1978) *op. cit.*, p. 143.
71 ARONOWITZ, S. (1977) *op. cit.*, p. 771.
72 BOWLES, S. and GINTIS, H. (1976) *op. cit.*, p. 14.
73 FREIRE, P. (1978) *op. cit., passim;* see also MCLAUGHLIN, A. (1976) 'From student-centered to dialogic teaching' *Radical Philosophers' News Journal* No. VI, April, pp. 31–39.
74 See BERNSTEIN, B. (1977) *op. cit.*, pp. 174–199. Also ROSSANDA, R., CINI, M. and BERLINGUER, L. (1977) 'These on education' in KARABEL, J. and HALSEY, A.H. *op. cit.*, p. 654. An unusually brilliant analysis cn be found in WARTOFSKY, M. (1975) 'Art and technology: Conflicting models of education. The uses of a cultural myth' in FEINBERG, W. and ROSEMONT, H. (Eds.) *Work, Technology and Education* Urbana, University of Illinois Press, pp. 166–185.
75 BOWLES, S. and GINTIS, H. (1976) *op. cit.*, p. 40.
76 FREIRE, P. (1978) *op. cit., passim.*
77 CAGEN, E. (1978) *op. cit.*, p. 28.
78 ROSSANDA, R., CINI, M. and BERLINGUER, L. (1977) *op. cit.*, p. 657.
79 MISGELD, D. (1975) 'Emancipation, enlightenment and liberation. An approach toward foundational inquiry in education' *Interchange* No. 3, p. 34.
80 WARTOFSKY, M. (1975) *op. cit.*, p. 179.
81 BEVERLY, J. (1978) 'Higher education and capitalist crisis' *Socialist Review* No. 42, November/December, p. 85.

# 3 Beyond the Correspondence Theory: Notes on the Dynamics of Educational Reproduction and Transformation*

As I have tried to indicate in the previous chapters various forms of radical scholarship have in the last two decades played an important role in stripping schools of the ethical and political innocence attributed to them by functionalist social theorists. Inspired by the dream rather than the reality of liberal democracy, functionalist accounts of schooling echoed the cheery harmony of Talcott Parsons and described schools as socializing institutions designed to provide students with the values and skills necessary for them to function productively in the larger society.[1] Steeped in the logic of consensus and 'role' socialization, functionalist theory left unexamined questions concerning the relationship of schools to issues of power, class conflict, and social control. Radical critics rejected the apolitical and consensus-based model of the functionalists; instead, they attempted to illuminate the political nature of schooling. They did this by pointing to the role that schools played in reproducing the inequities of wealth and power that characterized the existing society.

At the core of these critiques of schooling is what can be called a 'theory of correspondence'. The theory was first formulated by Herbert Gintis in his critique of Ivan Illich in 1972.[2] Since that time, it has been articulated by a number of radical theorists,[3] and appears to have reached its most elaborate expression in Bowles' and Gintis' *Schooling in Capitalist America*. In spite of its many versions, the core of the correspondence theory remains relatively unchanged. In essence, it represents a model of reproduction, the causal and determining force of which is the structure, relations, and patterns of the workplace. Broadly speaking, the correspondence theory posits that the hierarchically structured patterns of values, norms and skills that characterize the work force and the dynamics of class interaction under capitalism are mirrored in the social dynamics of the daily classroom encounter. Schooling, in this view, functions through its clasroom relations to produce students with the attitudes and dispositions that make them docile and

---

* This chapter is an edited version of an article which first appeared in *Curriculum Inquiry* Vol. 10, No. 3, Fall, 1980, pp. 225–247. Copyright © 1980 by the Ontario Institute of Studies in Education. Published by John Wiley and Sons, Inc.

receptive to the social and economic imperatives of a capitalist economy. Within this perspective, the mode of production not only produces commodities, it also 'produces' people as well; moreover, the underlying needs that sustain the economy appear so powerful that they 'determine' the forms and functions of other institutions of the society, particularly the schools. Bowles and Gintis express this sentiment well when they write:

> The educational system helps integrate youth into the economic system, we believe, through a structural correspondence between its social relations and those of production. The structure of social relations in education not only inures the student to the discipline of the workplace, but develops the types of personal demeanor, modes of self presentation, self image, and social class identifications which are crucial ingredients of job adequacy. Specifically, the social relationships of education – the relationships between administrators and teachers, teachers and students, students and their work – replicate the hierarchical division of labor.[4]

### Important Insights in the Correspondence Theory

Embedded in the theory of correspondence are a number of important insights essential to a more comprehensive understanding of schooling. One such insight is that schools cannot be analyzed as institutions removed from the socio-economic context in which they are situated, for the essence of schooling lies within the nature of its relationship to those wider societal forces of which it is a part. This type of relational analysis, though vastly underdeveloped, does help us to focus on the normatively-based patterns of meaning and structure that give form and content to certain aspects of both the overt and hidden curicula of schooling. The latter insight is particularly valuable because the correspondence theory posits a class analysis of schooling, one that shifts the blame for educational failure from teachers and students to the structural dynamics of the dominant society. This is important because such a view helps to undermine various positions that support the ideology of education's neutrality. This becomes clear when it is recognized that liberal and conservative critics have focussed on the problematics of schooling through very different ideological perspectives. In their views, views that have deeply obscured the class nature of schooling, we are led to support either a version of the 'blaming the victim' thesis or are treated to the gratifying notion that whatever problems exist in schools are purely technical in nature and can be resolved with a bit of fine tuning derived from systems management theory. For example, Charles Silberman attributes the failure of schools to the mindlessness of teachers.[5] His conservative counterpart, Arthur Jensen would have us believe that the source of most educational problems lies in the genetic history of 'failing' students or incompetent teachers.[6] Systems management theorists suggest that we tune up on behavioral objectives in order to structure our educational experiences in ways that promote efficiency and prediction.[7] In all of these cases, schools curiously exist beyond the imperatives of class and power, and appear as self-contained islands, neatly severed from the socio-economic forces of the outside society. The case may appear a bit overdrawn, but the ideologies that fuel these perspectives exercise a powerful grip on existing educational theory and practice.[8] It is to the credit of exponents of the correspondence theory that some of the latter accounts have been exposed as pieces of ideology parading under the guise of 'informed' educational truths.

It should also be noted that the correspondence theory has at least demonstrated, though inadequately, that educational change has resulted from class conflicts rather than from elite domination.[9] Moreover, its exponents have often helped to expose schools as sorting and tracking institutions that treat and teach minorities of class and color in ways vastly different from their middle- and upper-class counterparts. The end result, according to this perspective, is that working-class students are socialized for low-level jobs that require minimal skills and cognitive competence, while middle- and upper-class students are trained in higher levels of cognitive skills and modes of self-presentation. The correspondence between schools and the workplace becomes clear in this type of analysis:

> Without question, the schools are a major socializing influence in preparing youth for the realities of the workplace. What must be emphasized in this context is the fact that all individuals are not socialized for the same work patterns . . . Accordingly, the schools serve to prepare workers to fill the work hierarchy by differentiating both the amounts of and types of schooling experience that they receive.[10]

In summary, the correspondence theory has provided a theoretical service by enlarging our comprehension of the relationship between capitalism and schooling. When viewed as a significant and valuable stage in the ongoing development of educational theory and practice, this theory is part of an important historical moment. But the praise must end here. As a theoretical measure of the complex and often contradictory role that schools play in mediating and reproducing the existing social order, the correpondence theory in its present form has become a historic relic. Not only has it exhausted its own theoretical mileage, but it also represents a watered-down form of Orwellian one-dimensionality, and presently serves to checkmate any hope of social struggle or emancipation. The argument advanced here is that the correspondence theory fails both as a theory of reproduction and as a theory for educational change.

### Shortcomings of the Correspondence Theory

In the last few years the correspondence theory has received considerable criticism. Critics have pointed to its overly-determined model of causality, its passive view of human beings, its political pessimism, and its failure to highlight the contradictions and tensions that characterize the workplace and school.[11] While most of these criticisms are valid, they fail to question the basic problematics and assumptions at the core of the correspondence theory. That is, most criticisms point to shortcomings in the theory, but they do little to provide a qualitatively different level of analysis regarding the relationship between schools, the workplace and the dialectical role these two institutions have to other agencies of social and cultural reproduction. The shortcomings of these critiques as well as the failure of the correspondence theory itself become clear when analyzed as part of a more comprehensive theory of cultural hegemony.

### Notion of Hegemony

Criticizing the traditional Marxist theory of the state for relying too heavily on the concept of direct force in explaining how a ruling class maintained its control over society, Gramsci stressed an equal concern with what he called rule by consent or ideological domination. In his view, there was a much greater need to understand how dominant world views as well as social practices were reproduced throughout society in order to mystify existing power relations and social arrangements.[12]

The notion of hegemony, as I have suggested before, refers to a form of ideological control in which dominant beliefs, values, and social practices are produced and distributed throughout a whole range of institutions such as schools, the family, mass media, and trade unions. As the dominant ideology, hegemony functions to define the meaning and limits of common-sense as well as the form and content of discourse in a society. It does so by positing certain ideas and routines as natural and universal. The complexity of hegemonic control is an important point to stress for it refers not only to those isolatable meanings and ideas that the dominant class 'imposes' on others but also to those 'lived' experiences that make up the texture and rhythm of daily life. Raymond Williams illuminates the latter point with his claim that hegemony has to be seen as more than ideological manipulation and indoctrination:

> It is a whole body of practices and expectations, over the whole of living: our senses and assignments of energy, our shaping perceptions of ourselves and our world. It is a lived system of meanings and values – constitutive and constituting – which as they are experienced as practices appear as reciprocally confirming . . . It is, that is to say, in the strongest sense a 'culture', but a culture which has also to be seen as the lived dominance and subordination of particular classes.[13]

One approach in analyzing how hegemony functions in the school curriculum would be to investigate these four separate, though interrelated, aspects of the schooling process: (1) the selection of culture that is deemed as socially legitimate; (2) the categories that are used *to classify* certain cultural content and forms as superior or inferior; (3) the selection and legitimation of school and classroom relationships; (4) the distribution of and access to different types of culture and knowledge by different social classes. Each of these aspects of the school curriculum points to areas in which the imposition of specific values and meanings can be used to support the dominant culture. Such an analysis can be applied to a number of institutions other than schools and in the broadest sense points to the complexity of existing modes of control and power. But hegemony does more than expose the fallacy of defining class power and control exclusively by rule of political coercion and physical repression; it also represents an important concept for understanding both the prevailing mode of domination exercised by the capitalist state and the ensuing contradictions and tensions that exist within such a mode of control. What I am arguing here is that, if used correctly, the notion of hegemony provides a theoretical basis for understanding not only how the seeds of domination are produced, but also how they may be overcome through various forms of resistance, critique, and social action.

At first glance, it appears that advocates of the correspondence theory support such a notion of hegemonic control. For example, Bowles and Gintis stress that the social relations of the school embody forms of consciousness, personality traits, and modes of interpersonal behavior which channel students into accepting the ethos and hierarchy of existing work roles.[14] However, on closer examination it becomes evident that a comprehensive notion of hegemony is absent from the correspondence theory. Instead we are treated to views of causality, domination, and consciousness that are framed solely within the logic of capitalist production. The locus of domination appears to exist primarily within the economic realm, i.e., the workplace. This is a crucial theoretical flaw because it tends to rest on a base/superstructure model of reproduction in which politics and ideological institutions such as schools appear epiphenomenal, secondary forces that have no autonomous or semi-autonomous existence of their own and which end up being absorbed by the imperatives of capitalist production. Michael Carter and others reflect this position when they write:

> The forms and structures of work and schooling act and react upon one another, but the importance of the work process so much outweighs the importance of the schooling process that the motion of the former ultimately determines the motion of the latter.[15]

This model of reproduction ultimately fails, as Jean Beth Elshtain points out, because in it 'politics is displaced onto economic concerns exclusively, and, paradoxically, depoliticized as a result'.[16] Thus, political action is subsumed within the reproductive functions of capitalist production and stripped of its possibilities as a form of resistance that originates in the contradictions and struggles in the cultural/ideological sphere. It is not surprising that the notion of consciousness within this perspective loses its capacity as an active force. Instead, it is reduced merely to a 'reflection' or 'imprint' of the forces of production. Not only is consciousness reduced to a passive rather than active force in this account, but the socio/cultural forces that mediate between the forces of production and consciousness are also lost. The strict correspondence between 'social relations' and consciousness found in much of the work of reproduction theorists does more than commit an intellectual error in failing to discuss 'culture' as a mediating force, it also ends up *vulgarizing* both the notion of consciousness and the concept of hegemony. In part, the latter failure is related to another basic flaw in the base/superstructure model of reproduction. Such a model separates productive forces from social relations, or, put another way, it separates economic activity from ideological considerations. In doing so, it ignores the fact that ideology is not a consequence of non-ideological factors, but is constitutive of productive forces themselves. In other words, economic activity like any other activity constitutes a social relationship infused and shaped by different forms of consciousness and ideology. To separate the ideological realm from the workplace is to lose sight of how the cultural and economic interpenetrate each other.

Various studies of the workplace, for instance, repudiate the notion that such contexts consist of a division between the material forces of production, on the one hand, and passive human beings simply obeying the imperatives of these forces on the other. Stanley Aronowitz in *False Promises* provides a vivid picture of how automobile workers at the General Motors Company's Lordstown plant operate on the shop floor out of social relationships that are filled with acts of resistance and rebellion. As Aronowitz points out, 'the struggle by the line workers to organize production themselves is a constant motif of daily life.[17] Workers at various levels of production attempt to modify and control the time, pacing, and demands made upon them. Moreover, they develop a complex set of social relationships and rituals to break the horrible monotony and boredom embedded in their work routines. Whether it be through humor, small acts of resistance, or outright acts of sabotage, workers are constantly challenging the pre-defined authority of the workplace. That these challenges often manifest themselves in culturally symbolic, rather than overtly political, ways speaks less of the passivity of the workers than it does of the system of domination that is capable of deflecting political opposition among workers.

In essence the correspondence theory has failed to develop a socio-cultural component that would redefine the meaning of domination and reproduction and point to the spheres of culture and ideology as important hegemonic elements that reach deeply into the crevices and texture of daily life. A more comprehensive theory of social and cultural reproduction would have to acknowledge the multiple forms of determination and disjunctions that characterize advanced industrial societies.[18] It would have to acknowledge that existing modes of ideological control, whether they be part of the schooling process or forms of hegemony contained in other institutions of everyday life, must be considered as something more than merely superstructural. This is important because such a perspective redefines not only the notion of class rule and domination, but also suggests extending the notion of political struggle beyond what has been considered the economic realm. This is a significant issue because the failure of the correspondence theory to extend the realm of political struggle beyond the workplace vitiates the possibility for political action in ideological institutions such as schools. Moreover, this truncated notion of the underlying dynamics of reproduction and political action reinforces assumptions about 'radical' pedagogy that have less to do with 'emancipatory' action in the schools than with the sterile precepts of functionalism.[19] Some of these assumptions can be detailed here.

## Resistance and Schooling

Lacking an adequate notion of hegemony and ideology, the correspondence theory fails to show how the school as an active cultural sphere functions both to sustain and resist the values and beliefs of the dominant society. One reason for this is that a dialectical notion of ideology is almost completely missing from this perspective. For example, Bowles and Gintis grossly ignore in their work the content of what is taught in schools. Emphasizing the form of classroom encounters that replicate the social relations of the workplace, they do not consider how the dominant culture is mediated in schools through textbooks, through the assumptions that teachers use to guide their work, through the meanings that students use to negotiate their classroom experiences, and through the form and content of school subjects themselves. Yet, as Basil Bernstein and Pierre Bourdieu and others have shown, the way in which knowledge is selected, distributed, and evaluated is intimately related to the principles of social control.[20] In his critique of this position, David Hogan captures what is lost in this version of the correspondence theory:

> . . . they neglect mechanisms other than the correspondence between the social relations of production and education. Other features of the educational processs besides the form of the social relations of education might also have been considered . . . the form of the relations between curriculum, pedagogy, and evaluation (that is, the nature of the 'classification' and 'framing' of educational transmission) embody important ideological messages and are a critical part of the process of cultural reproduction of class relations. Others have pointed out that the content of the educational process – the 'cultural capital' – is also a significant aspect of the cultural reproduction of class relations. In effect, Bowles and Gintis, by limiting their analysis of reproduction to the correspondence between the form of social relations of education and production, have a much too restricted theory of reproduction of class relations through schooling.[21]

Moreover, a notion of the correspondence theory that emphasizes social relationships to the exclusion of investigating classroom content and other possible modes of ideology runs the risk of mystifying the very nature of what it attempts to illuminate, i.e., social and cultural reproduction. In other words, the latter view lacks any explanatory power in analyzing how the lived reality of teachers and students in the school offers resistance to the institutionalized modes of domination, whether they be ideological or material in nature. Clearly, teachers and students do not interpret the curriculum-in-use in a passive way. Like workers on the production line, teachers and students, though in different ways, often reject the basic messages and practices of schools. Paul Willis, for instance, vividly documents how working-class students in secondary school in England constantly struggle against the forms of symbolic violence that are being inflicted upon them.[22] The institutional assault on their mode of dress, their language, their lifestyle, and their sensuality is not accepted passively by many of these students. In creative, though often self-defeating ways, these students reject and ridicule the messages and demands of the school's overt and hidden curricula. Similarly, teachers often challenge the practices and myths of the dominant ideology found in the school curriculum. In failing to analyze how schools sustain and produce meanings, the correspondence theory gives no attention to how human actors in such settings *produce* knowledge. Lacking a thought-out theory of ideology, we are left with no conceptual tools to unravel how knowledge is both consumed and produced in the school setting. Not only does such a posture reinforce for teachers the notion that there is little they can do to change their circumstances, it also smoothes over some of the basic contradictions and tensions in the schooling process itself.

In short, the undialectical nature of ideology found in the correspondence theory does not illuminate how ideological hegemony is mediated both within and between the schools and other ideological institutions. More specifically, it does not speak to how the dominant ideology is often resisted, rejected, and redefined by the set of meanings that students and teachers carry around with them. Consequently, this posture 'not only leaves teachers completely flattened and speechless, but it is likely to reinforce the idea that radical change is beyond their frames of reference'.[23] Even contradictions such as those often found between the content of what is being taught and the classroom social relations in use are overlooked by the correspondence theory.

### Myth of 'Total' Domination

Inherent in the correspondence theory, as I previously stated, is a monolithic view of domination and an unduly passive view of human beings. Both of these themes are interrelated and paint a picture of schools characterized by unremitting oppression and domination. In this view schools are often falsely compared to prisons, asylums, and other oppressive 'total institutions'. Students often are seen as inmates and teachers seen as prison guards within the 'wooden' metaphors employed by supporters of this view.[24] While the peculiarly strained quality of this type of analysis can be easily dismissed, its underlying assumptions about domination need to be critiqued. Of course, to challenge such an interpretation is not to argue that schools do not function as agents of domination; there is enough evidence to support that view. What is being contested is the oversimplified view of domination held by supporters of the correspondence theory. For instance, in Althusser's Hobbesian vision of schooling there is little recognition of the dialectical interplay of power, ideology, and resistance. In Althusser's view the school functions to transmit the necessary skills and discipline required to socialize students passively into their future work roles.[25] Domination appears so total in this type of perspective that teachers and students 'appear as unwitting servants of such an ideology and have little choice in avoiding the service of its interests'.[26] But hegemonic ideologies, while always dominant, are never totally overpowering. Raymond Williams makes this point cogently when he writes:

The reality of any hegemony, in the extended political and cultural sense is that while by definition it is always dominant, it is never total or exclusive . . . it does not just passively exist as a form of dominance. It has continually to be renewed, recreated, defended, and modified. It is also continually resisted, limited, altered, and challenged by pressures not all its own.[27]

The source and the nature of the challenging pressures to which Williams refers have to be flushed out if the dialectical nature of the dynamic of cultural hegemony is to be used as the basis for a critique of the reductionist and overly-determined view of domination in the correspondence theory. Hegemony as a specific historical moment has to be abstracted somewhat from the mechanisms of control that shape its form and content. Domination as a characteristic feature of a given historical period may be rather obvious, but as R.W. Connell points out the:

situations can vary in the mechanisms (of control) that are active, and in the depth of control that is achieved . . . Hegemonic situations range from a strongly established pattern of direct controls with only marginal dissidence, through situations where a working class has formed as an economic and social category but its mobilization is being aborted, to situations where mobilization has occurred, though only within decided limits.[28]

By highlighting the mechanisms of control we can get a better understanding of the complexity of the field of ideology itself, a field that speaks to both the nature of domination and the possibilities for overcoming it. By focussing on the causal relationship between the workplace and schools as the primary forces in the ideological state apparatus, the correspondence theory posits a notion of reproduction that is too limited i.e., it ignores the role of capital, and the role of other institutions in the socio-cultural sphere.[29] A more comprehensive theory of ideology and social reproduction occurs when hegemony is related to all the major spheres of social existence. Kellner demonstrates this by identifying four major ideological realms: (1) the economic realm, i.e., ideologies of production, exchange, distribution, etc.; (2) the cultural realm, i.e., ideologies of culture, values, science, technology, mass media, art, etc.; (3) the social realm, i.e., ideologies of the private sphere, family, education, social groups, etc.; (4) the political realm, i.e., ideologies of the state, democracy, civil rights, legal-judicial system, police and military, etc.[30] While the dominant ideology inhabits and functions in all of these realms, there are contradictions both within and among the institutions that transmit their various ideologies.

The contradictions that exist in the various ideological regions become evident when one looks at the competing ideologies that manifest themselves in struggles over the control of the school administration and the form and content of school curricula. For instance, among different factions of the upper and middle classes, schools have become highly politicized arenas of struggle. On the one hand, members of the technical intelligentsia in both classes voice strong support for a curriculum that will produce scientists and technically skilled workers. On the other hand, sections of the intelligentsia who work in the cultural realm often support progressive modes of education that call for a loosening of authority in the classroom and a greater opportunity for students to work with a relative amount of freedom in a broad-based integrated curriculum.[31] Conflicting claims on schools also come from competing ethnic, religious, and racial groups. Thus, schools often find themselves at odds with the needs of the dominant society. The present glut of unemployed college and university students highlights the contradiction between wider societal needs and the demands of a public who believes that education is still an important vehicle for social mobility. What is crucial about these contradictions is that they highlight the relative autonomy characteristic of cultural institutions such as schools. It is this relative autonomy that provides the space for institutions in the ideological realm to serve as more than agents of reproduction.

The concept of relative autonomy in educational theory represents a central dilemma for the correspondence theory. Advocates of the theory find themselves caught in a major paradox over this issue. On the one hand, they have recognized that at the core of liberal theories of schooling is the mystifying notion that schools exist independently from the wider nexus of social, economic, and political institutions. This view, they rightly argue, depoliticizes schools and obscures their role as agents of social control. On the other hand, radical theorists have posited a theory of correspondence which in its attempt to contextualize schooling in a reproductive thesis practically seals off the possibility for educational and social change. Instead of developing an emancipatory theory of reproduction, they have produced a notion of causality and domination that makes teachers and students appear merely as social puppets. As a result the correspondence theory ends up as a 'radical' version of mangement ideology in which human beings are seen as essentially malleable and acquiescent in the face of demands made by corporate interests. Michael Apple highlights this issue:

> I want to argue that such overly-deterministic and economistic accounts .
> . . are themselves elements of the subtle reproduction, at an ideological
> level, of perspectives required for the legitimation of inequality . . . By
> seeing schools as total reflections of unequal 'labor', a market where
> workers simply do what they are told and acquiesce to the norms of
> authority relations of the workplace, these analyses accept as empirically
> accurate the ideology of management.[32]

Tied to its economistic straitjacket, the correspondence theory is unable to account for the relative autonomy of ideological institutions such as schools or to lay the foundations for examining how the contradictions and tensions generated within such semi-autonomous realms can be used to promote educational and social change. By failing to develop an adequate understanding of hegemony and ideology, the correspondence theory reduces both schools and human beings to abstractions within a reified model of production. What must be acknowledged is that schools are not *only* agents of reproduction; it follows that they cannot be reduced to expressions of the dominant ideology when, in fact, they have only a particular relationship to it. Similarly, categories of political economy cannot be detached from the lives and practices of concrete individuals. When this happens, teachers and students become static expressions of political economy, and, as William Pinar points out, the abstract subsumes the concrete.[33] Under such circumstances, domination and alienation become impaled upon economic categories that overlook the fact that such conditions are felt by real human beings under specific historical conditions.

### Notes on a Theory of Reproduction and Transformation

I now want to outline briefly some basic suggestions for developing a more adequate theory of reproduction and transformation, particularly as this applies to classroom practice. Though I am limiting my analysis to schools, this is not meant to suggest that the struggle in schools be isolated from wider political struggles. To do so would leave intact the fundamental and social and economic structures that generated the need for initiating social reform movements in the schools in the first place.

The development of such a theory would have to be based on a dialectical notion of society in which the socio-cultural realm is seen as an active sphere of determination in reproducing and conradicting class-based institutional arrangements. This is not a call to abandon the workplace as an important mode of determination, but to reject the notion that it is the only one. What is at stake here is a more comprehensive understanding not only of what schools do, but how social reality is formed. Clearly, there is a need to develop a theory of reproduction capable of explaining how schools in their dialectical linkages with other institutions produce both stability as well as forms of resistance. Put another way, we need to develop a relational analysis of society that uses critical categories such as class, ideology, and hegemony to expose *how* the interconnections among specific kinds of social practices, meanings, and institutions constitute the ideological and material character of a society steeped in domination.[34] For example, we need to investigate the forces at work at both the institutional level and the daily level of classroom life that structure experiences in which different socio-economic groups of students are taught different types of knowledge and different social practices. Similarly, we must learn to understand how the meanings generated in different types of cultural settings such as family cultures, work cultures, and class-specific peer cultures generate their own forms of resistance when they come up against institutions that embody and disseminate hegemonic ideologies.

As the latter type of analysis is developed it will be easier to move away from one-sided notions of causality, and still be able to connect our investigations to a view of domination and social transformation that demands the study of individuals 'in the whole range of their social relations, their character, formation, and the articulation of their consciousness'.[35] It is important to stress that such a position does not deny the overall importance of the economic realm as an important mode of determination. On the contrary, the importance of the economic realm becomes meaningful only if we see it as 'the ultimate determinant' that is caught in a dialectical relationship with other institutions that both actively structure it and are structured by it. Thus, such an analysis does not deny either the notion of determination or the importance of the economic realm, it simply attempts to make concrete the non-mechanistic relationships that exist between the economic realm and other ideological spheres. Marx captured the nature of these relationships when he wrote that the economic realm provides 'a general illumination which bathes all the other colors and modifies their particularity'.[36] It is within the space offered by this 'illumination' that the simple and constant 'fit' between the institution of school and the imperatives of capital breaks down.

In summary, a theory of reproduction and transformation must attempt to unravel how dominant culture symbols and practices emerge and are sustained in schools. In addition, it is imperative to analyze how contradictions and disjunctions arise at the level of day-to-day classroom activities, and how these contradictions often end up serving the very forces of reproduction and domination that they oppose. Finally, such a theory needs to look more closely at the conditions of classroom practices in order to assess how contradictions can be addressed realistically to promote educational alternatives that will help to promote social and political reconstruction. It is to some of these issues that I will now turn.

## New Sociology of Education

The role that schools play on a day-to-day level in the ideological and cultural reproduction of class relations has received considerable attention from a number of educational theorists in recent years. Bourdieu, Bernstein, Young and others have explored how schools institutionalize hegemonic ideologies and cultural messages which set limits to the modes of discourse and social practices that mediate classroom experiences.[37] One theoretical paradigm that has gained prominence in light of the emerging critiques of schools has been what can be loosely called a 'new' sociology of education. This position has provided a valuable service in uncovering how the overt and hidden curricula of schools legitimize specific forms of cultural capital, i.e., those modes of knowing, styles, tastes, dispositions, linguistic competencies, and behavior that the dominant society considers the most valued.

A number of the assumptions underlying the new sociology of education provide important critical concepts for teachers who need to question the basic notions that guide the way they view and structure their classroom encounters.

Rejecting functionalist views of society, knowledge, and human behavior, the 'new' sociology of education takes as its starting point a deep-seated interest in understanding communicative and symbolic patterns of interaction that shape the social construction of reality. Society, in this view, is conceived of as an essentially dynamic ensemble of social relations structured through the actions of men and women who consistently attempt to shape and redefine their existence. Thus, a view of human beings as active subjects replaces a functionalist view in which people are portrayed as simply bearers of predefined societal roles. In addition, the 'new sociology rejects the arbitrary division between objective and subjective forms of knowing supported by various forms of positivist rationality. In place of the latter division, the 'new' sociology posits a view of epistemology that treats knowledge as problematic and human intentionality as the most valid *starting* point for reconstructing knowledge.

The 'new' sociology of education treats all aspects of the schooling process as problematic, that is, it rejects 'common-sense' notions of pedagogy and views school knowledge, classroom social relationships, and the notion of evaluation as ongoing social constructs that must be constantly negotiated, redefined, and challenged by teachers and students alike. By stressing the active nature of human understanding and a dialectical view of knowledge, the 'new' sociology has developed an important mode of critique which raises insightful questions concerning how teachers and students both perceive and respond to the day-to-day dynamics of classroom life.

The value of the 'new' sociology of education, one that has to be included in a theory of reproduction and transformation, is that it views teachers and students as producers as well as consumers of knowledge. In a limited but important way, it has helped to redefine the relationship between power and knowledge in dialectical terms. That is, it demonstrates that knowledge is a social construction and, in doing so, it lays the theoretical groundwork for understanding that the relationship between power and knowledge is not necessarily one that automatically guarantees hegemony or domination. In other words, the 'new' sociology has helped us to understand that the production of meaning represents not only a significant aspect of the process of social domination, it has also helped to illuminate the fact that the production of meaning by teachers and students can represent a positive instance in the relationship between knowledge and power. In contrast, correspondence theories have stressed only one side of the relationship between power and knowledge and as a result have failed to focus on analyzing how the dominant ideology in schools can be modified or reversed. At least the 'new' sociology provides a theoretical foundation for helping educators understand the concepts and structures needed to produce classroom knowledge. Moreover, and more importantly, it suggests the need to examine how the dominant ideology is both expressed and constructed in textbooks, school films, classroom social encounters, and other ideological artifacts. More concretely, the 'new' sociology 'speaks' to the need for a mode of critique which, on the one hand, is capable of identifying through content analyses how meaning is distorted in cultural artifacts which are used in the classroom; on the other hand, it acknowledges the importance of those classroom social relationships in which teachers and students have the possibility to affirm their own power by demonstrating ways of producing knowledge that is capable of revealing its own assemblage, genesis, and truth claims.

Thus, the 'new' sociology moves beyond the limits of the correspondence theory by challenging its one-sided view of power, knowledge, and domination. But in the final analysis, the 'new' sociology does not link its heuristic interests to more deeply rooted political considerations. Consequently, it fails to develop a comprehensive understanding of the relationship between knowledge and power on the one hand, and ideology and domination on the other. It is to some of these failings that I will now turn.

### Beyond The Tenets Of The New Sociology

The notion that teachers should continually question the 'taken-for-granted' in education is important, but it runs the risk of reducing all meaning to merely subjective modes of understanding. Not only does such a position tend to get bogged down in a notion of cultural relativism, it also fails to account for the ways in which reality is masked. Put another way, the 'new' sociology neglects the importance of issues such as ideology and 'false consciousness'. That is, the notion that reality is socially constructed is incomplete unless it can account for knowledge or modes of reasoning that 'remove from criticism the interpretation of life and the world on which rationalizations of the existing order are based'.[38] Intentionality alone tells us little about the truth value of socially-constructed knowledge; the former is simply a 'moment' in the production of knowledge. The real issue is whether the knowledge produced represents a view of reality that comprehends how knowledge itself can be distorted or falsified in the interest of a dominant ideology. Equally important are questions concerning how structural determinants in the wider society function to sustain and uphold forms of knowledge and modes of reasoning that mystify the nature of social reality. As I have mentioned, though the possibilities for dealing with these issues are inherent in the 'new' sociology, they have not been developed. A more adequate methodology would have to link the notion of interpretation with a critique of ideology; as such, it would have to develop as a form of historical and political critique. In this case, knowledge would be analyzed within a perspective that analyzes to what degree it conceals or distorts the social, political, and economic conditions of the existing society. Moreover, such a perspective would have to raise questions about not only how consciousness has been formed, but also what it could be, i.e., what possibilities exist for it to become more reflexive and critical.

In short, linking the interpretive with a critique of ideology plays a valuable role in unmasking hegemonic ideologies and indicating how they may reproduce themselves in schools, but an equally crucial issue resides in the task of constructing a theory that further explains why teachers and students do not develop a consciousness of domination even though they reject the precepts and values of the dominant ideology. In other words, unmasking an ideology and indicating how it continues to reproduce itself, in spite of the contradictions and tensions that challenge it, are not the same thing. Moreover, this strikes me as one of the most important issues that has to be developed in any theory of reproduction and transformation. Below are some tentative suggestions for moving in that direction.

### Constraints and Resistance At The Level Of Classroom Practice

A theory that can provide for educational change must recognize the extent to which it is bound by real constraints both within and outside specific school settings. 'Radical' educational prescriptions that call for teachers and students to reassert their individuality, to criticize existing definitions of knowledge, to defy determinism with freedom, actively to construct their own lived reality and true humanity tend to go up in metaphysical smoke if they do not speak concretely to the existential reality of schooling. That is, such a theory must recognize the social space in which students and teachers operate, the actual conditions and parameters of practice. Not to do so is to end up with an elitist notion of change, one that may mistake powerlessness for passivity, for it is only within the conditions of practice that specific educational strategies can be assessed with regard to both their possibilities *and* limits.[39] In addition, by locating teachers and students in specific settings and conditions of practice we can gain a better understanding of how the process of social control works in schools, and what its linkages might be to parallel processes that lie outside the schools and within the structures of society itself and to the wider distribution of power.[40]

As a focal point for examining the conditions of school practice, we can begin by investigating the contradictions within which teachers, students, and administrators work. A much better sense both of how reproduction works and how it can be contested is afforded through such an approach. For instance, the findings of Grace, Willis, and others illustrate how a variety of mediating forces work in schools to limit the power of the dominant ideology.[41] Willis, as previously noted, points to the structure and content of the informal counter-culture of working-class students. What is important about this work is that it illuminates how the cultural capital of oppositional groups 'contains elements of a profound critique of the dominant ideology . . . in our society'.[42] These elements are contained in the style and messages of the informal culture. In this case, there is a rejection of individualism, conformity, academic credentials, and other issues. Moreover, these messages are developed within modes of language, dress, habit, and styles of behavior that demonstrate opposition to the dominant ideology.

There are a number of mediating forces that, in part, support forms of resistance among teachers as well. Informal cultural and ideological factors such as ethnicity, race, world-view, and social class background often generate oppositional attitudes among teachers toward school authority, rules, predefined curriculum structures, and institutionally sanctioned forms of teacher accountability. The point here, often lost even in critiques of the correspondence theory, is that various individuals and groups of teachers interpret the role of schooling in different terms. Though these interpretations lack the political penetration and acuity to expose the nature of the underlying contradictions that schools both reproduce and act on, they do exist amidst certain ambiguities that provide room for further political analysis and insight. For instance, there are often deep-rooted disjunctions between what Sharp and Green have labelled a teaching ideology and a teaching perspective.[43] A teacher's ideology refers to relatively high level abstractions about the purpose and nature of teaching itself. The concept of teaching perspective, on the other hand, refers to those sets of beliefs and practices that manifest themselves under actual conditions of teaching. Recently, the work of

Keddie, Apple, Anyon, and others, documents the view that teachers operate under conditions that reinforce deep-seated and often unrecognized biases and myths.[44] Clearly, both the conditions that promote these ideological manifestations and the underlying source of their contradictions indicate the need to examine more closely the relationship between the existential reality of teachers' work and its relationship to objective structures of class control in the larger social reality.

## *Limits Of Cultural Forms Of Opposition*

The modes of opposition briefly analyzed above speak to the importance of certain mediations and the force of creativity among different social groups trying to affirm their individual and collective identities in structures and settings that are predefined for them. However, it is crucial to recognise that the modes of opposition and resistance used by these groups are not mediated through viable political categories. Consequently opposition which lacks this political quality often results in reproducing the dominant culture. This is particularly true where opposition plays itself out more as a matter of style and cultural rebellion than as a world view directed toward political and social transformation. Such opposition does not understand the political nature of its own resistance; it is resistance that does not call into question the deeper socio-political structures that generated it in the first place. For instance, while the working-class students in Willis' study rejected the middle-class mores of the school, they supported at a more fundamental level some of the basic assumptions of the existing division of labor and power in the dominant society. Though they rejected individualism, conformism, credentials, and other elements of the ideology of meritocracy, they supported notions of sexism, racism, and anti-intellectualism. In part, teachers find themselves in the same position. Though they may recognize that many of the meritocratic notions about curriculum and pedagogy are flawed, they support a range of myths and beliefs about class and power that prevent them from developing insights that point to the political nature of their own practice or to the political source of the structural limitations imposed on them by existing social and economic arrangements.

## *Structural Restraints In Schools*

The restraints that undermine recognition of the contradictions which emerge in the schooling process are primarily ideological. They are deep-seated images, ideas and values that make the social construction of reality appear as an eternal part of the reality of society and schooling. The existential reality of teachers and students is also shaped by specific structural and social processes at the day-to-day level of schooling. While the practical conditions of the schooling experience differ from school to school, they do share underlying features that link them to each other and to wider societal forces. All school settings generate in non-mechanical ways pressures, constraints, and limits on the nature and feasibility of what teachers and students can do to 'shape their own reality'. Class size, the use of school authority, community influences, and the ideology and strength of a school board all play a crucial role in determining how politically vulnerable human actors might be if they 'innovated' or tried something different in their classrooms. The question of the overt and covert 'rules and meanings' that govern teacher decision making cannot be excluded from consideration when analyzing the relationship of theory to practice. To do so runs the risk of creating theoretical models that ultimately 'serve to neutralize their critical potential by imposing further constraints upon teachers in their already contradictory work'.[45] The acknowledgement of these structural and social circumstances is an important and necessary complement to a critical understanding of the ideological and structural forms of reproduction and resistance that characterize the contexts of schooling. But ideological and structural forms do more than complement each other, they interpenetrate each other as well. We get a sense of what this means if we view structures not just as limiting phenomena but as enabling phenomena as well. Structures in this sense can be seen as ideologically-based social relationships expressed in an objectivized form. They are concrete but they are not static, they can be changed. Giddens calls this notion the duality of structures, and defines it thus:

> . . . structures can always in principle be explained in terms of their structuration as a series of reproduced practices . . . [ Thus the task is] to explain how structures are constituted through action and reciprocally how action is constituted structurally.[46]

### Critique And Concrete Classroom Experiences

What this means for educational theory and practice is that structures of reproduction do not exist outside of the actions of educators to change them. For instance, writers such as Althusser see teachers and students as no more than products of structures. What is needed to offset this type of unwarranted determinism is a view of social reality in which structures are seen in their geneses and historical development. The source of such an account would be grounded in the consciousness and actions of human beings shaping and restructuring their own histories under specific historical conditions and at a specific moment in time. This issue brings us back to the question of why a consciousness of domination does not develop among teachers and students who are alienated by the pedagogical conditions in which they find themselves.

Whitty provides one answer when he criticizes those educational theoreists who believe that only a 'permanently critical approach to "reality"' is necessary to transform the oppressive conditions of schooling. What is absent from such a view according to Whitty:

> . . . is the recognition that even when pupils are aware that 'alternative' structures are possible, they may not experience the transcendence of existent realities as a living possibility . . . no strategy is likely to prove

meaningful to the teacher or pupil who, while aware of the theoretical possibility of actually shaping his world, still feels shaped and oppressed by it.[47]

Clearly, any theoretical stance that does not examine the nature and strength of the ideological and structural constraints that shape the parameters in which teachers and students operate runs the risk of defeating itself. But there is another issue here that is equally important, one that suggests a redefinition of ideology itself. Alternative educational strategies that highlight the distorting beliefs and values that are embedded in the official and covert school cultures contain a seriously flawed definition of ideology. The central point here is that the dominant ideology does not just refer to modes of reasoning which serve to mask reality. It also refers to forms of practices and routines that are often so deeply entrenched in the structure of the human personality that they congeal into what Russell Jacoby calls 'second nature'. As he puts it:

> Ideology that has hardened into nature . . . becomes accumulated and sedimented history. It is ideology so long unliberated, so monotonously oppressive that it congeals . . . It becomes history that surfaces as nature.[48]

To put it another way, ideology is something other than 'false consciousness', i.e., 'the repression of society in the formation of concepts . . . a confinement of experience, a restriction of meaning'.[49] This view of ideology points to a deep structure of domination, one that suggests that if the divisions of labor that characterize the wider society are going to be dealt with in the schools then educators will have to go beyond exposing the submerged meanings which underlie both the dominant ideology and the forms of resistance exhibited by both teachers and students. These must be recognized and dealt with, but only within classroom social relationships that illuminate, concretize, and demonstrate a more radical notion of liberation. In other words, it is not enough to act on the contradictions and tensions in schools by providing students and teachers with a theoretical analysis which reveals the political source of such contradictions. Theoretical work in the cultural realm must be supplemented in schools by fighting for concrete social encounters that generate ongoing experiences which illustrate, in as much as the context will allow, new and tanscendent ways of thinking and behaving that interpenetrate each other. Such a task will have to be grounded in the cultural capital that teachers and students bring with them to the school setting. For, as Pinar points out, such 'praxis' (thought and action) can occur only as the contradictions are understood in the context of immediate individual and social life.[50]

As this chapter indicates, there is no easy route for changing the political substance and character of schools. This is simplified by the fact that any struggle for social justice must also take place in the wider society, and that educational theory and practice, though significant, is only one part of that struggle. But the struggle for viable educational alternatives will move forward more quickly once we locate human agents within the center of such a task. To do so is to move beyond a theory of correspondence by recognizing that reproduction is a complex phenomenon that not only serves the interest of domination but also contains the seeds of conflict and transformation. To recognize this is to begin the task of developing an educational theory informed by indictment which is found at the heart of all forms of resistance, an indictment whose central message is that things must change. It is with this task in mind that we turn to the next chapter.

## Notes and References

1 PARSONS, T. (1959) 'The school class as a social system: some of its functions in American society', *Harvard Educational Review*, Vol. 29, No. 4, pp. 297–318; DREEBEN, R. (1968) *On What is Learned in Schools* Reading, Mass., Addison–Wesley Publishing Co., Inc.

2 GINTIS, H. (1972) 'Toward a political economy of education: A radical critique of Ivan Illich's Deschooling Society' *Harvard Educational Review*, Vol. 42, No. 1, pp. 70–96.

3 See GRUBB, W.N. and LAZERSON, M. (1975) 'Rally 'round the workplace: Continuities and fallacies in career education' *Harvard Educational Review*, Vol. 45, No. 4, pp. 451–474; CARNOY, M. and LEVIN, H.M. (1976) *The Limits of Edcuational Reform* New York, David McKay; SCRUPSKI, A. (1975) 'The Social System of the School' in SHIMAHARA, N.K. and SCRUPSKI, A. (Eds.) *Social Forces and Schooling*, New York, David McKay, pp. 141–186; BOWLES, S. and GINTIS, H. (1976) *Schooling in Capitalist America: Educational Reform and the Contradictions of Economic Life* New York, Basic Books.

4 BOWLES, S. and GINTIS, H. *op. cit.*, p. 131.

5 SILBERMAN, C. (1971) *Crisis in the Classroom* New York, Vantage Books.

6 JENSEN, A.R. (1969) 'How much can we boost I.Q. and scholastic achievement' *Harvard Educational Review*, Vol. 39, No. 1, pp. 1–123.

7 POPHAM, J.W. (    ) 'Objectives-based management strategies for large educational systems', in YEE, A. (Ed.) *Perspectives on Management Systems in Education* Englewood Cliffs, New Jersey, Educational Technology Publications, pp. 32–45.

8 See for instance, the commentaries on 'traditional' ideologies in education by PINAR, W.F. (1978) 'The reconceptualization of curriculum studies' *Journal of Curriculum Studies*, Vol. 10, No. 4, pp. 205–214; EISNER, E. (1979) *The Educational Imagination* New York, Macmillan; GIROUX, H.A. (1980) 'Teacher education and the ideology of social control' *Journal of Education* Vol. 162, No. 1, Winter, pp. 5–27.

9 Though Bowles and Gintis, *op. cit.*, make this point, they are repeatedly attacked for not doing so. This has resulted in a number of misguided critiques of their work. One example of this genre is KEEFE, D. (1978) 'Profit and control: The Bowles and Gintis thesis', *Journal of Curriculum Studies*, Vol. 10, No. 3, pp. 252–261.

10 BEHN, W.H. *et al.*, (1976) 'School is bad; Work is worse' in CARNOY, M. and LEVIN, H. (Eds.) *The Limits of Educational Reform*, p. 229.

11 Some of the better critiques include: SARUP, M. (1978) *Marxism and Education* Boston and London, Routledge and Kegan Paul; BERNSTEIN, B. (1977) *Class, Codes and Control: Vol. III* Boston and London, Routledge and Kegan Paul, particularly Chapter 8; TUNNELL, D.R. (1978) 'An analysis of Bowles' and Gintis' thesis that schools reproduce economic inequality' *Educational Theory*, Vol. 28, No. 4, pp. 334–342; MACDONALD, M. (1977) *The Curriculum and Cultural Reproduction* Milton Keynes, England, Open University Press; BOWERS, C.A. (1978) 'Educational critics and technocratic consciousness: Looking into the future through a rear-view mirror' *Teachers College Record*, Vol. 80, No. 2, pp. 272–286; GLESSON, D. (1979) 'Curriculum development and social change' in EGGLESTON, J. (Ed.) *Teacher Decision Making in the Classroom*, Boston and London, Routledge and Kegan Paul, pp. 193–302; APPLE, M. (1980) 'The other side of the hidden curriculum: Correspondence theories and the labor process', *Journal of Education*, Vol. 162, No. 1, Winter, pp. 47–66.

12 GRAMSCI, A. (1971) *Selections from Prison Notebooks,* (Editors and Translators, Quinten Hoare and Geoffrey Smith) New York, International Publishers.

13 WILLIAMS, R. (1977) *Marxism and Literature* New York, Oxford University Press, p. 110: KELLNER, D. (1978) 'Ideology, Marxism and advanced capitalism' *Socialist Review,* Vol. 8, No. 6, pp. 30–65.

14 See in particular Chapter 5 in BOWLES, S. and GINTIS, H. *op. cit.*

15 CARTER, M.A. (1976) 'Contradictions and correspondence: Analysis of the relation of schooling to work' in CARNOY and LEVIN (Eds.) *The Limits of Educational Reform,* p. 58.

16 ELSHTAIN, J.B. (1979) 'Feminists against the family' *The Nation* Vol. 229, No. 10, November, 17, pp. 481, 497–499.

17 ARONOWITZ, S. (1973) *False Promises* New York, McGraw-Hill; BENSON, S.P. (1978) 'The clerking sisterhood: Rationalization and the work culture of saleswomen in American department stores' *Radical America,* Vol. 12, No. 2, pp. 41–55; EDWARDS, R. (1979) *Contested Terrain* New York, Basic Books.

18 See MANDEL, E. (1972) *Late Capitalism* London, New Left Books; Wright carries Mandel's analysis further and talks about six modes of determination. These include (1) structural limitation, (2) selection, (3) reproduction/non-reproduction, (4) limits of functional compatibility, (5) transformation, (6) mediation. WRIGHT, E.O. (1978) *Class, Crisis and the State* London, New Left Books, pp. 1–29.

Since *Schooling and Capitalist America* was published, Bowles and Gintis have attempted to unravel some of these criticisms. For instance, they admit that they may be 'Faulted for passing from "social relations" to "consciousnes" without discussing their mediation by "culture" . . .' in GINTIS, H. and BOWLES, S. (19   ) 'Reply to Sherry Gorelick', *Monthly Review,* Vol. 30, No. 6, p. 62.

19 LaBRECQUE, R. 61978) 'The correspondence theory' *Educational Theory,* 28, No. 3, pp. 194–201. Some aspects of Sherry Gorlick's review also deal with this issue. See GORELICK, S. (1977) 'Undermining hierarchy: Problems of schooling in capitalist America' *Monthly Review,* 29, No. 5, pp. 20–36.

20 BERNSTEIN, B. (1977) *op. cit.;* BOURDIEU, P. and PASSERON, J.-P. (1977) *Reproduction in Education, Society, and Culture* London, Sage Publications.

21 HOGAN, D. (1979) Capitalism, Liberalism, and Schooling', *Theory and Society,* Vol. 8, No. 3, November, pp. 387–413.

22 WILLIS, P. (1977) *Learning to Labor: How Working-Class Kids get Working-Class Jobs* Lexington, D.C., Heath.

23 ERBEN, M. and GLEESON, D. (1977) 'Education as reproduction: A critical examination of some aspects of the work of Louis Althusser' in YOUNG, M. and WHITTY, G. (Eds.) *Society, State and Schooling,* Barcombe, England, The Falmer Press, p. 75.

24 The conceptual foundations for much of this writing is taken from Erving Goffman's work, particularly GOFFMAN, E. (1961) *Asylums* New York, Anchor Books. A more recent example of this genre can be found in FREIDENBERG, E.Z. (1979) 'Children as objects of fear and loathing' *Edcuational Studies,* Vol. 10, No. 1, Spring, pp. 63–75.

25 ALTHUSSER, L. (1971) 'Ideology and Ideological State Apparatuses', in ALTHUSSER, L. *Lenin And Philosophy and Other Essays,* (trans. B. Brewster) London, New left Books, pp. 121–173.

26 ERBEN, M. and GLEESON, D. *op. cit.,* p. 77.

27 WILLIAMS, R. (1977) *op. cit.,* pp. 112–113.

28 CONNELL, R.W. (1977) *Ruling Class Ruling Culture* Cambridge, England, Cambridge University Press, p. 207. The essential dynamics of this issue are cogently explored in APPLE, M.W. (in press) 'Analyzing determinations: Understanding and evaluating the production of social outcomes in schools', *Curriculum Inquiry.*

29 See DEBORD, G. (1970) *Society of the Spectacle* Detroit, Black and Red; APPLE, M. (in press) 'Analyzing Determinations . . .'; BRENKMAN, J. (1970) 'Mass media: From collective experience to the culture of privatization' *Social Text* Vol. 1, No. 1, Winter, pp. 94–109; A more comprehensive theory of reproduction would have to be concerned with more than the reproduction of cultural symbols or class relationships; it would have to address itself to the reproduction of all the conditions which support the relations of domination. Rachel Sharp's treatment of this issue is helpful here.

> It is not simply agents who have to be reproduced as workers, capitalist, etc., with the appropriate dispositions and motivations, but also the material and other means for reconstituting the capitalist process . . . a study of reproduction involves among other aspects, the study of the economic preconditions for the reproduction of capitalist production . . . analysis involves an understanding of the dynamics of the circuit of capital

and the various stages and forms of that circuit. In addition, reproduction also involves the reproduction of a class relationship in which economic, political, and ideological conditions are involved.
From SHARP, R. (1978)'The Sociology of the Curriculum: A Marxist Critique of the Work of Basil Bernstein, Pierre Bourdieu, and Michael Young', unpublished m/s, p. 30.

30  KELLNER, D. (1978) 'Ideology, Marxism, and advanced capitalism', *Socialist Review*, 8, No. 6, pp. 57–58.

31  BERNSTEIN, B. (1977) *op. cit.*, pp. 174–200.

32  APPLE, M.W. (1980) 'The other side of the hidden curriculum: Correspondence theories and the labor process', *Journal of Education*, Vol. 162, No. 1, Winter, pp. 50–51.

33  PINAR, W.F. (in press) 'The abstract and the concrete in curriculum theorizing' in GORDON, M. and MACDONALD, J. (Eds.) *Liberation and Curriculum*, Berkeley, Calif., McCutchen Publishing.

34  GIROUX, H.A. 'Dialectics and the development of curriculum theory' (see Chapter IV).

35  LICHTMAN, R. (1978) 'Marx's theory of ideology' *Socialist Review* Vol. 8, No. 6, pp. 56–75.

36  MARX, K. (1973) *Grundrisse* New York, Vantage Publishing, p. 107.

37  BERNSTEIN, B. (1977) *op. cit.*; BOURDIEU, P. and PASSERON, J.-P. (1977) *Reproduction in Education, Society, and Culture* London, Sage Publications; YOUNG, M.F.D. (1971) *Knowledge and Control* London, Collier–Macmillan; DALE, R., ESLAND, G. and MACDONALD, M. (1976) (Eds.) *Schooling and Capitalism: A Sociological Reader* London, The Open University Press; KARABEL, J. and HALSEY, A.H. (1977) (Eds.) *Power and Ideology in Education* New York, Oxford University Press.

38  MCCARTHY, T. (1978) *The Critical Theory of Jürgen Habermas* Cambridge, M.I.T. Press, p. 86.

39  Whitty makes a creditable point here when he states that 'It may therefore prove valuable . . . for those concerned to challenge prevailing notions of education, to consider more thoroughly the nature of the parameters within which redefinitions of knowledge may or may not be feasible . . .It may, for instance, be important to make distinctions between (a) those features of knowledge which may not be subject to relativization in any conceivable circumstances; (b) those features which conceivably might be different in substantially different historical circumstances; and (c) those features which might be altered by the legitimizing activities (of different) interest group(s) . . . I am suggesting that a more careful attention to such distinctions might permit us to be less ambiguous about what are and what are not "open human possibilities" for teachers surveying the school curriculum and desiring change . . . I want to suggest that recent approaches to the study of school knowledge . . . lay too little stress on the parameters within which redefinitions of education might prove possible and, that in doing so, they may unwittingly imply that the failure to redefine situations is a purely personal one'. In WHITTY, G. (1977) 'Sociology and the problem of radical educational change: Notes toward a reconceptualization of the "new" sociology of education', in WHITTY, G. and YOUNG, M.F.D. (Eds.) *Society, State, and Schooling* Barcombe, England, The Falmer Press, p. 40.

40  *ibid.*, p. 29

41  WILLIS, P. (1977) *op. cit.*; GRACE, G. (1978) *op. cit.*; a particularly interesting study of this issue can be found in LUNDGREN, U.P. and PETTERSSON, S. (1979) (Eds.) *Code, Context, and Curriculum Processes* Stockholm, Sweden, CWK Gleerup.

42  WILLIS, P. (1977) *op. cit.*, p. 129.

43  SHARP, R. and GREEN, A. (1975) *Education and Social Control* London and Boston, Routledge and Kegan Paul, pp. 68–69.

44  APPLE, M.W. and KING, N. (1977) 'What do schools teach?' in WELLER, R. (Ed.) *Humanistic Education*, Berkeley, Calif., McCutchen Publishing, pp. 341–358; KEDDIE, N. (1971) 'Classroom Knowledge' in YOUNG, M.F.D. (Ed.) *Knowledge and Control*, London, Collier–Macmillan, pp. 133–160; ANYON, J. 'Social Class and the Hidden Curriculum of Work' *Journal of Education*, Vol. 162, No. 1, p. 67–72; GIROUX, H.A. (1080) 'Teacher education and the ideology of social control' *Journal of Education*, Vol. 142, No. 1, Winter, pp. 5–27.

45  GRACE, G. (1978) *op. cit.*, p. 197.

46  GIDDENS, A. (1976) *New Rules of Sociological Method*, New York, Basic Books, p. 161; It is impossible within the confines of this paper to do justice to the debate that exists among various Marxist persuasions concerning the relationship between structuralism, ideology, and consciousness. For a detailed look at such arguments see: COWARD, R. and ELLIS, J. (1977) *Language and Materialism: Developments in Semiology and the Theory of the Subject* Boston and London, Routledge and Kegan Paul; ALTHUSSER, L. (1976) *Essays in Self-Criticism* London, New Left Books; 'Marxism and Structuralism', theme of a special issue of *The Insurgent Sociologist*, Vol. 9, No. 1, (Summer 1979).

47 WHITTY, G. and YOUNG, M.F.D. (1977) *op. cit.,* p. 35.
48 JACOBY, R. (1971) *Social Amnesia* Boston, Beacon Press, p. 31.
49 MARCUSE, H. (1964) *One Dimensional Man* Boston, Beacon Press, p. 208
50 PINAR, W.F. (in press) *op. cit.,* p. 11.

# 4 Dialectics and the Development of Curriculum Theory

One of the major tasks of the curriculum field is to demonstrate in consistent fashion the process of self-criticism and self-renewal. Unfortunately, such a task is more easily stated than accomplished. Yet, while the reasons for the loss of this critical capacity are varied and complex, the underlying source for the atrophy of self-reflection in the curriculum field may be traced to a general failure, particularly among members of the dominant tradition, to understand how the interface of ideology, dominant institutional interests, and curriculum theory contribute to the latter's incomplete development.

Walter Benjamin provided one clue when he wrote, 'in every era the attempt must be made to wrest tradition away from a conformism that is about to overpower it'.[1] This implies that no field of inquiry, including the curriculum field, is immune from the complacency that threatens it once the field gains status as an 'acceptable' mode of discourse and inquiry. Thus, the institutionalization of the curriculum field points to the need to develop a mode of analysis that educates its members to the language and logic of its own political and ideological center of gravity. What this means is that if the curriculum field is going to resist the conformity that threatens to overtake it, its members will have to reassess its possibilities for critique and growth against the influence and mediations of those dominant institutional forces that often work to limit the curriculum field's power as a mode of critical discourse and inquiry.

The role of curriculum theory as a vehicle of critique and vision has a long and valued tradition. If that tradition is to be maintained, we will have to begin with an acknowledgement of its decline within the last few decades. At the core of this acknowledgement is the notion that such a tradition consistently needs to replenish itself in the face of changing historical situations and the development of new social formations. This suggests that we must consider new forms of discourse and practice in order to maintain the field's critical posture as well as its ability for

* This chapter is a revised version of an article which first appeared in *The Journal of Curriculum Theorizing* Vol. 2, No. 2 (1980). Copyright © (1980) JCT.

self-renewal. This chapter represents one step in the process of self-renewal by attempting to show the significance of the concept of the dialectic for curriculum theory and practice. It posits a general framework that points to new ways to examine the relationships and ensuing questions that result when we use a different conceptual model to critique the curriculum field. The model used here is neither altogether new, nor is it intended to be complete. In part, it modestly demonstrates both the strengths and weaknesses of the dialectic itself: the dynamic of an unfolding process whose very existence points to an incessant struggle against a series of conflicts and contradictions that underscore the curriculum field, the wider society, and the perceptions that shape our understanding of the world in which we live and work. Moreover, these conflicts and contradictions are rooted in real life situations, and if they are to be understood by educators, they will have to be examined at their source, for only then can they be overcome. The concept of the dialectic helps to shake us from the boredom and indifference that accompanies the belief that we live in the best of all worlds. In essence, it speaks to the existence of contradictions that are a part of every age. Its message is neither a celebration of relativity nor cynicism, but rather an acknowledgement that the search for the truth must begin by seeing beyond the false harmony between subject and society. Such 'harmony' must be seen for what it is: a piece of ideology that smoothes over the existence of those contradictions that call into question the meaning and consequence of our work as educators and the role that such work has in reproducing the inequities that mark the larger society.

The meaning of the dialectic has an elusive quality. Variations on its meaning and application extend from Plato to Hegel to Mao Tse Tung. The concept has been defined in purely idealist terms by Hegel as well as in vulgar materialist terms by a score of orthodox Marxists.[2] In its many versions, it has been used as a rationale to support repressive ideologies and social systems as well as radical world views and social orders. Given the mixed history of the concept, it will be a major goal of this chapter to delineate what I believe are the most useful and central categories of the dialectic.

Instead of being viewed as a universal method, characterized by rigid rules and magical qualities, the concept of the dialectic is defined here as a critical mode of reasoning and behavior, one that represents both a part as well as a critique of the conflicts and solutions that define the nature of human existence. In effect, the real meaning of the concept of the dialectic is rooted in the major assumptions that give its categories their driving and critical power. Similarly, the categories themselves both reflect and develop from those aspects of human knowledge that reflect and critically penetrate 'the process of natural and social development'.[3] But if these categories of the dialectic are to become functional, the assumptions that reveal both their interests and intent must be clarified. It is to the latter task that I will now turn.

It is my belief that the notion of the dialectic becomes important only within a commitment of the notion of emancipation, one that seeks to liberate human beings in both subjective and objective terms. In other words, a notion of emancipation that penetrates the world of everyday life with critical concepts that link the pre-conceptual, the ritualized experiences and the routine practices of daily existence with forms of reflection that reveal their objective and social roots. It is in the tension between the recognized oppression that underlies our daily lives and the critical understanding that demands a call to rectify it that the dialectic becomes more than a neutral social science category.[4]

Given this context, it would be inappropriate to reduce the dialectic to a form of epistemology that functions solely as a tool of rational understanding. Nor can the dialectic in this case be viewed simply as a ready-made formula or 'method' whose laws exist outside of history or human action. Both positions strip the dialectic of its critical force. In the first instance, the dialectic is reduced to mere cognition. Lost here is the concreteness of the dialectic, a concreteness rooted in the very basis and origins of being itself.[5] In other words, the dialectic is more than a comprehension of reality, it is the 'designation for aspects of being within being itself . . . human existence in its reality, in its events, within the world as it is conceived and formed'.[6] Karol Kosik captures this point in his claim that 'dialectics does not enter cognition from without as an afterthought . . . rather cognition is dialectics itself, in one of its forms'.[7] Cognition, in this sense, is not simply contemplation, it is the understanding of reality insofar as humankind shapes it in the process of living it.

On the other hand, it is important to understand that the dialectic is not simply a methodology governed by universal laws. Such a perspective has more to do with 'frozen' ideology than a critical concept of the dialectic. Removed from the necessity of constant self-renewal through the process of reflective criticism, this view of the dialectic becomes synonomous with a petrified, omniscient system of universal laws. Not only does methodology stand alone as a measure of truth in such a view, it also denies the notion of human intentionality and the interplay between human consciousness and specific historical circumstances. Such a position has more to do with vulgar forms of positivism than with the dialectic. T.W. Adorno has noted that the latter position can only degenerate into a form of ideological shorthand that extends unqualified support to the status quo. He writes:

> A rigorous dialectical thinker should not in fact speak of method, for the simple reason – which today has almost entirely disappeared from view – that the method should be a function of the object, not the inverse. This notion, which Hegel elaborated very convincingly, is one which has been all too simply repressed by the positivistic spirit, such that the overvaluation of method is truly a symptom of the consciousness of our time. Sociologically speaking, it is truly closely related to the general tendency to substitute means for ends. In the last instance, this tendency is related to the nature of the commodity: to the fact that everything is seen as functional, as being-for-another and no longer something which exists in itself.[8]

Of course, this is not meant to imply that methodological reflections should be dispensed with. It does mean that method should allow educators to get a clear perception of how they should resolve pre-defined issues; but the ultimate meaning of such issues must be dealt with before methodological considerations can be taken into account. Thus, the dialectic does not begin with a methodology, it begins with the fact of human existence and the contradictions and disjunctions that, in part, shape it and make problematic its meaning in the world. This is not meant to suggest that the concept of the dialectic does not have its limitations. In some cases, the dialectic is useful, in others it is not. It is clear that there are microphenomena and projects that under certain conditions yield valuable insights when analyzed according to the rules of formal logic, rules which are distinctly undialectical. For example, there are laws of formal logic such as the law of exclusion – i.e., either A, or non-A – that are more applicable to a specific problem than the concept of the dialectic might be. Yet, while formal logic has a certain valuable specificity and application, in the final analysis it is the dialectic that helps us to understand the limitations of formal logic. To ignore the limitations and strengths of the dialectic is to expand it into its opposite: an empty concept with no boundaries or possibilities for self-reflection and correction. In the final analysis, it can be said that the dialectic represents an interpenetration of reasoning and method, an interpenetration that belies both an abstract objectivism and abstract subjectivism. If the driving power of the dialectic is not to dissolve into metaphysical smoke, it must be seen as a form of radical critique and action, each of which act on and penetrate the other.

This brings us to another assumption that gives critical power to the concept of the dialectic. Any emancipatory notion of the dialectic has to be grounded in the process of critique and praxis. In general terms this means that the dialectic functions so as to help people analyze the world in which they live, to become aware of the constraints that prevent them from changing that world, and, finally, to help them collectively struggle to transform that world. As a form of critique, the dialectic functions to bring to awareness underlying contradictions that support existing forms of alienation. It is based on the use of a language and discourse that are incapable of looking at the world in a different way: that is, from a perspective that transcends the world of 'facts' and 'natural' laws that serve to smother reality and to flatten contradictions. Although it must be recognized that as a first step towards praxis, critique is as difficult as it is necessary. In other words, critique in itself is a difficult task. This is particularly true in the United States since the dominant social science paradigm eschews critical categories of social thought.[9] It comes as no surprise to find that categories like social class, ideology, false consciousness, and class conflict are either missing from the language of mainstream social science or conveniently stripped of any analytical power. Under such circumstances, the relationship between dialectical reasoning and critical thought becomes lost.

In brief, a critical concept of the dialectic moves beyond mainstream social analysis by presenting itself as both the form and experience of critique. As an epistemology it gives power to the concept of negative thinking. Herbert Marcuse illuminates the latter with his claim that 'dialectical thought starts with the experience that the world is unfree; that is to say man and nature exist in conditions of alienation, exist as other than they are'.[10] Thus, the driving force of negative thinking resides in its ability to penetrate reality and to search and reveal the source and genesis of the contradictions that give it meaning. Put another way, negative thinking is an attack on the pseudoconcrete, i.e., the collection of phenomena that reproduce and support forms of mystification and ideology that conceal the essence of reality. Kosik describes the pseudoconcrete as 'the collection of phenomena that crowd the everyday environment and routine atmosphere of human life, and which penetrate the consciousness of acting individuals with a regularity, immediacy and self-evidence that lend them a semblance of autonomy and naturalness . . .'.[11] Clearly, there is no room in this type of analysis for those positivistic assumptions that suggest: (1) that the relationship of theory to practice is primarily technical; (2) that there is only one scientific method; (3) that knowledge is inherently neutral; and (4) that scientific inquiry itself is value free.[12] The importance of critique as a fundamental dimension of the dialectic rests with its ability to peel away the layers of meaning that give shape to our everyday lives; moreover it serves as a guide to action designed to alter those life forces that embody the power of an oppressive reality. As such, the concept of the dialectic used here is closely tied to an acknowledgement of the importance of a critique that embraces critical categories which serve to illuminate the intersection of the social and the personal, history and private experience. This allows us further to extend our definition of praxis as a guiding assumption of the dialectic.

Praxis as I use it has a number of important moments, all of which overlap and interpenetrate. Praxis, as one moment, represents the transition from critical thought to reflective intervention in the world. Paulo Freire captures the importance of this general conception of praxis when he writes:

> Men will be truly critical if they live in the plenitude of praxis, that is if their action encompasses a critical reflection which increasingly organizes their thinking and thus leads them to move from a purely naive knowledge of reality to a higher level, one which enables them to perceive the causes of reality.[13]

Praxis, as another moment, suggests more than a struggle against the forces of oppression; it further suggests a struggle that defines freedom in social and not merely personal terms. Emancipation is linked in this case to groups of people struggling against the social forces that oppress them. It also suggests that the struggle affirms the power of human agents to act in a self-determining fashion out of a context that is as deeply historical as it is critical. Praxis, then, typifies a conception of freedom that analyzes the content and form of existing struggles within the context of their historical genesis and development.

Praxis, as a third moment, translates an historical sensibility into a critical sensibility.[14] The point made in the previous chapter is worth repeating here: modes of reasoning, interpretation, and inquiry develop a critical capacity to the degree that they pay attention to the flow of history. In the absence of an attentiveness to history, criticism is often muted by the dominant ideology, which often parades under the banner of absolute verities and 'natural' laws. This type of 'assault' on historical sensibility is no small matter. Marcuse rightfully claims that this represents a form of false consciousness.[15] Understandably, a critical notion of the dialectic grounds itself in historical sensibility because not to do so represents an attack on the very process of thinking itself. In more specific terms, the dialectic incorporates an historical sensibility in the interest of liberating human beings not only from those traditions that legitimate oppressive institutional arrangements, but also from their own individual history, i.e., that which society has made of them. This is the critical point that links praxis and historical consciousness. For we must turn to history in order to understand the traditions that have shaped our individual biographies and intersubjective relationships with other human beings. At the core of the dialectic is the notion that underlying the mediations that form the intersubjective space in which we live, work, study and dream are social relationships, relations between people and not things. All the material things around us, whether it be the buildings we live in or the money that we use to pay our rent, represent the objectification of human labor and social formations operating under specific socio-historical conditions. These are both part of the dialectic and serve as well as an object of study and analysis through one form of the dialectic, i.e., dialectical reasoning.

In short, if the concept of the dialectic is to become useful in the service of radical pedagogy, it will have to be grounded in assumptions that give its central categories an emancipatory purpose. I have specified what these assumptions are by arguing: (1) that the dialectic is a form of praxis that links critical reasoning with a critical intervention in the world; (2) that the dialectic is not guided by absolute laws but is a process of critique and praxis that under different historical circumstances takes different forms; (3) that the dialectic necessitates human agents acting collectively to transform the world in which they live; (4) that the dialectic is grounded in a vision that links historical and critical sensibilities as modes of reasoning that inform and enrich each other; (5) that the dialectic is not value-free, but rests on interests that oppose oppression in all of its forms.

This section will briefly spell out what the central categories of the dialectic are, and attempt at the same time to provide brief examples of how these categories relate to educational theory and practice.

Totality represents one of the central categories of the dialectic. Its meaning is based on the insight that for any fact, issue, or phenomena to become meaningful it must ultimately be examined within the context of the social totality that gives it meaning. This respresents one of the fundamental tenets of the dialectic, one that underscores context in the methodological sense as well as in the sense of grasping the importance of 'historical totality'. For instance, as one observer writes:

> To comprehend an historical object completely in its concrete reality, one has to grasp the totality of events. Such a comprehension is impossible if the historical object is considered rigid and isolated from its historical

context, and treated as an identity free of contradictions 'throughout time', instead of seeing it as a many-faced coming into being, acting and passing away in time. Not only its positive moments should be brought into view but also its negative moments which equally belong to it – what the historical object has been – and what it is becoming, and what it is not contributes to its reality, since this is what determines it and moves it.[16]

Moreover, the category of totality stresses that the 'irreducible unit of reality is the relation and not the thing'.[17] Within the context of human history and understanding, socio-political reality is seen as the 'unity of production and products, of subject and object, of genesis and structure'.[18] Thus, the category of totality speaks to the importance of seeing things rationally in their many-sided development, moreover, it points to a world in which things, meanings, and relations are not conceived as objects removed from human history and action, but rather are seen as products of human praxis. Within the notion of totality there is little room for a reified, positivistic vision of the world, one that celebrates a posture that is at once fragmented, isolated, and ahistorical.

In concrete, pedagogical terms this means that the role of schools, curriculum development, and pedagogy itself must be examined within a context that reveals their development historically as well as their relationship to the larger social order. Michael W. Apple has voiced this concern with his claim that:

> . . . education as a field of study does not have a strong tradition of such 'situating'. In fact, if one were to point to one of the most neglected areas of eduational scholarship, it would be just this, the critical study of the relationship between ideologies and educational thought and practice, the study of the range of seemingly commonsense assumptions that would lay bare the political, social, ethical, and economic interests and commitments that are uncritically accepted as 'the way life really is' in our day-to-day life as educators.[19]

As a mode of reasoning, the category of totality in the dialectic allows educators not only to beome more critically interpretive, it also suggests new ways of acting in the world. It helps teachers and students alike to link knowledge with specific normative interests, with specific frames of reference. The latter point necessitates one important qualification about the category of totality, and that is, for this category to become viable it must be connected to notions of causality and ideology. The category of totality ceases to be dialectical when it becomes nothing more than a methodology for asserting that everything is connected with everything else. The importance of totality lies in its value in helping us answer fundamental questions about the truth content and nature of reality.[20] If focuses on the ideological and objective structures of society and looks at how they function in their contradictions and correspondence to distort as well as reflect reality. Totality in this sense points to causal relationships as part of an effort to ascertain the truth. This leads us to the next category, the notion of mediation.

Mediation is a core category of the dialectic that enriches and deepens the notion of totality. It does this by dispensing with the trivial notion that reality is merely a reflection of the sum of forces that make up the world in which we live. In essence, mediation rejects simple 'reflection' theories by claiming that 'all active relations between being and consciousness are inevitably mediated . . .'.[21] This suggests two important points: (1) mediation is a process that embodies the object itself, i.e., those forces that shape our perceptions of the world are not just in our minds, but are a material and constitutive part of our everyday routines and practices; (2) pure immediacy in its various forms: perception, commonsense, 'facts', and sensation is an illusion. Mediation is thus a process, an internalized force, and a critical category. It can be used to reveal how the mechanisms of social and cultural reproduction both determine and legitimate the meaning of various socio-cultural institutional arrangements, modes of knowing, ways of behaving, patterns of interaction, etc. In short, the category of mediation provides the framework for looking at various cultural phenomena in terms of their essences and not in terms of their 'legitimated' commonsense meanings. Thus, mediation indicates a search for the essence of a phenomena, a peeling away of its different layers of meaning until one finds the combination of objective and subjective forces that made it what it is and therefore constitute its true nature. Mediation is both a process and a statement against the notion that phenomena reveal themselves immediately. It posits the need for human beings to look for the structure of meaning beyond the distorting fabricated 'reality' of ideology. It points to another level of reality, one that suggests not distortion but reality in its unmasked form.[22]

The value that the category of mediation has for educators is noteworthy. It calls into question the static and petrified commonsense assumptions that underlie much of our thinking about curriculum and classroom pedagogy. It forces us to think relationally about the nature of knowledge, classroom social relationships, and values. Similarly, it points to ever-widening levels of mediation and correspondence between schools and the larger society. Not only does it continually prod us to make problematic the selection, organization, and distribution of meanings and values that structure classroom learning, it also serves to open to examination the very belief and values that guide for actions in and out of the classroom.

In brief, the category of mediation is crucial to the dialectic because it lifts our commonsense perceptions and experiences to new levels of understanding, complexity, and concreteness. In doing so, it serves to illuminate the way in which specific social and political forces mediate between ourselves and the larger society. As a critical category, it replaces the myth of the autonomous individual with the problem of what one has to do to struggle to become a self-determining social agent acting on rather than responding to the world in which we live.

The next category of the dialectic I have labelled is the category of appropriation. Unlike the Hegelian version of the dialectic, the unfolding process at work in history, in my view, is not abstractly spiritual, it involves a subject. This means that at the heart of the dialectic is a human agent who is never merely a passive being removed from the historical arena, but instead is an acting subject who with qualitatively different levels of reasoning and action appropriates and penetrates the reality in which he or she lives. Appropriation, as it is used here, refers to human beings who in varying degrees both reproduce and act upon the socio-cultural matrix in which they find themselves.[23] The driving force of appropriation is the recognition of the value of consciousness and action in the service of praxis. Appropriation rejects the overly-determined and passive view of man inherent in various forms of behaviorism and vulgar Marxism. But appropriation represents more than a celebration of subjectivity, it further represents a rejection of all world views and social formations that support an objectified, and oversocialized model of human behavior. In other words, it both rejects and struggles against forms of objectivism that deny human consciousness, subjectivity, and action.[24]

Within the context of radical pedagogy, the category of appropriation posits reflective thought and action as a central concern of both teachers and students. This points to forms of classroom interaction that promote critical dialogue and communicative patterns stripped of unnecessary institutional control. In addition, it helps us to focus on the way in which various aspects of the schooling process reproduce in both material and ideological terms the mechanizations of social conformity and control. Thus, it helps us to focus more critically on questions concerning the nature of the hidden curriculum, the patterns of social control underlying student-teacher relationships, and the forms of ideology embedded in the use of specific types of knowledge and modes of classroom evaluation.[25] But if appropriation is to move beyond a hermeneutic function, it will have to be linked to a notion of transcendence, and this leads us to the final category of the dialectic.

As the final category of the dialectic, transcendence (Aufhebung) subsumes a number of other characteristics that are often associated with the dialectic, i.e., the driving force of contradictions, the unity of opposites, and the negation of the negation.

The essence of the category of transcendence lies in its refusal to accept the world as it is. Its posture is based on the political and moral imperative that things must change. Inherent in its aforementioned nature is a commitment to a world view that calls for the 'emancipation of sensibility, imagination, and reason in all spheres of subjectivity and objectivity'.[26]

Transcendence distinguishes itself by its acknowledgement that the contradictory forces that steer, shape and characterize specific historical moments and social formations must be measured against their emancipatory and repressive possibilities. They must be seized by human beings acting as subjects in the intervention and shaping of history and dealt with as part of a 'struggle for their liberation'.[27]

On one level, transcendence represents what Agnes Heller has called:

> . . . the simple consciousness of alienation, the recognition that the social relations are alienated: from this there follows (or this constitutes the base for) the need to overcome alienation, to overturn the alienated social and productive relations in a revolutionary way, and to create general social and productive relations which are not alienated.[28]

Thus, transcendence as a category of the dialectic is a call to action informed by an emancipatory vision. It is a call to develop an awareness of our own historically conditioned self-formative processes as well as an awarenes of those socially un-necessary modes of domination that shape the larger society. In different terms it is a call to reveal how the antagonistic character of social reality manifests itself in both personal and social terms and how both of these realms affect, change, and reproduce each other.

Put another way, transcendence is more than an explanatory concept, it is a categorical demonstration of the negation of the negation. That is, it traces the contradictions that characterize existing society to their fractured source and tries to overcome them.[29] As the negation of the negation, transcendence is at first a form of refusal and secondly an act of reconstruction. Resistance gives way to the search for qualitatively better modes of existence. The medium of transcendence is informed consciousness and reflexive action, and its goal is a society free of alienating and oppressive social institutions and life forms.

While it is impossible to detail here how this overarching category of the dialec-tic might specifically shape the process of schooling, one aspect of its pedagogical application can be clarified. The category of transcendence forcefully supports an educational philosophy based on the assumption that the purpose of education should be to educate youth not for the present 'but for a better future condition of the human race, that is for the idea of humanity'.[30] Transcendence posits the need for all educational workers to examine their most fundamental assumptions about pedagogy next to a clearly delineated set of emancipatory intentions. In this case, commitment is substituted for objectivism, and a critical and visionary posture toward the world is substituted for a 'professional' noncommital manner. Thus, what all of this means is that we need a critical pedagogy that links pedagogical processes to radical modes of reasoning, both of which support each other and act as a catalyst for students and teachers to fight against those ideological and material forces that prevent such a synthesis from manifesting itself, whether it is inside or outside the school. A number of radical educators have already begun to lay the foundations for such a pedagogy.[31]

The concept of the dialectic as presented in this chapter is both a conceptual tool as well as a mode of experience that is useful in developing pedagogical theory and practice. Its basic categories are not universals, but social processes steeped in specific assumptions about schools, society, human nature, and freedom. Moreover, these categories provide a powerful analytical scheme for analyzing, modifying, and changing the complex mediations that influence the many levels of human consciousness and action, both in schools and in the wider society. The dialectic points not only to the contradictions of schooling, but also to the need for tracing and resolving those contradictions in the larger society. I will now complete this chapter by suggesting a few specific ways in which the concept of the dialectic can be applied to classroom pedagogy.

If the concept of the dialectic is to become relevant to classroom pedagogy, teachers can begin by using its central categories to examine the curriculum as a selection from the larger culture. By doing so, they can begin to look at their own educational philosophy within a particular social, cultural, and historical context. The notion of schooling as a cultural phenomenon not only calls into question the basic assumptions that structure one's view of classroom pedagogy, it also forces teachers to examine the role schools play as agents of social and cultural reproduction. The dialectic, in this case, illuminates for teachers the way in which the dominant beliefs and values in the wider society and their own world views interpenetrate. Schooling, in this case, is stripped of its innocence. The foundation for a progressive form of classroom pedagogy can be now developed since schooling can be understood as a study in ideology and values. Questions concerning totality, mediation, and appropriation now become essential in developing a form of pedagogy in which teachers carefully examine how the structural and ideological determinants of the dominant society affect the behavior, attitudes, and speech of all those involved in the classroom encounter.

The concept of the dialectic is particularly useful in making teachers attentive to the specific ways in which cultural forms in the classroom reproduce, redefine, and affect the selection of meanings and social relationships that receive institutional support. One major task of classroom teachers will be to help students understand the social and economic meanings that stand behind various forms of classroom knowledge and pedagogical encounters. This means that we have to make clear to students, depending upon the levels we are working with, the valuative underpinings and limitations of different forms of knowledge. Just as teachers must come to recognize the theoretical assumptions that underlie their own pedagogical concepts and practices, students must also learn to recognize the meaning of 'frame of reference', and how the latter concept is instrumental in deciding, selecting, and organizing the 'facts' that go into everything from their social studies texts to their health textbooks.[32] The foundation for such an approach can begin by developing classroom pedagogy around social processes and conceptual models that raise and demonstrate questions which probe the nature of classroom knowledge and its ensuing social relationships.

Classroom pedagogy of this sort would have to develop a view of students that recognizes them as appropriators or self-conscious agents in the classroom encounter. This means teachers would have to take seriously those cultural experiences and meanings that students bring to the day-to-day process of schooling itself. Making knowledge problematic becomes meaningful only if students are allowed to explore such knowledge within their own modes of knowing and understanding. The important notion of schooling as a selection from the wider culture becomes meaningful when teachers begin by acknowledging not only the source and meaning of their own cultural capital, but also the importance and meaningfulness of the cultural capital that characterizes their students. If we take the experiences of our students as a starting point for dialogue and analysis, we give them the opportunity to validate themselves, to use their own voices. Once students become aware of the dignity of their own histories and perceptions, they can then make a leap to the theoretical and begin to examine critically the truth value of their meanings and perceptions, particularly as they relate to the dominant culture.[33]

William Pinar has written of the need for students to be able to formulate questions that will help them to capitalize on, use, and learn within their own experiences.[34] This is an important point. Teaching students to step outside the somewhat reified world of schooling represents more than supplying them with critical modes of reasoning. Critical reasoning becomes an empty exercise if students do not learn how to both reflect on, as well as transform, the nature and meaning of their own lived-worlds. In other words, students must be given the opportunity to learn how to use and interpret their own experiences in a manner that reveals how the latter have been shaped and influenced by the dominant culture. Subjective awareness becomes the first step in transforming those experiences.

One important step in helping teachers develop a pedagogy that will assist students to move beyond the taken-for-grantedness that shapes part of their view of the world lies in providing them with a new language and conceptual scheme through which they can view the world more critically. It goes without saying that dialogue and supportive interaction represent crucial vehicles for the development of a dialectical pedagogy, but they become meaningful only if students have a language which allows them to move towards a critical stance, 'a way of looking at the world which can serve as the foundation of subsequent analysis and criticism . . .'.[35] In concrete terms this means that students must learn a language that is both hermeneutic and emancipatory. Such a language would help both teachers and students to become more interpretive, but it would also reveal the structures and limitations present in different modes of language. For instance, a distinction should be made between a dialectical and non-dialectical approach to language. The latter can be designated as a language that is confined to the boundaries of a given subject, confined to the operations, principles, and inner space of a given topic. This is the 'inside' language of technocratic rationality, i.e., the language of means, techniques, etc. We often hear it among lawyers, music theorists, mathematicians, etc. A more dialectical language is characterized by the way it draws from a variety of subjects to examine any given topic. It draws upon the 'languages' of psychoanalysis, sociology, history, psychology and a wide variety of other subjects in order to examine a specific problem or issue. It is the language of connections and mediations. It refuses to support a mode of reasoning that reinforces the artificial constructs between the various disciplines and subjects.

The use of a dialectical language will make it easier for teachers to enable students to understand the meaning of frame of reference. By looking at issues from a variety of perspectives, students can learn something about the interpretive screens that people use in constituting and creating reality. The latter is of profound insight and has enormous political significance. When applied to the content and process of classroom pedagogy, it 'tells us that our most basic thought-processes and our very image of reality are neither natural, inevitable, or fixed but merely the product of the particular society in which we live'.[36] The link between human knowledge, values, and the nature of truth becomes an operational pedagogical principle within this approach. One qualification must be made here. Teaching students critical conceptual categories that help them to confront their own unexamined and implicit views of the world should not be reduced to a mere celebration of subjectivity, i.e., 'you have your views and I have mine'. The latter is a form of 'bad subjectivity' and can be avoided by teaching students to challenge and test the relationship between what they know and reality as it objectively exists. The world does not necessarily correspond to the way people view it. Not to understand this is to ignore the importance and meaning of false consciousness and to end up supporting a mystifying form of cultural relativism. Students must be taught to look beyond the immediate, they must learn how to test the truth claims inherent in any interpretation, including their own.

It is my hope that this chapter has demonstrated successfully the need for curriculum theorists and other educators to reexamine the most basic assumptions and values that guide their work. It has provided a rationale and some suggestions for using the concept of the dialectic as a step towards the process of renewal and self-criticism in our field. If the spirit of critique and social commitment is to be kept alive in the curriculum field, we are going to have to work hard to sustain such a tradition. This suggests not just developing new conceptual models through which to view our work, more importantly it means committing ourselves to a notion of truth and justice that makes our view of what we do and who we are meaningful.

### Notes and References

1 BENJAMIN, W. (1969) 'Theses on the philosophy of history' in *Illuminations* New York, Schocken, p. 255.
2 CORNFORTH, M. (1962) *Historical Materialism* New York, International Publishers. The classic example is STALIN, J. (1939) 'Dialectical and historical materialism' *History of the Communist Party of the Soviet Union* New York, International Publishers. For an insightful analysis of Stalin's purging of the dialectic, see MARCUSE, H. (1961) *Soviet Marxism* New York, Vantage Books. Two interesting general critiques of the orthodox Marxist positions can be found in ALBERT, M. and HAHNEL, R. (1978) *Unorthodox Marxism* Boston, South End Press; MILLER, J. (1979) *History and Human Existence: From Marx to Merleau-Ponty* Berkeley, University of California Press.
3 SHERMAN, H. (1976) 'Dialectics as method' *The Insurgent Sociologist* 3, Summer, p. 62.
4 FREIBERG, T.W. (1979) 'Critical social theory in the American conjuncture' in *Critical Sociology* New York, Halstead Press, pp. 1–21.
5 MARCUSE, H. (1976) 'On the problem of the dialectic' *Telos* 27, Spring, pp. 12–39. MERLEAU-PONTY, M. (1973) *On the Adventures of the Dialectic* (trans. Joseph Bien) Evanston, Northwestern University Press. ADORNO, T.W. (1973) *Negative Dialectics* New York, Seabury Press.
6 MARCUSE, H. (1976) *op. cit.*, p. 22.
7 KOSIK, K. (1976) *Dialectics of the Concrete* Boston and Dardrecht, Holland, D. Reidel Publishing Co.
8 ADORNO, T.W. (1977) 'Goldman and Adorno: To describe, understand and explain' in GOLDMAN, L. (Ed.) *Cultural Creation in Modern Society* (trans. Bart Grahl) St. Louis, Telos Press, pp. 130–131.
9 FREIBERG, T.W. (1979) *op. cit.*, pp. 7–8. See also BERNSTEIN, R. (1976) *The Reconstruction of Social and Political Theory* Philadelphia, University of Pennsylvania Press, pp. ix–54.
10 MARCUSE, H. (1970) *Reason and Revolution* Boston, Beacon Press, p. ix.
11 KOSIK, K. (1976) *op. cit.*, p. 2.

12 DALLMARY, F. and McCARTHY, T.A. (1977) 'Introduction: The positivist reception' in *Undestanding and Social Inquiry* Notre Dame, University of Notre Dame Press, pp. 77–78. See also ADORNO, T.W., ALBERT, H., DAHRENDORF, R., HABERMAS, J., PILOT, H. and POPPER, K. (1976) *The Positivist Dispute in German Sociology* London, Heinemann Educational Books.

13 FREIRE, P. (1973) *Pedagogy of the Oppresed* New York, Seabury Press, p. 125.

14 GIROUX, H.A. See Chapter One.

15 MARCUSE, H. (1964) *One Dimensional Man* Boston, Beacon Press, p. 204.

16 MARCUSE, H. (1976) *op. cit.*, pp. 20–21.

17 OLLMAN, B. (1976) 'On teaching Marxism' *The Insurgent Sociologist* Summer, p. 42.

18 KOSIK, K. (1976) *op. cit.*, p. 7.

19 APPLE, M.W. (1979) *Ideology and Curriculum* Boston and London, Routledge and Kegan Paul, pp. 17–18.

20 KOSIK, K. (1976) *op. cit.*, p. 19.

21 WILLIAMS, R. (1977) *Marxism and Literature* London, Oxford University Press, p. 98.

22 LUKACS, G. (1968) *History and Clas Consciousness* Cambridge, Mass. MIT Press.

23 WILLIS, P. (1977) *Learning to Labour: How Working-class Kids get Working-class Jobs* Lexington, Mass., Lexington Books.

24 GIROUX, H.A. See Chapter Five.

25 ANYON, J. (1979) 'United States history textbooks and ideology: A study of curriculum content and social interest' *Harvard Educational Review* and (1979) 'Education, social "structure" and the power of individuals' *Theory and Research in Social Education* Vol. 7, No. 1, pp. 49–59. GIROUX, H.A. and PENNA, A.N. (1979) 'Social education in the classroom: The dynamics of the hidden curriculum' *Theory and Research in Social Education* Vol. 7, No. 1, Spring, pp. 21–42.

26 MARCUSE, H. (1978) *The Aesthetic Dimension* Boston, Beacon Press, p. 9.

27 FREIRE, P. (1973) *op. cit.*, p. 33.

28 HELLER, A. (1975) *The Theory of Need in Marx* London, Allison and Busby, p. 95.

29 JACOBY, R. (1975) *Social Amnesia* Boston, Beacon Books, p. 61.

30 MARCUSE, H. (1972) *Counterrevolution and Revolt* Boston, Beacon Books, pp. 27–28.

31 This list is far from inclusive: See the collection of writings in PINAR, W.F. (1975) (Ed.) *Curriculum Theorizing* Berkeley, McCutchen; PINAR, W.F. and GRUMET, M. (1976) *Toward a Poor Curriculum* Dubuque, Kendell/Hunt; GREENE, M. (1978) *Landscapes of Learning* New York, Teachers College Press; KARABEL, J. and HALSEY, A.H. (1977) (Eds.) *Power and Ideology in Education* New York, Oxford University Press; APPLE, M.W. (1979) *op. cit.*; WILLIS, P. (1977) *op. cit.*

32 GIROUX, H.A. (1978) 'Writing and critical thinking in the social studies' *Curriculum Inquiry* Vol. 8, No. 4. pp. 291–310.

33 GREENE, M. (1975) Curriculum and consciousness' in PINAR, W.F. (1975) *op. cit.*, p. 304.

34 PINAR, W.F. (1975) 'Currere: Toward reconceptualization' in PINAR, W.F. (1975) *op. cit.*, pp. 396–414.

35 ELSHTAIN, J.B. (1976) 'The social relations of the classroom: A moral and political perspective' *Telos* 27, Spring, p. 108.

36 DOLBEARE, K. (1976) 'Alternatives to the new fascism' *The Massachusetts Review* Vol. 17, No. 1, Spring, p. 77.

# 5 Paulo Freire's Approach to Radical Educational Theory and Practice*

As I explained in Chapter Two, radical pedagogy in North America appears to be suffering from a kind of schizophrenia. Caught between the imperatives of radical content and radical classroom social relationships, radical educators in general have settled for one at the expense of the other. The result has been illegitimate forms of pedagogy that bear little resemblance to the radical label under which they parade. Lost in such approaches is a critical awareness of how sociology and psychology, process and content, as well as knowledge and human action merge to form the dialectical dynamic at the heart of what constitutes radical pedagogy.[1]

As I pointed out in Chapter Two, we are often treated to truncated notions of radical pedagogy which end up celebrating one-sided and ideologically frozen dimensions of the educational experience. On the one hand, radical educators treat us to a potpourri of encounter group happenings and process-based interpersonal activities designed to enrich our existential selves with moments of collective warmth and cheery solidarity. Removed from the necessity of a critical mode of reasoning through which to mediate these classroom social relations, educators who support this perspective appear to be practicing a form of depthless psychology rather than a form of radical praxis.[2] Within this perspective, the social mechanisms that generated the need for a radical pedagogy in the first place get lost amidst a sterile celebration of feelings and self.

On the other side stand those radical educators who are staunch defenders of what might be termed 'liberating' content. Appearing less in the guise of Karl Marx than Jerome Bruner, this group either ignores classroom social relations altogether or plays down their importance. This version of radical pedagogy becomes enshrined in the forms of information, issues, and alternative world views designd to break through the ideological encrustations that hold the 'oppressed' in a helpless state of political ignorance. Missing here is the insight that ruling-class domination rests on something other than ideology and false

* This is an edited version of an article which first appeared in *Curriculum Inquiry* Vol. 9, No. 3 (Fall 1979). Copyright © by The Ontario Institute for Studies in Education. Reprinted by permission of John Wiley and Sons, Inc.

consciousness. What cannot be explained by this perspective is how domination reaches into the inner recesses of the psyche; or as Christopher Lasch put it, 'how this internalization of authority reconciles the lowly man to the "idea of a necessary domination of some men over others . . ."'.[3] Liberation under such circumstances becomes synonomous with entrance into a privileged epistemology, free from the constraints of ideology, repression, and false consciousness. In one sense, this version of radical pedagogy reduces the 'oppressed' to the status of victims patiently waiting to be saved from an ignorant schoolmaster.[4]

Absent from both of these perspectives is a critical understanding of the complex interplay that exists between pedagogy, ideology, and social change. Neither view has developed a theory of liberation that could provide a foundation for educational theory and practice in the most radical sense. Instead, each of these views support forms of pedagogy that are both reductionistic and incomplete. More specifically, both forms of pedagogy end up objectifying and in some cases depoliticizing, though in different ways, the very people they intend to liberate. It is only recently that these versions have been challenged and criticized.[5]

Paulo Freire, the Brazilian educator in exile, now working with the World Council of Churches in Geneva, stands out as an educator who has helped to bridge and bypass those unnecessarily dichotomized strands of pedagogy that characterize much of what passes as radical education in North America. Working with the oppressed in Brazil and Africa, Freire has forged a pedagogy that, in the best tradition of radical praxis, unites theory and practice; moreover, Freire himself represents a concrete embodiment of his own call for such a unity. Freire is, of course, not unknown in North America. Since his exile from Brazil in 1964 and the publication in English of *Pedagogy of the Oppressed* and *Education for Critical Consciousness,* Freire has become something of a cult-hero among a minority of North American liberals and radicals. But like other major thinkers, his reputation has not always been followed by a clear understanding or rightful application of his ideas. One reason might be the difficulty of Freire's writing style, which some critics claim is not only abstruse, but also at odds with his claim to a demythologizing humanism.[6] Anti-intellectualism aside, a more arguable reason is that Freire's pedagogy has been developed and used in Third World countries that bear little resemblance to the advanced industrial countries of the West. This point is defensible only if one attempts to impose Freire's methodology like a grid upon a vastly different, socio-political cultural experience. Moreover, the criticism appears less as an indictment of Freire's pedagogy than of those educators who unknowingly follow in the positivist tradition of elevating 'methodology' to the status of a truth.

This should not imply that Freire's pedagogy is without its flaws, or that its core assumptions are readily adaptable for use in countries far removed from sociopolitical conditions that generated it in the first place. There can be little question that his pedagogy has its share of over-simplifications and theoretical sloppiness, which will be examined in the last section of this chapter. But more importantly, it contains several concepts and theoretical insights that provide the fundamental building blocks for a radical pedagogy applicable to the North American experience.

Freire's theoretical roots bear little resemblance to those of his colleagues in North America. Instead of relying heavily upon the positivist tradition that pervades the social sciences in North America he has developed his educational theory and practice from a variety of radical sources drawn from history, philosophy, sociology, phenomenology, existentialism, and Neo-Marxism.[7] Freire is deeply indebted to Marx, Husserl, Buber and Sartre, among others, for his intellectual heritage. At the center of his pedagogy is a dialectical understanding of the connections between school and the larger universe of socio-political meanings and beliefs that legitimates the dominant society. Fortunately, Freire is not a structuralist with the intent of propping up a functional sociology and barren form of pedagogical behaviorism that denies subjectivity and *Verstehen*. Instead, he acknowledges the false ideological distinctions between public and private and searches for the objective forces that shape the individual and collective consciousness of the oppressed. Freire is well aware of the political implications of Russell Jacoby's claim that we not only live in society but society also lives in us.[8] Capitalizing upon Marx's critique of ideology and Freud's psychoanalytical model, Freire attempts to examine the nature of domination within specific socio-historical conditions. He is well aware that individual and collective consciousness can constitute either a domesticated force that acquiesces in the face of political domination or an emancipatory force engaged in the shaping of hisory. Freire rejects the notion that domination is an exclusively private affair and looks at the multifaceted ways in which schooling functions to structure and shape the subjective perceptions and identities of the oppressed.

In essence all pedagogy, according to him, is essentially a political issue and all educational theories are political theories. Inherent in any educational design are value assumptions and choices about the nature of humankind, the use of authority, the value of specific forms of knowledge and, finally, a vision of what constitutes the good life. Freire's work represents a critical attempt to illustrate how ideologies of various means and persuasions reflect, distort, and prevent men and women from becoming socio-political actors in the struggle against an oppressive society. Thus, to understand his pedagogy one must begin with a recognition that it is both a call for liberation and an ongoing process of radical reconstruction. All of his major themes follow from this premise.


## Culture and Schooling

Freire never tires of insisting that schooling is not neutral. In fact, he points out that the proclaimed 'neutrality' of schooling is in itself nothing less than a mystification, a convenient ideology that hides the political function of schooling. Fortunately, Freire does not cling to the type of wooden analysis echoed by various mechanistic Marxists who see the school as a mere transmission belt that simply 'processes' students into the alienating realms of leisure and work. Freire rejects this 'oversocialized' and deterministic model of pedagogy and views the process of schooling in more complex terms. Thus, he not only helps us to focus on schooling as a process designed to reproduce and legitimate the prevailing, dominant consciousness in the existing culture, he also points to the contradictions and problems that accompany that process. Moreover, Freire supports the view that meaning can be constructed by actors whose perceptions do not always conform to the perceptions of the oppressed.

Like Pierre Bourdieu in France, Freire sees culture as doing more than passing on the heritage of a given country.[9] For Freire, culture is not an all-embracing neutral category of social science. Instead, it is a 'dependent but nevertheless special sphere within the social process as a whole',[10] and its function is political in essence. The *dominant* culture functions to legitimize existing modes of social relations and production. It also functions to provide the motivational structures that link individual needs with social needs and, finally, culture provides a society with the symbolic language for intepreting the boundaries of individual and social existence.[11] The connection between culture and education is a crucial theme in Freire's work and represents a powerful critique of the positivist approach to schooling that prevails in the United States, particularly as a result of the long-standing influence of what William F. Pinar has called the strict practitioners and the conceptual-empiricists in the curriculum field.[12]

Only by viewing schooling as a semi-successful agency of legitimation within the context of larger socio-economic forces can one begin to understand the source of the problems and contradictions that in large part plague the schools. The prevailing forms of knowledge, values, social relationships and forms of evaluation that are used in schools do not exist in precious isolation from the larger society. They are linked, for the most part, either directly or indirectly to the prevailing cultural hegemony and dominant economic arrangements. This relationship between culture and politics leads to another theme in Freire's work that is useful to radical educators in the West: Freire's theory of knowledge, particularly its relationship to the concepts of domination and emancipation.

### Theory of Knowledge

If Freire believes that schooling is to be grounded in political and ideological choices, liberation then becomes more than a matter of technique, (i.e., providing people with a few skills). What is at stake in Freire's notion of liberation is that people should be able to generate their own meanings and frame of reference and be able to develop their self-determining powers through their ability to perform a critical reading of reality so that they can act on that reality. He makes this clear when talking about the assumptions behind the literacy campaign he inaugurated in Guinea–Bissau:

> The act of learning to read and write, in this instance, is a creative act that involves a critical comprehension of reality. The knowledge of earlier knowledge, gained by the learners as a result of analyzing praxis in its social context opens to them the possibility of new knowledge. The new

knowledge going far beyond the limits of earlier knowledge, reveals the reason for being behind the facts, thus demythologizing the false interpretations of these same facts. And so, there is now no more separation between thought-language and objective reality. The reading of a text now demands a 'reading' within the social context to which it refers.[13]

Knowledge, according to Freire, is not neutral; it should be regarded not as the acquisition of a body of information, but as the result of a human activity situated in human norms and interests. Similarly, just as there is a distribution of economic capital in society, there is also a distribution of cultural capital, of which knowledge is a crucial part. What is at stake here is to recognize that the act of knowing is more than a technical issue, it is, in part a political issue. Knowing is not a matter of the best way to learn a *given* body of knowledge, but a theoretical-practical issue designed to distinguish between essence and appearance, truth and falsity. Knowledge parading under the guise of objectivity, has for too long been used to legitimate belief and value systems that are at the core of bondage. 'Objective' knowledge not only mystifies, but it also turns people into spectators by removing the norms, values and interests underlying it from public debate. Reality, for Freire, is something other than that which is codified in the established language and 'facts'. Liberation begins with the recognition that knowledge, at its root, is ideological and political, inextricably tied to human interests and norms. The latter is not a call for a Cartesian notion of the truth, one that denies the truth claims of the objective world. Instead, the correlation between knowledge and human interest should be viewed as the theoretical foundation or beginning for going beyond what Nietzsche has called the dogma of the immaculate perception. At the core of Freire's notion of knowledge is a recognition of the dialectical interconnections between the doer, the receiver, and the objective world itself. Knowledge is seen as an active force that is used by the learner to make sense of his 'life-world'. Herbert Marcuse captures this dialectical dynamic in his statement:

> Dialectical thought invalidates the *a priori* opposition of value and fact by understanding all facts as stages of a single process – a process in which subject-object are so joined that truth can be determiend only within the subject-object totality. All facts embody the knower as well as the doer; they continuously translate the past into the present. The objects thus contain subjectivity in their very structure.[14]

Within Freire's model, knowledge becomes a liberating tool only when it can be released from reifying social and political relationships. Knowledge, in this case, is more than a social construct, it also represents the basis for social action. A radical conception of knowledge does not rest simply on the ability to demystify the ideological hegemony of the dominant order. That is important, but incomplete. A radical conception of knowledge also rests on how well it can be used by the oppressed themselves to question the very processes used to constitute and legitimate knowledge and experience in the first place. Divorcing knowledge from the processes that constitute it, represents not only a crude pedagogical simplification, but a reactionary political act that in the final analysis maintains a division of labor that prevents radical educational praxis. Freire's concept of knowledge as a liberating tool easily speaks to a number of ways in which such a concept could be employed to enrich radical educational theory and practice in the West. A specific analysis of those elements of Freire's theory of knowledge that seem valuable for use in advanced industrial countries will be touched upon in the following brief analysis.

At the core of the act of knowing is both a questioning attitude and a specific set of social relationships. On one level, knowing demands understanding 'dialectically . . . the different forms in which human beings know their relations with the world . . . knowing demands the curious presence of subjects confronted with the world'.[15] On another level, knowing means looking at knowledge from a perspective that enables men and women to transcend the realms of intellectual habit and common sense. Only then can the oppressed recognize the ideological distortions that influence and shape their understanding of social and political reality. In the phenomenological sense, Freire urges that radical educators learn to 'bracket' and make problematic the knowledge they present to their students. Thus, every effort must be made to avoid forms of pedagogy and knowledge that provide a mechanistic and deterministic view of the world. In a more specific sense, this suggests that all educational experience begin with questions concerning the meaning and nature of knowledge itself. For example, as previously mentioned, the relationship between knowledge and ideology could be pursued through such questions as: 'whose reality is being legitimated with this knowledge?'; 'why this knowledge in the first place?'; 'whose interests does this knowledge represent?'; 'why is it being taught this way?'; 'does this knowledge have meaning for the learner?' and 'is this knowledge part of the learner's cultural capital?'.[16]

Freire goes futher than arguing that educators must constantly discover and rediscover ways to help the learner view knowledge as problematic. Any radical theory of knowledge must also give equal emphasis to the processes by which we learn to know, the methods by which we constitute meaning. Like Ludwig Wittgenstein, he is convinced that how we come to know presupposes intersubjective agreements and standards and that knowing is shaped and influenced by specific forms of intentionality and intersubjective norms which cannot be separated neatly from social relations.[17] Freire focuses on the essence of the issue with his claim that 'the knowledge of how to define what needs to be known cannot be separated from the why of knowing . . . the practice of thinking about practice is the best way to think correctly'.[18] If Freire is right, and I think he is, we need as educators to develop a pedagogy designed not only to help students generate their own meanings, but also to help them reflect on the process of thinking itself. Questions that teach students how specific structures of thought are both used and embodied in particular types of world views, ideologies, and experiences must be translated into viable pedagogical practices. Because it is then that students will be able to use knowledge as part of a self-determining process that helps them to distinguish false from true knowledge claims.

Another component of Freire's theory of knowledge centers around his view of knowledge as fundamentally linked to the question of social relationships. As a social construct, knowledge has to be defined through the social mediations and roles that provide the context for its meaning and its mode of distribution. This is a central concept in Freire's pedagogy. Knowledge becomes the *mediator* of communication and dialogue among learners. Needless to say, for Freire this means that the mediation of knowledge demands classroom social relationships radically different from the top-to-bottom models of socialization that characterize traditional modes of schooling. In other words, the critical pursuit of knowledge has to be paralleled by a quest for mutual humanization among those engaged in such a pursuit. Unlike 'banking education' that inhibits creativity and domesticates students, a radical pedagogy requires non-authoritarian social relationships that support dialogue and communication as indispensible for questioning the meaning and nature of knowledge and peeling away the hidden structures of reality.[19]

### Theory of Domination

While Freire does not provide a theory of domination that explores class-rule and exploitation in all of its manifestations, he does provide a useful analysis of how the mechanics of domination operate within pedagogical settings. Though he used broad theoretical sweeps to illustrate his position, he does manage to focus on traditional forms of pedagogical theory and practice that have remained unexamined for too long. For Freire, domination is the prevailing theme for most of mankind. Like the Italian social theorist, Antonio Gramsci, Freire pays less attention to the use of force as the basis of ruling-class domination than he does to the question of how the loyalty and obedience of a population is maintained primarily through ideological means.[20] According to Freire, it is the cultural institutions of the dominant elite that play a major role in inculcating the oppressed with myths and beliefs that later become anchored in their psyches and character structure. To the degree that repressive institutions are successful in universalizing the belief system of the oppressor class, people will consent to their own exploitation and powerlessness. This should not suggest that Freire is either a reductionist or a fatalist. The engine of ideological repression does not run, in Freire's analysis, so smoothly or a successfully as some other social theorists have suggested.[21] There are contradictions that help the oppressed see through the transparent claims and norms of the given social order, particularly in Third World nations. Moreover, there is hope, and the basis for a radical vision embedded in the objective fact of oppression and alienation itself. Domination evokes its opposite. Yet there is no guarantee that the structures of domination will automatically produce revolutionaries. But there is hope that a change in individual and collective consciousness within radical educational structures will provide the subjective preconditions for the basis for radical struggle.

Freire provides a useful insight in his recognition that the passivity of the oppressed, i.e., students, is social and deliberate. The objective conditions of oppression, economic and political impoverishment, only provide part of the answer in understanding the constitutive nature of oppression. Freire believes that a more fruitful answer to the 'culture of silence' that characterizes the oppressed can be found in analyzing the subjective basis of oppression. But domination for Freire is not to be found in *either* the subjective realm *or* the objective conditions of oppression, limited either to the realm of consciousness or the realm of material exploitation. Instead, domination is rooted in a subjective-objective dialectic. The point of interest in that dialectic, for Freire, is how objective socio-political forces shape one's subjectivity. This perspective can best be illuminated in the form of the following question: 'What are the objective forces that shape our consciousness and character in the interest of the oppressor?'. The answer to this question underlies Freire's starting point for working with the oppressed in understanding and changing the socio-political reality in which they live.

Within traditional pedagogical practices, Freire identifies modes and structures of domination that function to reproduce those divisions between work and play, mental and manual labor, and theory and practice that appear to reinforce the powerlessness of students. The content, pedagogical styles, and forms of evaluation within the educational setting all function, in part, as message systems to distribute and reinforce the self-depreciation, fatalism, and misdirected violence characteristic of the oppressed. As a result, domination is often met with passivity, confusion, and socially diverted anger. Freire clarifies this with his comment that, 'the more completely they accept the passive role imposed upon them, the more they tend to adapt to the world as it is and to the fragmented view of reality deposited in them'.[22]

What emerges from Freire's notion of domination is a set of pedagogical practices designed to overcome the oppressive conditions in which students find themselves. He places a heavy emphasis in his design for liberation on what he terms dialogical communication. Dialogical communication represents developing pedagogical structures in which dialogue and analysis serve as the basis for individual and collective possibilities for reflection and action. In this way the oppressed:

> . . . see and analyze their own way of being in the world of their immediate daily life, including the life of their villages, and when they can perceive the rationale for the factors on which their daily life is based, they are enabled to go far beyond the narrow horizons of their own village and of the geographical area in which it is located, to gain a global perspective on the world.[23]

Dialogical communication, in this case, is both a theoretical and strategic concept for political action. In Freire's previous works, the concept was heavily indebted to how radical educators could use the cultural capital, the language and life style of the oppressed, in an effort to promote among them an interest and critical reading of reality on both the local and larger levels. Educators who ignored the cultural capital of the oppressed practiced cultural invasion. Freire clearly understood and explained the concept of cultural invasion and warned strongly against using the methods of the oppressor to teach the oppressed. For instance, in quoting Amilcar Cabral, Freire stressed that, if the 're-Africanization of mentality' is to take place, radicals would have to begin with the 'concrete reality of the learners and their own experience in this reality'.[24] Accordingly, it was only under such circumstances that the creative power of the people would emerge with the guidance rather than domination of radical teachers and leaders. He suggests that the reasons for the educational failures of minorities of class and color is not to be found outside but inside the institutionalized nature of schooling. As mentioned in previous chapters, schools generate the cultural capital of the upper classes and in doing so 'teach' the dominated classes to devalue their own culture.[25] While we are often told that the educational system does this, we are rarely offered an in-depth explanation of how it is done. Freire helps to fill this gap for English speaking audiences.

Freire emphasizes the need for radical educators to develop both content and methodologies that are consistent with a progressive political stance. In *Pedagogy in Process,* his latest book, he enriches this perspective by providing an amplified picture of what political views, processes, and organizational structures were necessary for the liberation of the oppressed. In writing about his experiences in Guinea–Bissau, he spells out in concrete terms what forces had to be overcome before the oppressed could translate dialogical communication into political action. This was the most positive moment in Freire's history since 1964, for it forced him to speak, though in general terms, to those contradictions in the socioeconomic realm that had to be overcome before radical pedagogy could be transformed into action. Freire has often talked about 'limit-situations' that radicals must overcome but he has not spelled out, in a specific or compelling way, that these socio-economic situations might look like or what kind of response they would necessitate.

Freire's most recent work might cost him his liberal supporters. His attack on the division of labor between work and schooling calls for radical reconstruction and not liberal rhetoric. Thus, his newly stated radical position crosses over the line of compromising liberal politics. But in the end, Freire's stronger political stance and theoretical incisiveness give those who support his work a clearer perspective on the political assumptions and values behind his pedagogy. With the publication of *Pedagogy in Process,* it will be difficult to misinterpret the political assumptions behind Freire's theory and practice. Critics and detractors have either seen Freire as hopelessly lost in dehistoricized utopian categories or have considered and used his concepts such as 'conscientization' as a neutral, multi-functional pedagogical device.[26] Freire's exposition of his work in Guinea–Bissau clearly demonstrates the true nature of conscientization: learning through reflection and action to overcome the social, economic and political contradictions of an oppressive reality.

Freire's work can be useful to educators in North America in a number of distinct ways. It not only serves to politicize the notion of schooling, but reveals the normative and ideological underpinnings that exist at the various levels of the classroom encounter. In addition, Freire extends the notion of radical educational praxis by exposing those facets of the 'hidden curriculum' that exist in both the selection and distribution of knowledge as well as in the use of pedagogical styles designed to transmit that knowledge. Moreover, his work reinforces the necessity of understanding the cultural capital of the oppressed and analyzing its treatment within the dominant culture, particularly the way in which the schooling process serves to legitimate the cultural hegemony of the dominant class. In many respects, Freire's pedagogy provides concrete examples of how the work of theorists such as Basil Bernstein and Pierre Bourdieu can serve radical purposes within historically determined and culturally shaped pedagogical situations. William Pinar has recently claimed that it is imperative that the curriculum field in the United States shift its 'attention from the technical and practical, and dwell on the notion of emancipation'.[27]

Though Friere provides the broad theoretical framework needed to help bridge some of the gaps that plague radical education in North America, his analysis in key places warrants further substantiation and depth. In the section that remains, I will provide a brief critique of some of these areas and point to other sources that might be useful in supplementing Freire's work, thus making it more adaptable and useful for educators.

It is indeed one of Freire's strengths that he addresses educational issues as political ones, particuarly in his strong emphasis on the relationship between schooling and the dominant culture. For him, the fact of domination in Third World nations, as well as the substantive nature of that domination, is realtively clear. Consequently, his analysis of the socio-political conditions of domination are confined to both an acknowledgment and a strong rhetorical indictment. While such a stance may be justifiable for Third World radicals who need spend little time documenting and exposing the objective conditions of domination for the oppressed, the situation is vastly different in North America. The conditions of domination are not only different in the advanced industrial countries of the West, but they are also much less obvious, and in some cases, one could say more pervasive and powerful. Even Freire appears to have misconstrued the extent and nature of the ideological hegemony that exists in North America, particularly in the United States. For instance, while visiting the United States in the early seventies, Freire claimed:

> this is one of the most alienated of all countries. People know they are exploited and dominated, but they feel incapable of breaking down the dehumanized wall.[28]

The alienation, exploitation, and domination to which Freire refers is certainly an objective fact, but it is far from a subjective perception recognized by most Americans. Not only the content and nature of domination need to be documented in this case, but the very *fact* of domination has to be proven to most Americans. In North America, technology and science have been developed so as to create immeasurably greater conditions for the administration and manipulation of individuals. Jurgen Habermas has made this point succinctly:

> The quasi-autonomous progress of science and technology then appears as an independent variable on which the most important single system variable, namely economic growth, depends. Thus arises a perspective in which the development of the social system seems to be determined by the logic of scientific-technical progress. The immanent law of this progress seems to produce objective exigencies, which must be obeyed by any politics oriented toward functional needs . . . It is a singular achievement of this ideology to detach society's self-understanding from the frame of reference of communicative action and from the concepts of symbolic interaction and replace it with a scientific model. Accordingly, the culturally defined self-understanding of a social life-world is replaced by the self-reification of men under categories of purposive-rational action and adaptive behavior . . . The manifest domination of the authoritarian state gives way to the manipulative compulsions of technical-operational administration.[29]

Any radical pedagogy would have to examine closely how the forces of science and technology in North America are used to conceal class-specific interests, value systems, and the nature of domination. Moreover, such an analysis would have to reveal the historical genesis of these forces as new forms of legitimation and make clear how they have been applied within schools to obscure the political interests that they serve.

Given this criticism, it is imperative that Freire's notion of ideology and socialization be both qualified and enlarged for use by Western educators. With respect to the notion of ideology, Freire is not clear about whether he supports a definition of ideology derived from Marx, in which ideology is seen as a distortion of reality, or if he supports a view of ideology similar to one articulated, in different ways, by Louis Althusser and Alvin Gouldner. Althusser and Gouldner do not view ideology as an aberration that will disappear in a socialist society, but rather as a constitutive medium, different in degrees, in all societies.[30] The distinction is subtle but crucial enough to be qualified. If Freire is suggesting that the 'end of ideology' will come with a classless society, then he may be unwittingly supporting a version of the very positivism he insists on criticizing, i.e., ideology in this case is replaced by 'science' with its concomitant claim to absolute truth.

While Freire spends some time in providing a substantive description of the ideologies he criticizes as well as an analysis of the material and psychological forces that sustain them, he fails to provide a clear analysis of the historical forms of political and social life that produced them. Freire, like many phenomenologists and Marxists before him, performs a theoretical service in helping us to 'bracket' the social and political meanings that tacitly structure educational encounters. But if we are going to be able to understand the relationship that exists between the dominant and minority cultures, particularly as that relationship manifests itself in schools, we must explore the dominant culture so as 'to lay bare the complex relationship between knowledge and power';[31] the strength of such an analysis rests with its ability to explore the political nature of what has come to count as school knowledge both in terms of its contemporary usage and its historical development. Moreover, it is not enough to raise questions about the interests that certain types of knowledge or ideologies serve; the real question is what type of compulsions maintain the false claims that these ideologies attempt to hide from public view.[32]

Another aspect of Freire's work that warrants criticism is his notion of dialogical communication. Missing from his perspective on reflexive discourse is an analysis of how *historically* changing socio-economic conditions have placed specific limits on the connections between emancipatory discourse and action consistent with that discourse. In other words, the relationship between communication and action in Freire's pedagogy is not always clear. What are the objective and subjective forces of resistance that prevent the transition from radical communication to radical action? Freire touches on this issue most directly in *Pedagogy of the Oppressed* but the analysis is too general. Even more important, how will the oppressed evaluate their teachers if both the limits and possibilities for generating and implementing radical discourse cannot be measured against a set of socially defined norms which define the conditions that support non-repressive communication and public discourse?

Implicit in all pedagogy is a vision of society. In Freire's pedagogy, dialogical relationships and reflexive discourse play a central part. But what Freire fails to do is to make clear that modes of communication which are free from domination only become meaningful when measured against socio-political arrangements next to which *all* institutions and social relationships in the larger society must be measured. By doing this, Freire ends up with a pedagogical model for communication that appears abstracted from institutionalized discourse and social relations in a larger society. Thus it appears that Freire truncates the power of his own pedagogy by limiting its application to specific pedagogical contexts.

The political nature of language is revealed in its use to structure and shape the communicative process. Similarly, the political function of language is revealed in its role as an integrating or differentiating factor that mediates one's understanding of reality. Claus Mueller states this position clearly. 'The symbolic and conceptual interpretations embedded in . . . acquired language become a mediating factor that shapes one's view of the environment';[33] He further clarified the political function of language by pointing out that 'it is an important factor which is determined, not only by the social context of a society but by political institutions and interests as well . . . both socially restricted language and politically manipulated language can function as agents promoting the stability . . . of a political order'.[34]

In political terms, this means that the basis for effective communication cannot be reduced to an analysis of the structural mechanisms and linguistic competencies at work within specific pedagogical contexts. As mentioned above, larger political interests and institutions play a multi-faceted role in restricting and influencing communication. What is needed as a supplement to Freire's notion of dialogical communication is a broader critique and elucidation of the concepts of distorted and non-distorted communication. One such attempt has been made by Jurgen

Habermas who believes emancipation is inextricably linked to making 'un-distorted communication' the basis for the development and critique of all forms of social organization.[35] Such a task demands at its outset an analysis of how historically changing ideology, forces of production, and forms of political authority have limited the conditions for spirited and non-distorted communicative interaction. Constraints on communication could then be explored in the following terms suggested by Dieter Misgeld:

> (1) conditions of economic scarcity; (2) conditions of social and political inequality (to be examined with reference to the presence or absence of conditions of economic scarcity and its magnitude and quality); and (3) psychologically operative repressions such as the censoring of need interpretations, dependent of variations of the first two points.[36]

An understanding of these constraints provides the foundation for the development of norms guided by emancipatory interests, norms that can become the theoretical building blocks for *a priori* elements of an ideal speech situation capable of functioning as a social ideal. Once again, the peculiar character of such an ideal speech situation can be grasped in Freire's insistence that liberation begins with the recognition that in a free society there is no room for manipulation, cultural invasion, conquest, and domination; and that there can be only participants and subjects in the shaping of a liberated society.[37] Both Freire and Habermas speak of the dialogue that ought to be rather than the dialogue that is. The radical insight here is that the conditions that make such a dialogue possible lie at the heart of a social order and not just at the core of a pedagogical encounter.[38]

It would be misleading as well as dangerous to extend without qualification Freire's theory and methods to the industrialized and urbanized societies of the West. But to acknowledge this should not suggest dismissing Freire's work outright. Instead, if one looks closely at Freire's efforts I think one will find specific themes and practices that will help to enrich and broaden radical pedagogy in North America. Freire's work demonstrates that the dynamic of progressive change stems, in part, from working *with* people rather than *on* them. It is in the latter spirit of respect for human struggle and hope, that an emancipatory pedagogy can be forged, one in which radical educators can consolidate and use the insights of Freire within the context of our own historical experience in order to give new shape to the meaning of radical praxis.

### Notes and References

1 This issue is more fully explored in Chapter 2 of this book.
2 See KOHL, H. (1969) *The Open Classroom* New York, Vintage Books; BREITBART, V. (1974) *The Day Care Book* New York, Knopf; NEIL, A.S. (1960) *Summerhill* New York, Hart; KOZOL, J. (1922) *Free Schools* Boston, Houghton Mifflin; For an excellent critique of this position, though done with a bit of overkill, see ELSHTAIN, J.B. (1976) 'The social relations of the clasroom: A moral and political perspective' *Telos* No. 27, Spring, pp. 97–110.
3 LASCH, C. (1978) *Haven in a Heartless World* New York, Basic Books, p. 87.

4 A radical justification for this approach can be found in GRAMSCI, A. (1971) 'On education' in *Selections from the Prison Notebooks,* (edited and translated by Quinten Hoare and Geoffrey Nowell Smith) New York, International Publishers, pp. 24–43. For one example of this approach see MEEROPOL, M. (1978) 'A radical teaching a straight principles of economics course', in *Studies in Socialist Pedagogy;* NORTON, T.M. and OLLMAN, B. New York, Monthly Review Press, pp. 131–145.

5 BERNSTEIN, B. (1977) *Class, Codes and Control Vol. 3* London, Routledge and Kegan Paul; CAGEN, E. (1978) 'Individualism, collectivism and radical educational reform', *Harvard Educational Review,* Vol. 48, No. 2, May, pp. 227–266; RAVITCH, D. (1978) *The Revisionists Revised: A Critique of the Radical Attack on the Schools* New York, Basic Books; GORELICK, S. (1977) 'Schooling problems in capitalist America' *Monthly review* October, pp. 20–36.

6 BOSTON, B.D. (1977) 'Paulo Freire: Notes of a loving critic' Geneva, World Council of Churches Publication, pp. 83–92.

7 For a concise overview of this tradition see BERNSTEIN, R.J. *The Restructuring of Social and Political Theory* New York, Harcourt Brace Jovanovitch, pp. 3–54.

8 JACOBY, R. (1975) *Social Amnesia* Boston, Beacon press.

9 BOURDIEU, P. and PASSERON, J.-C. (1977) *Reproduction in Education, Society and Culture* London, Sage Publications.

10 HORKHEIMER, M. (1972) 'Authority and the family' in *Critical Theory: Selected Essays* New York: Seabury Press, p. 59.

11 An excellent analysis of the political nature of culture can be found in DREITZEL, H.P. (1977) 'On the political meaning of culture' *Beyond the Crisis,* BIRNBAUM, N. (Ed.) New York, Oxford University Press, pp. 83–129.

12 PINAR, W.F. (1978) 'The reconceptualization of curriculum studies' *Journal of Curriculum Studies,* Vol. 10, No. 3, July–September, pp. 205–214.

13 FREIRE, P. (1978) *Pedagogy in Process: The Letters to Guinea-Bissau* New York, Seabury Press, p. 24.

14 MARCUSE, H. (1960) *Reason and Revolution* Boston, Beacon Press, p. viii.

15 FREIRE, P. (1978) *Education for Critical Consciousness* New York, Seabury Press, p. 101.

16 FREIRE, P. (1978) *op. cit.,* p. 101; See also YOUNG, F.D. (Ed.) *Knowledge and Control* London, Collier-Macmillan.

17 WITTGENSTEIN, L. (1953) *Philosophical Investigations* New York, Macmillan.

18 FREIRE, P. (1978) *op. cit.,* p. 102, 148.

19 FREIRE, P. (1973) *Pedagogy of the Oppressed* New York, Seabury Press.

20 For a clear explanation of Gramsci's notion of hegemony see BOGGS, C. (1976) *Gramsci's Marxism* London, Pluto Press, pp. 36–84.

21 MARCUSE, H. (1964) *One Dimensional Man* Boston, Beacon Press; For a critique of this position see PICCONE, P. (1978) 'The crisis of one dimensionality' *Telos,* No. 35, Spring, pp. 43–54. Also WILLIS, P. (1977) *Learning to Labour: How Working-Class Kinds Get Working-Class Jobs* Lexington, D.C., Heath; GORNICK, S. (1977) *op. cit.*

22 FREIRE, P. (1973) *op. cit.,* p. 60.

23 FREIRE, P. (1978) *op. cit.,* p. 57.

24 *ibid* p. 115.

25 BOURDIEU, P. and PASSERON, J.-P. *op. cit.,* passim.

26 NASAW, D. (1974) 'Reconsidering Freire', *Liberation* September/October, pp. 33–36. Also DE LEON, S. (1977) 'Radical approaches to literacy' *New York Times* May 1, p. 36. De Leon tells the story of how Consolidated Edison in New York adopted (?) Freire's notion of literacy and conscientizaco to teach 'skills' to the uneducated to they might beome 'employable and promotable'!!

27 PINAR, W.F. (1977) 'Notes on the Curriculum Field, 1978' Paper presented to the American Educational Research Association in New York in April 1977, p. 11. For a similar critique of the field in England see SARUP, M. (1978) *Marxism and Education* London, Routledge and Kegan Paul, pp. 51–67.

28 EGERTON, J. (1973) 'Searching for Freire' *Saturday Review of Education* April, p. 33.

29 HABERMAS, J. (1969) *Toward a Rational Society: Student Protest, Science and Politics* Boston, Beacon Press, pp. 105–107.

30 ALTHUSSER, L. (1970) *For Marx,* (trans. Ben Brewster) New York, Vintage Press, pp. 231–236; ALTHUSSER, L. (1971) *Lenin and Philosophy,* (trans. Ben Brewster) New York, Monthly Review Press, pp. 127–186; GOULDNER, A.W. (1976) *The Dialectic of Ideology and Technology* New York, Seabury Press.

31 SINBA, C. (1977) 'Class, language, and power' *Ideology and Consciousness* May, p. 91.

32 SCHROYER, T. (1973) *The Critique of Domination* Boston, Beacon Press. One important point here is that domination in the advanced industrial countries of the West transcends the conventional notion of ideology as a set of social cultural, and political ideas that are merely imposed on the oppressed. Of course, Freire recognizes this, but his analysis needs to be extended if it is to be used by radical educators in North America. Freire places a strong emphasis on demythologizing the world of the oppressed. But in the West, this must take a form consistent with a view of domination that is understood in the hegemonic sense, i.e., as a form of domiantion that is deeply felt, lived, and experienced at the level of everyday life. As Raymond Williams points out, hegemony must be seen as deeply saturating the consciousness of a given society. And any viable strategy designed to counter this mode of domination will have to recognize it as something totally embedded and reproduced in a wide range of social processes, the process of schooling representing only one agency of social control. What must be analyzed and studied then are the various ways in which different agencies of legitimation perform what Williams calls the process of incorporation; the issue here is that this analysis cannot be limited to schools. See WILLIAMS, R. (1973) 'Base and superstructure in Marxist cultural theory *New Left Review* Vol. 82 November/December, pp. 3–16.
33 MUELLER, C. (1973) *The Politics of Communication* New York, Oxford University Press, p. 15.
34 *ibid* p. 19.
35 WELLMER, A. (1976) 'Communications and emancipation' in *On Critical Theory* NEILL, J.O. (Ed.) New York, Seabury Press, p. 262.
36 MISGELD, D. (1975) 'Emancipation, enlightenment, and liberation: An approach toward foundational inquiry into education' *Interchange* Vol. 6, No. 3, p. 35.
37 FREIRE, P. (1973) *op. cit.,* pp. 3–31.
38 For an excellent summary and critique of Habermas' work see MCCARTHY, T. (1978) *The Critical Theory of Jurgen Habermas* Cambridge: The MIT Press, passim.

# 6  *Teacher Education and the Ideology of Social Control*[*1]

## Introduction

This chapter examines the relationship between teacher education and the ideology of social control. It does this by looking at the dialectical tension that exists between teacher-education programs and the dominant society through a set of concepts that link as well as demonstrate the interplay of power, ideology, biography, and history. It further illuminates this interplay by analyzing the rationality that presently dominates these programs. Finally, it not only examines the implications of this rationality for teacher-education programs, it also points to ways in which it can be overcome.

Teacher-education programs are caught in a deceptive paradox. Charged with the public responsibility to educate teachers to enable future generations to learn the knowledge and skills necessary to build a principled and democratic society, they represent a significant agency for the reproduction and legitimation of a society characterized by a high degree of social and economic inequality.[2] Unfortunately, the source of this paradox remains an enigma to most educators. In part, the 'hidden' meaning of the paradox can be explained by the ambiguous position that teacher-education programs occupy in this country. On the one hand they, along with the entire educational system, speak to a very real need on the part of all socio-economic classes to learn about and to transform the nature of their existence. On the other hand, schools and their various programs exist within a constellation of economic, social, and political institutions that make them fundamental part of the power structure.[3]

As public and private institutions, teacher-education programs and their respective schools of education provide the appearance of being neutral,[4] yet they operate within a social structure that disproportionately serves specific ruling interests.[5] Thus, teacher-education programs embody structural and ideological contradictions that are related to a larger social order caught in a conflict between the imperatives of its social welfare responsibilities and its functional allegiance to the

---

\* This chapter is a revised version of an article which first appeared in *The Journal of Education* Vol. 162, No. 1 (Winter 1980). Copyright © 1980 by the Trustees of Boston University.

conditions of capitalism. Such a posture testifies not only to the political nature of these programs, it also points to the necessity to unravel the multi-faceted ways in which they both serve and contradict the latent as opposed to the overt functions of the existing society.

It is within this political and economic framework that I want to examine the relationship between teacher education and the ideology of social control. I believe that the nature, function, and the possibility for reforming such programs can only be grasped through an analysis of ways in which power, ideology, biography, and history mediate between schools and the social and economic determinants of the dominant social order. Through such an analysis, I want to begin to lay the theoretical groundwork for a theory of ideological and material constraints. At the core of this theoretical scheme is an acknowledgment of the importance of the dialectical interplay between human consciousness and objective reality. There is also a further concern with institutional structures as representations of social relationships that are both shaped by and in turn shape human actions.

## Social and Cultural Reproduction

The starting point for understanding the above perspective rests with the assumption that the principles governing the organization of social practices, knowledge, and normative criteria in teacher-education programs represent a selection from corresponding principles in the wider society. Within this context teacher-education programs, like the universities and colleges of which they are a part, embody collective traditions and social practices that are linked to notions of meaning and control that can be traced in both historical and contemporary terms to specific economic and social intrests. If questions of meaning can be associated with notions of authority and control, the issue can be raised as to whose sets of meaning stalk behind and legitimate the organization and structure of teacher-education programs. In more specific terms, how are these meanings sustained? How are they modified and altered? What are the value assumptions that lie hidden beneath the form and content of such programs? And, finally, what material and ideological forces obscure the latent functions of these programs?

It is important to stress that while there are a number of contradictions between teacher-education programs and the wider society, these contradictions only point to the 'relative autonomy' of such programs and fail, in the final analysis, to posit a convincing case for examining them as 'free-floating', existing outside of the imperatives of class and power in which they are embedded.

More recently a number of educational theorists have attempted to analyze education and history within a political and ideological context that functions in the interest of social and economic reproduction. In essence they have attempted to discover how institutions that serve as agencies of socialization function to help reproduce the division of labor that permeates existing social and institutional arrangements. Representing one mode of analysis, political economists such as Bowles and Gintis[6] have analyzed and demonstrated how the varied ideological and economic outcomes of schools reproduce social and economic inequality. Rejecting the consensus view of functionalist sociology, neo-Marxists have interpreted educational change as the outcome of class conflict and struggle. Moreover, they have explored how schools utilize certain selective principles such as testing, I.Q. scores, and tracking in order to discriminate against minorities of class and color. In this view, the educational system through its differential distribution of knowledge and non-academic skills, awarded along class, racial, and sexual lines, functions to legitimate rather than ameliorate the injustices of the larger society. Representing a similar concern, but using a different mode of analysis, a number of social theorists, influenced by the new sociology of education in England, have examined the political function of schools through an analysis of how social reality is constructed and negotiated at the day-to-day level of the classroom encounter.[7] Both positions provide important conceptual insights and new critical categories for examining teacher education and the function of schooling. Yet neither position is without its respective flaws, flaws that must be overcome in order for educators to develop a more comprehensive framework for the study of educational theory and practice.

The economistic view, as I have argued in this book, often presents an overdetermined model of correspondence between schooling and the economic structures of society.[8] Moreover, in this view men and women appear to be eliminated as active, interpretive agents, and the institutions under analysis appear to be abstracted from the specifically conditioned social relationships they represent. Consequently, what we sometimes get from this perspective is a kind of melodrama in which a unified and 'wicked' ruling class imposes its will on the complacent masses. Thus, while it is to the credit of economistic theorists that they have politicized the notion of schooling while similarly providing a theory of *class* reproduction, their analysis fails in the end because concrete individuals and social groups have a way of disappearing and schools end up being treated like 'black boxes'.[9]

On the other hand, as I have suggested before, the new sociology of education theorists have illuminated the concrete ways in which teachers, students, and educational researchers both produce and work through socially constructed definitions of curriculum, pedagogy, and evaluation.[10] But this perspective also has serious shortcomings. In effect the new sociologists have failed to ground their view of domination in an adequate theory of class and social reproduction.[11] Similarly, the new sociology, in many cases, seems so intent on concentrating on how students and teachers construct and negotiate meanings in daily classroom encounters that both groups appear to 'get lost' in the myriad of everyday classroom life. Consequently, we are often left with the notion that liberation can simply be willed into being, i.e., objective structural and ideological forces that limit one's choices and actions become merely paper barricades to be blown away with a little gust of intentionality. In summary, both views posit an unwarranted division between the subject and the object, and in so doing eliminate the subject from reality.[12]

### Beyond Methodology Madness

It is essential to understand that questions about meaning and purpose in teacher-education programs are political in nature. Such questions provide teacher educators and their students with value-laden 'paradigms' that establish the foundation for addressing everyday school practices. In the most general sense, teacher-education programs represent socializing agencies that embody rules and patterns for constructing and legitimizing categories regarding competence, achievement, and success. Moreover, they serve to define specific roles (teacher, student, principal) through the language they use and the assumptions and research they consider essential to the teaching profession. Unfortunately, the basic premises and rules that underlie such programs are usually viewed as commonsense perceptions; they go unquestioned and often result in many problems in the teaching arena to be defined as basically technical ones.[13] Popkewitz captures both the spirit and consequence of this when he writes:

> The technical definitions of educational problems and the procedural responses to reform in teacher education are legitimated by much of the research in the field. Most research tends to view teaching as a problem of human engineering and teacher education as the most efficient way to provide new recruits with the specific behaviors and attitudes of the people who practice teaching . . . the conduct of schooling, the system of status and privilege of the occupation, and the social and political implications of institutional arrangements are obscured through a process of reification. Teaching and teacher education are treated administratively . . . What is ignored are the ways in which teacher education imposes work styles and patterns of communication which guide individuals as to how they are to reason and to act in their relationships in the setting of schooling. The language, material organization, and social interactions of teacher education establish principles of authority, power and rationality for guiding occupational conduct. These patterns of thought and work are not neutral and cannot be taken for granted.[14]

The overall effect on teacher education of the social engineering approach has been considerable and is far removed from the vision of John Dewey, George Counts, and other progressive educators who stressed the ethical, experiential, and emancipatory dimensions of such programs. A number of educators such as Stanley Aronowitz[15] have recently decried the rampant 'methodology madness' that appears to dominate the field of teacher education. Overly anxious about presenting students with 'seven' approaches to empirical research, 'six' dimensions of curriculum, and endless approaches to constructing behavioral objectives, too many courses in these programs are silent about the assumptions embedded in these varied approaches, not to mention the interests they serve or the ethical consequences of their use. The results suggest not a more comprehenseive level of thought, but the debasement of thinking itself. As Aronowitz points out:

> The stress on critical thinking . . . offering the student a chance to construct his own reality, has been debased by the emphasis on 'methods' rather than content in the preparation of teachers by teachers colleges. This approach to the curriculum has contributed to the training of several generations of elementary and secondary school teachers whose main skill has become maintaining control over the class rather than understanding the cognitive and effective process of learning. Moreover, thousands of young teachers suffer from intellectual ignorance; they bring few resources to their work and often fall back on police-like behavior toward students to compensate for their inability to teach.[16]

While there are numerous exceptions to Aronowitz's charge, the question of whether teacher-education programs are based on valuative and cognitive principles that undermine critical thought and take for granted that which its task is to explain is no small matter. If educators have been blind to the role and function of teacher education, it is in part due to the study by mainstream educators of such programs under micro-social categories that ignore the historical and political context in which they exist. Thus, we are treated to studies that suggest that the quality of teacher-education programs can improve only if they select students with higher SAT test scores.[17] In the same vein, it has been suggested that we can improve teacher education if a process of psychological screening for entrants is built into the admission policies of such programs.[18] Such responses are characteristic of the rationality that dominates educational theory and practice. Divorced from the language of power, history, and critical sociology these positions appear deaf to the assumptions that generate the questions they formulate, not to mention the answers they provide. The basic, constitutive nature of these programs seems to disappear in studies of this sort. The basis assumptions that give meaning and legitimacy to teacher education are relegated to the realm of common sense.

A more worthwhile approach to examining teacher education will have to begin by utilizing macro-social categories that reveal hows the underlying economic and political structures of the larger society influence the 'here and now' ideology and culture that are part of the tissue of everyday life in these programs.

### New Critical Categories for Examining Teacher Education

The form and content of teacher education are inextricably linked to notions of power, culture, ideology, and hegemony. A further investigation of these concepts provides the basis for examining not only how such programs function as agencies of economic and cultural reproduction, but also how the conradictions and tensions in these programs point to possible reforms and modifications.

It has been pointed out[19] that mainline curriculum theorists rarely understand what the linkages are between curriculum theory and cultural reproduction, and that this leads to some puzzlement on their part as to why the notion of culture should be bracketed in the first place. Part of the problem lies with the depoliticized notion of culture that permeates mainstream social science. In this view culture is defined as simply a people's total way of life, the entirety of those goods, services, and labor produced by human beings. Adorno sums up this definition well when he writes, 'culture is viewed as the manifestation of pure humanity without regard for its functional relationship to society'.[20] Divorced from notions of class, power, and ideology, such a definition becomes an empty social science category that relegates *'culture'* 'to the atmosphere of a presumably harmonious Olympus'.[21] A less mystifying approach would subsume 'culture' within the category of society so as to reveal its functions as a legitimating, motivational structure that provides members of the dominant society with symbolic message systems and institutions to 'lay the psychological and moral foundations for the economic and political system they control'.[22] Culture as used in this book suggests not the existence of one 'whole social process' happily produced by all members of society, but different layers of meanings and practices mediated by the inequitable distribution of wealth and power. Thus, one cannot speak of one culture or of a multiplicity of cultures; it is more accurate to speak of a dominant culture (with its own contradictions, of course), and of the existence of minority cultures, all mediated by considerations of power and control.[23]

The concept of dominant culture takes on a particular clarity in the writings of Korsch[24] and Gramsci.[25] In their view, the state wields its power through a combination of force and *consent.* In this context the notion of cultural reproduction becomes more clearly linked to the state's political and economic functions. That is, state power relies less upon the use of physical repression than it does upon the use of belief and value systems to organize public consent for its policies and practices. Hegemony is an ideology that defines the limits of discourse in a society by positing specific ideas and social relationships as natural, permanent, rational, and universal. Hegemony, then, is an ideology that has been institutionalized by the state.[26] But again it must be stressed the hegemony refers to more than dominant belief and value systems, it also refers to those routines and practices that saturate people's daily experiences.

The concept of hegemony and its implications for studying the ideology of social control in teacher education would be incomplete without a definition and analysis of ideology. First, I want to reject outright the orthodox Marxist notion of ideology as a set of illusions or lies. The concept recaptures its critical spirit if it is viewed as a form of social reconstruction. This means that ideology is a set of beliefs, values, and social practices that contain oppositional assumptions about varying elements of social reality, i.e., society, economics, authority, human nature, politics, etc.[27] Moreover, ideology is now seen as a critical view of the world that is value-laden, a view which points to the contradictions and tensions in a society from the perspective of its own world view: i.e., libralism, communism, socialism, anarchism, and others.[28] Ideologies become hegemonic when they are institutionalized by the dominant society.[29] At this point, they are stripped of their oppositional power and serve to legitimize existing institutional arrangements and social practices. 'Hegemonic ideologies smooth over the rough edges of reality and provide an idealized view . . . Hegemonic ideology presents private interests as public goods.[30] Through its structured silence about what ought to be, hegemonic ideology elevates 'common sense' to a universal truth.

The concept of hegemonic ideology strips teacher-education programs of their purported innocence. This becomes clear if we raise questions about how hegemonic ideologies are created and distributed in a society. Social theorists such as Gramsci and Althusser[31] have attempted to answer such questions by pointing to the 'ideological state apparatus' as the primary reproducer of hegemonic ideology.

Agencies considered part of the ideological state apparatus act as vehicles of socialization, either directly or indirectly, and while trading in ideas and values, they function to mediate beween the summits of power and eveyday life. The ideological state apparatus includes churches, schools, trade unions, media, workplaces, and the family. At the core of this perspective is the insight that advanced industrial countries such as the United States inequitably distribute not only economic goods and services but certain forms of cultural capital as well, i.e., 'that system of meanings, abilities, language forms, and tastes that are directly and indirectly defined by dominant groups as socially legitimate'.[32] If we view the distribution of knowledge and social practices as a form of capital linked (though not mechanistically) to the concept of hegemony, I think we can get a clearer understanding of the role that schools play in this society. Bernstein[33] and others have argued that schools are the primary agents of ideological control. This raises specific questions about teacher-education programs since they 'train those intellectuals' who play a pervasive and direct part in socializing students into the dominant society. The implications of the view would certaintly dispel the perspective voiced by educators such as Tyler[34] and R.S. Peters[35] that schools simply 'transmit' culture. The term 'transmit' hides the reality that lies behind the notion of 'reproduction'. As was mentioned earlier, schools do not transmit culture, instead they play a fundamental role in reproducing the dominant culture.[36] This has led a number of critics to raise substantive questions about schools and their relationship to the dominant culture.[37] These inquiries focus on questions such as: Whose culture gets distributed in the schools? Who benefits from such culture? What are the historical, social, and economic roots of this culture? How is this culture distributed? How is is sustained in the curriculum?

In short, teachers at all levels of schooling are part of an ideological region that has enormous importance in legitimizing the categories and social practices of the dominant society. Hence, the fundamental question now becomes, 'How does the dominant ideology manifest itself in teacher-education programs?'. I believe we can answer that question by first pointing to the rationality that dominates such programs; secondly, we can examine how this rationality ties these programs to wider societal interests. Through such an analysis, the theoretical framework will be developed for examining how this type of rationality can be countered in order to restructure teacher education as it presently exists.

### The Dominant Rationality in Teacher Education

Any attempt at defining the dominant rationality underlying teacher education has to begin with an essential qualification. The rationality described below is portrayed in ideal-essence terms. In the extended political and cultural sense, it represents a form of dominance, but it is not all-engulfing, total, or exclusive. There are many contradictions and permeations that merge with the dominant rationality and give it a different 'face' or 'texture'. Various forms of system-management pedagogy, or knowledge-based curriculum approaches are but two examples of so-called innovative approaches to classroom instruction that at heart are simply recycled and repackaged forms of the existing rationality that has dominated schools and teacher-education programs since their inception. Similarly, different contexts produce varied responses to such a rationality. For instance, rural and small teachers colleges may embrace such a rationality with a different degree of intentionality than schools of education that are part of metropolitan university systems. Moreover, this rationality as a form of hegemonic ideology does not represent a set of categories or 'rules' – it is much more than that. At its core it represents the ideological expression of real social relationships and human encounters. As such, it is not static but constantly changing and modifying itself in the face of changing socio-historical conditions.

The strength and pervasiveness of the rationality that presently dominates educational theory and practice can be grasped in the increasing national support of competency-based systems of instruction, behavioristic models of pedaogy, and the various versions of systems theory models in curriculum development and evaluation. At first glance, this mode of rationality, hereafter referred to as technocratic rationality, appears to be a post-sputnik trend. A closer examination reveals that such is not the case. Technocratic rationality has a long history in curriculum theory and practice, and was initiated by many of the curriculum field's early founders, Franklin Bobbitt, W.W. Charters, Edward L. Thorndike, Charles Peters and others. What is significant about the history of this form of rationality is that it reveals its roots in models of industrial psychology and control patterned after the scientific managment movement of the 1920s.[38] Not only does the language of this mode of rationality conceptualize the nature and function of schooling in industrial terms (that is, schools are seen as factories, students as raw material), it also supports modes of behavior and goals premised on the need for a form of social control dedicated to social homogeneity and group conformity. The historical record shows that the demands of industrialization for cheap and docile labor provided the school with the 'ideal' task of instilling 'the immigrants with specific values and standards of behavior'.[39] While the interests behind the historical devlopment of technocratic rationality are rather clear, it appears that the historical roots of its more contemporary versions have been forgotten by many teacher-educators. This form of 'social amnesia' not only characterizes technocratic rationality, it also shapes the conditions under which it sustains itself. The consequences for teacher education are no small matter.

The importance of what passes as a legitimating rationality in teacher education cannot be overstated. Any form of rationality suggests specific limits and boundaries on the areas one sees fit for investigation, the questions one deems important for study, and the modes of investigation to be used. All forms of rationality, in one sense, provide *both* the definition and legitimation for the categories and assumptions that give expression and create opportunities for investigating the world. As Popkewitz points out, 'What passes as reason and rationality in teacher education has important implications to the meaning held in larger society'.[40] This becomes evident when the basic assumptions that characterize technocratic rationality are made clear.

### Assumptions Behind Technocratic Rationality

In broad general terms, a number of assumptions characterize technocratic rationality or what I have referred to in Chapter 1 as the culture of positivism. (1) Educational theory should operate in the interests of lawlike propositions which are empirically testable. A major asumption here is that empirical analytic research can identify lawlike regularities in the social world 'which can be identified and manipulated as with objects in the physical world'.[41] (2) The natural sciences provide the 'proper' model of explanation of the concepts and techniques of educational theory, design, and evaluation. This becomes clear in the work of Suppes,[42] Popham[43] and other major educational researchers in the field who decry methods of investigation not based upon the technical principles or interests of prediction, control, and certainty. Variables which cannot be formally expressed in quantitative terms, i.e., philosophical analyses, historical inquiry, mystery, awe, forms of transcendence are seen as 'soft' data, not fit for serious inquiry. Elliot Eisner brings this point out in claiming that 'the belief that educational research is a form in inquiry whose conclusions can be couched only in numbers is so pervasive that, of the 47 articles published in the *American Educational Research Journal* during 1974–1975, only one was non-statistical.[44] The failure to appreciate that there are fundamental interests in teacher education other than those of explanation, prediction, and technical control is what ties most educators to this rationality that shapes their view of pedagogy and teacher education. (3) Knowledge in this form of rationality is reduced to those concepts and 'facts' that can be operationally defined, that is, they have precise meanings and definitions. This had led to a celebration of techniques whose aim is to identify the different subsets of knowledge and put them together in order to produce knowledge about the whole. Knowledge defined this way sets the stage for separating the knowing subject from the known object. One consequence of this is that it becomes difficult to conceptualize how the subject and object are mutually influenced and transformed in the 'act of knowing'. On the other hand, the notion of value-free knowledge speaks to knowledge that has to be discovered and transmitted. There is a certain dogmatism here, reinforced by the assumption that knowledge is the exclusive province of those who know; human consciousness and activity appear to surrender themselves to the guardians of the 'truth'. (4) Finally, educators can and must separate statements of value from the 'facts' and 'modes of inquiry' which ought to be objective.

These assumptions represent the driving force of a form of rationality that views itself as scientific, objective, and functional to the demands of teacher-education programs. Of course, the notion of functional becomes meaningful only when measured next to how this perspective views the larger relationship between teacher education and wider institutional arrangements. This view has been expressed quite well by Talcott Parsons[45] who saw such programs as fitting the existing needs of the present society; thus the relationship was a functional one. Inherent in this form of rationality is a definition of society that stresses consensus, equilibrium, and order. Consequently, the value of teacher-education programs is measured in terms 'of their contributions to basic system requirements'.[46] Lost from this type of analysis is the language of power and control. For example, society may be held together less by shared values than by ideological and material restraints. To ignore the latter is to accept as a given the basic norms and assumptions that shape existing socio-economic institutions. Moreover, this perspective sees the socialization of prospective teachers as primarily a technical one, i.e., 'to transform the human raw material of society into good working members'.[47]

Absent from such a view is any attempt to question the nature and quality of the society that teacher-education programs so cheerfully support. Similarly, the underlying emphasis on consensus and control in these programs generates models of socialization and role performance that downplay notions of social conflict and competing socio-economic interests. In addition, by failing to make problematic the basic beliefs, values, and structural socioeconomic arrangements characteristic of American society, technocratic models of socialization and role performance depoliticize the nature of the teaching experience as well as the relationship between teacher education, schooling, and wider societal interests. Anyon illuminates the nature of the problem when she writes:

> [Theories] . . . of school socialization that do not make problematic relationships between the reproduction of an unequal socio-economic order, practical and symbolic ideologies in school, and the construction of personal opportunity and identity, not only circumvent analysis of education and U.S. society, but trivialize our notions of childhood socialization.[48]

Within the theoretical boundaries of technocratic rationality the concept of socialization supports a passive view of students and an overly integrated perception of society.[49] The role of the teacher is often seen as one that can be universally defined in measurable terms and generally applied to any class or school, notwithstanding different levels of schooling. Roles for the prospective teacher are often viewed as 'fixed' and objectively given. In this case, teacher roles are treated like 'things', and the socialization process simply provides students with the skills and requirements to carry out these predefined roles efficiently.[50] The hidden curriculum here is that role theory becomes 'a refinement of conformity theory';[51] characteristically, the teacher is not viewed as a creator of values but simply as the receiver and transmitter of 'institutional' norms.[52] Consequently, the teacher's own existential reality becomes lost amidst a form of socialization and role theory that is blind to its own ideology. This position fails to acknowledge that there are no universally acceptable 'roles' and 'methodologies' that can be placed in gridlike fashion on any context. Gerhard Arfwedson points to the reason for the latter in his statement:

> The contextual setting of teacher situations varies in so many different dimensions and directions that what is a 'good' personality, role or method in one situation may be almost the 'worst' in another situation . . . These active contextual factors, which define the limits and possibilities that characterize the teacher's working situation, are found not only within the school as a place of work or within the educational system. The actual local society, too, as well as society in a broader sense (i.e., the state and the country) have to be taken into account when a survey of determining factors in teachers' work is to be made.[53]

### Theory and Teacher Education

Unfortunately, the nature and role of theory in many teacher-education programs provide little or no explanatory power for students to reflect critically on how pedagogy is informed by theory or on how specific ideological and material conditions inside and outside of the schools play a determining part in shaping as well as constraining different pedagogies. The contours of the technocratic notion of theory are too one-dimensional. What is missing is a theory in which the relational structure of teacher and context, school and society, can be explained in terms of the possibilities and limitations that exist in correspondence and tension with each other. The contours of such a theory have been explained by Ulf Lundgren:

> What we have is the contours of a theory in which the development of an educational system and of a curriculum can be explained in relation to processes for cultural reproduction, the need for qualification, the development of educational systems as a part of the state apparatus, and the demands on education for differentiation of labour.[54]

Steeped in the language and assumptions of the strict sciences, most teacher-education programs operate within parameters in which 'problems that do not lend themselves to measurement or to scientific solution (are) considered intellectually ill-conceived'.[55] This message is not only verified in the research models that dominate the educational field but also in the curriculum models that dominate teacher education and public school pedagogy.[56]

The political and ethical function of theory is subsumed in this perspective amidst a trivializing concern with methodology and models. Supported by claims of objectivity and impartial scientific research, students in teacher education find themselves operating out of predefined categories and styles of thought that make curriculum appear to have a life of its own. Instead of being seen for what it is, a specific social reality expressing a distinct set of social relations and assumptions about the world, curriculum appears as something which exists in a suprahistorical vacuum.[57] The claims to objectivity and science which support this view are both false and mystifying. They are false because any notion about curriculum and pedagogy is value-laden and historically grounded, and unavoidably so. They are mystifying because by claiming to be objective such assertions falsify the meaning of 'science' in order to be silent about the underlying politics and interests in which they are grounded.[58] By not making its basic assumptions problematic, technocratic rationality places itself beyond the realm of criticism and debate. Thus its posture has little to do with objectivity and a great deal to do with 'objectivism', which as Gouldner describes it, is 'communication that conceals the presence of the speaker, . . . thinking that ignores the language or theory about which thought is taking place'.[59]

While it is impossible to detail fully how technocratic rationality promotes conformity and social control in teacher education, it is important to attempt to illuminate in concrete terms the effect it has had on the way teacher-education programs view knowledge and classroom pedagogy.

### Knowledge and Classroom Pedagogy

A major criticism of both teacher education and public schooling has focused on how specific forms of knowledge and meanings are selected and distributed in their respective settings. These criticisms are not meant to imply that discussions about the selection, form, and content of knowledge go unexamined. Such is not the case. It is the criteria used in such programs that warrant criticism. For instance, Harris[60] claims that teacher educators give high priority to variables involved in trying to answer the question 'What knowledge is of most worth?' The problem lies with the restricted assumptions and criteria used in formulating and answering such a question. The assumptions that shape the criteria and ensuing questions support the notion that knowledge is objective, 'out there' to be learned and mastered. As Popkewitz points out, 'These discussions are often related to questions about the structure of knowledge'[61] or to the technical organization of content. The language used in this case represents the language of internal criticism, it is confined to solving the 'puzzles' within its own symbolic space, and as such cannot step outside of the assumptions that legitimate it. Put another way, it is not a dialectical language, one that can choose among competing paradigms and disciplines in order to think about the subject or processes in use.[62]

It has been argued that such a static view of knowledge and students is both elitist and conservative. This view fails to provide a theoretic stance for analyzing the way teacher-education knowledge is selected, organized, distributed, and evaluated.[63] Instead of perceiving knowledge as a study in ideology, linked to socially constructed human interests, technocratic rationality ignores the relationship between power and school knowledge and often ends up celebrating, in both the overt and hidden curricula, knowledge that supports existing institutional arrangements. Popkewitz,[64] Anyon,[65] Apple,[66] and others have done extensive studies illuminating the biases and ideologically laden categories and assumptions that permeate textbooks and classroom practices. The responsibility for the latter cannot be placed on teachers' shoulders exclusively. In many respects teacher-education programs have simply not given teachers the conceptual tools they need in order to view knowledge as problematic, as a historically conditioned, socially constructed phenomenon. Similarly, the objectification of knowledge is usually accompanied by the objectification of the classroom social encounter. Knowledge is not just content; its use also suggests specific kinds of classroom social relationships. When knowledge is seen as objective and 'out there', it is usually accompanied by top-to-bottom forms of pedagogy in which there is little dialogue or interaction.[67] But the way pupils construct meaning, the importance of subjectivity, and the value of knowledge outside of the 'rationality' of strict science are important dimensions of the process of curriculum and instruction. These modes of knowing represent important pedagogical principles that future educators need to understand in order to be able to shape their *own* lives in a self-determining manner.

This leads to one final criticism. Knowledge in the technocratic rationality view is defined and used so as to be separated from the lived histories and biographies not only of teachers but of students.[68] Thus knowledge is used not only to mask the role that it plays in shaping how people view themselves and others, it also serves to ignore how important the relationship is among knowledge, context, and learning. For instance, knowledge that goes unexamined does more than hide the social interests it supports; it also militates against the use of social relationships that generate meanings from the perceptions and voices of different cultural actors involved in the 'learning' process. This means that teachers are trained neither to recognize nor use the cultural capital of others as a central category for dialogue and personal affirmation in their teaching. The result is a form of pedagogical violence that prevents teachers from establishing conditions which allow students to speak with an authentic voice.[69] Similarly, the notion of 'objective' knowledge not only fails to reveal how knowledge is culturally bound, it also serves to buttress normative and intellectual support in teacher-education programs for the ethos of 'professionalism'.[70] The latter refers to the cult of 'experts and 'professionals' who become avatars trained to guard as well as 'transmit' the sacred knowledge and language to prospective educators, who in turn make *their* expertise available to members of the public. If the metaphor seems overdrawn, it is only because there is a real necessity to break down the pompous and dangerous ideology of professionalism that is so ingrained in teacher education. As Lasch,[71] Bledstein,[72] and Edelman[73] have pointed out, the growth of professionalism in education has done little to benefit the public and a great deal to serve the narrow interests of educators themselves. The latter interests include: increased hierarchical differentiation in the teaching profession, a growing standardization of school practices, and an increasing call for the legitimation of the value of 'certified' knowledge. In general, the growth of the ideology of professionalism has only been matched in the field of education by the tendency of its members 'to work toward inertia'.[74]

### Implications for Teacher-Education Programs

Teacher-education programs, it has been argued in this essay, function as agencies of social control. They do the latter to the degree that they directly or indirectly 'educate' future generations of teachers to accept uncritically those skills, attitudes, and dispositional qualities that support the dominant social order. Of course, this is not meant to suggest that such programs mechanistically and awesomely reproduce the social and cultural imperatives of the state. Nor does this position suggest that students are so malleable and powerless that they willingly submit to their own victimization. Teacher-education programs operate within parameters that are severely constraining, but they also contain options for creating new possibilities and social realities. In other words, the seeds exist within teacher education for developing 'critical intellectuals' who can begin the task of generating a more radical and visionary consciousness among their fellow workers, friends, and students. It is crucial to recognize that teacher-education programs not only exist in dialectical tension with the rest of society; they also mediate tensions and contradictions specific to their own interests and concerns. Teacher-education programs, then, both embody and demonstrate contradictions and correspondences with wider societal interests.[75] It is the tensions and contradictions in these programs that testify to their relative autonomy, and it is within the context of this relative autonomy that 'radical' teachers can find the political space to develop innovative courses and alternative modes of pedagogy. It is an opportunity that should not be ignored.

Prospective reform in teacher education must begin by giving students the theoretical and conceptual tools to combat all forms of mystification and alienation. In both stuctural and intellectual ways, students should be able to penetrate beneath the commonsense, surface realities that, in part, shape their day-to-day experiences. Similarly, students should be given the opportunity to generate their own meanings, speak with their own voices, and come to understand 'that there is always more to see and hear and feel, that the quality of our enjoyment is to some degree a function of what we know'.[76] Students in teacher education must learn that knowledge is a socially constructed phenomenon and that methodological inquiry is never value-free. Moreover, they must be given the opportunity to learn how specific classroom social relationships not only are value-laden, but, in part, represent material-ideological configurations characteristic of the workplace and other agencies of socialization and social control. But these heuristic devices are incomplete unless they are coupled with an affirmation of the importance of social justice and social action. With the latter in mind, a deepening attitude of self-awareness and justice must link the biographical with the social, the private with the sense of community. Maxine Greene perceptively captures the importance of such a dialectic when she writes:

> There must be a perception of the ways in which persons locate themselves in the world in the light of their own particular biographical situations, the experiences they have built up over time. Every individual

inteprets the realities he or she confronts through perspectives made up of particular ranges of interests, occupations, commitments, and desires. Each one belongs to a number of social groups and plays a variety of social roles. His or her involvements – the work he or she has done, the schools he or she has attended, his or her race and class membership – affect the way 'the stock of knowledge at hand' is used. Particular persons make use of it to order, to interpret from particular vantage points; as they do so, a common meaning strucure is built up among them; they share a common world. . . . Whatever efforts can be made to enable teachers-to-be to speak for themselves and confront the concreteness of their lives ought to play into the critique that challenges mystification. And in time, this might be carried into the classrooms of the schools or wherever such problems finally work.[77]

If teacher educators and their students are encouraged to think about the self-formative processes that underlie their own thinking, this may also help them to reflect critically on the constraints that limit the possibilities they are attempting to develop and implement. It is a theory of ideological and material constraints that requires the need for the heuristic to be complemented by the political.[78] Furthermore, empirical investigations in education can only be useful when they are subordinated to the heuristic and political questions that determine their meaning and function. Adorno[79] clearly expressed this point when he wrote 'but one must not confer autonomy upon them or regard them [empirical investigations] as a universal key. Above all, they must themselves terminate in theoretical knowledge'. The existence of material and ideological constraints should not be viewed as a limit situation, but as a starting point from which teacher educators can assess and act on those beliefs and strucural forces that both legitimate and reproduce the worst dimensions of technocratic rationality. In more specific terms I will point to some broad suggestions that teacher educators might want to consider.

Teacher educators and their students must learn to think dialectically.[80] This means that they must develop a satisfactory theory of totality. Schools must be seen as part of a wider societal process. But to posit the importance of interconnections is merely a valuable methodological precept. More important,

> to ask for a theory of totality is to ask how a society reproduced itself, how it perpetuates its conditions of existence through its reproduction of class relationships and its propagation of ideologies which sanction the *status quo*.[81]

The dialectic involved here is a crucial one. The interplay of power, norms, and value will have to be connected with a more relational view of academic knowledge. The artificial constructs that characterize the ordering and boundaries of subject matter must give way to more fluid interconnections. But this must be preceded by an understanding that *both* knowledge and people are 'processed' in schools, and if such an understanding is to become a viable starting point for a critical sociology of education, then the central task of teacher education will be 'to relate those principles of selection and organization that underlie curricula to their institutional and interactional setting in schools and classrooms to the wider social structure'.[82] The latter task demands that teacher educators reconstruct more critical categories for educational theory and practice. For instance, categories such as social class, ideology, false consciousness, and hegemony must be linked to others such as oppression, emancipation, freedom, and indoctrination.[83] Similarly, teacher educators and their students must draw as much as possible from other disciplines in order to examine social reality. As Greene writes: 'they must be enabled to look through the perspectives opened by history, sociology, anthropology, economics and philosophy; they must learn how consciously to order the materials of their experience with the aid of such perspectives'.[84]

It is also crucial that students in these programs learn to use in their work theoretical models not based exclusively on the interests of prediction and control. Needed are theoretical models that flush out the political and ethical questions that implicitly or explicitly provide the foundation for educational theory, development, and evaluation. One approach would be to provide students with theoretical models that support interests such as human understanding, contextual inquiry, aesthetic literacy, and social reconstructionism. Such models can be drawn from fields such as hermeneutics, symbolic interactionism, phenomenology, semiotics, and neo-Marxism. Classroom and curricula activities that allow students to examine issues from a variety of perspectives, and to test the truth claims of these perspectives, at least provide the climate for dialogue and critique, and the latter are important pedagogical principles.

Another crucial point centers around providing students with heuristic devices based on different languages and different modes of rationality. It is imperative that future teachers be able to understand the 'full range and varieties of rationality of which humans are capable, that are not limited to one set of assumptions about how we come to know'.[85] For instance, Huebner[86] suggests five modes of rationality that should play an integral role in both understanding and shaping educational theory and practice – technical, political, scientific, aesthetic, and ethical. Each not only has its own language, but calls for a different and complex mode of interpretation. Pioneering examples of the attempt to link educational theory with modes of rationality in the arts and in critical psychology can be found in the work of Grumet[87] and Pinar.[88] The more students in teacher-education programs learn to understand both the distinctiveness as well as the interconnections among these modes of rationality, the greater will be their range of heuristic and political abilities.

In addition, I think it is imperative that teacher educators and their students develop pedagogical approaches that enable them to understand the value and experience that each brings to the classroom experience. Teaching must be viewed, in part, as an intensely personal affair.[89] This suggests that prospective teachers be given the concepts and methods to delve into their own biographies, to look at the sedimented history they carry around, and to learn how one's own cultural capital represents a dialectical interplay between private experience and history. Methods of curriculum design, implementation, and evaluation must be seen as a construction in values and ideology. This approach provides the foundation for future teachers to analyze how their own values mediate the classroom structures and student experiences they work with.

Finally, teacher-education programs must stress as well as demonstrate the importance of historical sensibility as a tool for critical thinking. The value of making educational theory and practice problematic represents one important step towards deymystifying the ideology of technocratic rationality, but it is not enough. If the 'death trap' of pedagogical relativism is to be avoided, educators must turn to history to trace how school knowledge, modes of school organization, modes of evaluation, and classroom social relationships have developed out of specific social assumptions and political interests. Teachers, students, even the forms and shapes of schools themselves, carry the weight of history. And it is this 'weight' that breaks into the moment as an objective and universal consideration. If teacher education is to move in the direction of a critical science, it will have to trace the interests and historical roots of the fields that it supports. Every field, whether it be curriculum, social education, or reading and language, is steeped in dominant paradigms that can only be understood and analyzed if their respective social and politial assumptions and orientations are placed in a historical context. By doing so, it becomes relatively clear that the study of 'the field' quickly becomes the study of the historical development of specific social relationships operating at particular conjunctures during specific socio-historical periods. The historical sensibility represents an attempt to trace the self-formative genesis of any field. Thus it is at once historical and crtitical. Such a sensibility raises new questions and provides new possibilities. Questions such as 'How did systems management get into the curriculum field? What are the historical roots of the existing testing paradigm? Whose interests does the testing paradigm serve? How does technocratic rationality work in the interest of the state? What were the conditions under which it changed its form and content? What is the history of educational psychology in the curriculum field? What were the social theories and beliefs of the founders of the curriculum movement?' help students to unravel the multiple socio-economic and ideological connections that mediate between schools and the wider social structure. Moreover, they point to the possibility of both critique and transformation.

These suggestions are meant to be no more than tentative guidelines that can be used to illuminate the limits of teacher education as well as establish the conditions for a dialogue over possible reforms. They argue strongly for recognizing the political nature of teacher education and the schools of which they are a part. Moreover, these suggestions represent a call to both students and teachers in such programs to redefine their roles and to work toward making teacher education, in the Kantian spirit, a 'battleground' where future generations of teachers can be educated to a 'fight' for the building of a better and more just society for everyone.

## Notes and References

1 This chapter is dedicated to John di Biase (d. 1973) and Armand Giroux (d. 1978) each of whom knew something about the 'dark' side of culture and ideology. It is also dedicated to Jeanne Brady whose very existence makes me believe in the future.

2 BOWLES, S. and GINTIS, H. (1976) *Schooling in Capitalist America: Educational Reform and the Contradictions of Economic Life* New York, Basic Books.

3 ALTHUSSER, L. (1971) 'Ideology and ideological state apparatuses' in *Lenin and Philosophy and Other Essays* (trans. Ben Brewster) New York, Monthly Review Press; BOURDIEU, P. and PASSERON, J.-P. (1977) *Reproduction in Education, Society and Culture* Beverley Hills, Calif., Sage.

4 For instance, this idea can be found in the work of educators such as Arthur Jensen and Charles Silberman. Jensen believes that problems with schooling can be traced to the intellectual capacities of the students. Silberman traces the source of school problems to the mindlessness of teachers. Both views treat schools in a decontextualized fashion; such perceptions are ahistorical, as well as apolitical, and end up abstracting schools from the society in which they exist.

5 JENCKS, C. (1979) *Who Gets Ahead?* New York, Basic Books.

6 BOWLES, S. and GINTIS, H. (1976) *op. cit.*

7 BERNSTEIN, B. (1977) *Class, Codes and Control Vol. 3: Towards a Theory of Educational Transmission* (2nd ed.) London, Routledge and Kegan Paul; YOUNG, M.F.D. (1971) (Ed.) *Knowledge and Control* London, Collier Macmillan; MACDONALD, M. (1977) *The Curriculum and Cultural Reproduction* Milton Keynes, England, The Open University Press.

8 LEOPARTE, C. (1974) 'Approaches to school: The perfect fit' *Liberation* September/October, pp. 26–32; GORELICK, S. (1977) 'Schooling problems in capitalist America' *Monthly Review Press* No. 29, pp. 20–36.

9 MEHAN, H. (1979) *Learning Lessons: Social Organization in the Classroom* Cambridge, Mass. Harvard University Press.

10 YOUNG, M.F.D. (1971) *op. cit.;* KEDDIE, N. (1971) 'Classroom knowledge' in YOUNG, M.F.D. (Ed.) *op. cit.*

11 SHARP, R. and GREENE, A. (1975) *Education and Social Control* London, Routledge and Kegan Paul.

12 ISRAEL, J. (1979) *The Language of Dialectics and the Dialectics of Language* London, Harvester Press.

13 GRACE, G. (1978) *Teachers, Ideology and Control: A Study in Urban Education* London, Routledge and Kegan Paul; APPLE, M.W. (1979) *Ideology and Curriculum* Boston, Routledge and Kegan Paul.

14 POPKEWITZ, T. (1979b) 'Teacher education as socialization: Ideology or social mission'. Paper presented at the American Educational Research Association Annual Meeting, San Francisco, April, pp. 1–3.

15 ARONOWITZ, S. (1973) *False Promises* New York, McGraw-Hill.

16 *ibid* p. 314.

17 WEAVER, T.W. (1979) 'In search of quality: The need for talent in teaching' *Phi Delta Kappan* September, pp. 29–32, 46.

18 LORTIE, D.C. (1975) *Schoolteacher* Chicago, University of Chicago Press.

19 APLE, M.W. (1970) *Ideology and Curriculum* Boston, Routledge and Kegan Paul.

20 ADORNO, T.W. (1978) 'Culture and administration' *Telos* No. 37, pp. 93–111.

21 FERRAROTTI, F. (1976) 'The struggle against total bureaucratization' *Telos* No. 27, pp. 157–159.

22 DREITZEL, H.P. (1977) *Beyond the Crisis* New York, Oxford University Press, p. 88.

23 SINBA, C. (1977) 'Class, language and education' *Ideology and Consciousness* No. 1, pp. 77–92.

24 KORSCH, K. (1970) *Marxism and Philosophy* New York, Monthly Review Press.

25 GRAMSCI, A. (1971) *Selections from the Prison Notebooks* (trans. and ed. Hoare, Q. and Smith, G.) New York, International Publishers.

26 FREIBERG, J.W. (1979) 'Critical social theory in the American conjuncture' in FREIBERG, J.W. (Ed.) *Critical Sociology* New York, Irvington Press.

27 KAUFMAN, B. (1978) 'Piaget, Marx and the political ideology of schooling' *Journal of Curriculum Studies* No. 10, pp. 19–44.

28 GOULDNER, A. (1976) *The Dialectic of Ideology and Technology* New York, Seabury Press.

29 KELLNER, D. (1978) 'Ideology, Marxism and advanced capitalism' *Socialist Review* No. 8, pp. 36–55.

30 *ibid* p. 54.

31 GRAMSCI, A. (1971) *op. cit.;* ALTHUSSER, L. (1971) *op. cit.*

32 APPLE, M.W. (1979) *op. cit.*, p. 496.
33 BERNSTEIN, B. (1977) *op. cit.*
34 TYLER, R. (1949) *Basic Principles of Curriculum and Instruction* Chicago, University of Chicago Press.
35 PETERS, R.S. (1966) *Ethics and Education* London, Allen and Unwin.
36 ANYON, J. (1979a) 'Ideology and United States history textbooks' *Harvard Educational Review* No. 49, pp. 361–386; GIROUX, H.A. (1979) see Chapter One; BOURDIEU, P. and PASSERON, J.-P. (1977) *op. cit.*
37 MACDONALD, M. (1977) *op. cit.*; APPLE, M.W. (1979) *op. cit.*
38 VALLANCE, E. (1973/4) 'Hiding the hidden curriculum' *Curriculum Theory Network* No. 4, pp. 5–21; FRANKLIN, B. (1976) 'Technological models and the curriculum field' *The Education Forum* pp. 303–312.
39 APPLE, M.W. (1979) *op. cit.*, p. 73; KATZ, M.B. (1968) *The Irony of Early School Reform* Boston, Beacon Press.
40 POPKEWITZ, T. (1979b) *op. cit.*, p. 21.
41 POPKEWITZ, T. (1979c) 'Paradigms, in educational science: Different meanings of social theory and implications' Speech prepared for the American Educational Research Association Annual Meeting at San Francisco.
42 SUPPES, P. (1974) 'The place of theory in educational research' *Educational Researcher* No. 3, pp. 3–10.
43 POPHAM, J.W. (1973) 'Objectives-based management strategies for large educational systems' in YEE, A. (Ed.) *Perspectives on Management Systems in Education* Englewood Cliffs, New Jersey, Educational Technology Publications.
44 EISNER, E. (1979) *The Educational Imagination* New York, Macmillan, pp. 10–11.
45 PARSONS, T. (1959) 'The school as a social system: Some of its functions in American society' *Harvard Educational Review* No. 29, pp. 279–318.
46 SHARP, R. and GREEN, A. (1975) *op. cit.*, p. 2.
47 POPKEWITZ, T. (1979b) op. cit., p. 6.
48 ANYON, J. (1979a) *op. cit.*, p. 39.
49 BOWERS, C.A. (1976) 'Curriculum and our technocracy culture: The problem of reform' *Teachers College Record* No. 78, pp. 53–67.
50 POPKEWITZ, T. (1979b) *op. cit.*
51 TURNER, R.A. (1962) 'Role-taking: Process versus conformity' in ROSE, A. (Ed.) *Human Behaviour and Social Processes* London, Routledge and Kegan Paul.
52 GRACE, G. (1978) *op. cit.*
53 ARFWEDSON, G. (1979) 'Teachers' Work' in LUNDGREN, U.P. and PETTERSSON, S. (Eds.) *Code, Context and Curriculum Processes* Stockholm, Liber.
54 LUNDGREN, U.P. (1979) 'Background: The conceptual framework' in LUNDGREN, U.P. and PETTERSSON, S. *op. cit.*, p. 33.
55 EISNER, E. (1979) *op. cit.*, p. 15.
56 PINAR, W.F. (1975) 'Currere: Towards a reconceptualization' in PINAR, W.F. (Ed.) *Curriculum Theorizing: The Reconceptualists* Berkeley, Calif., McCutchen.
57 YOUNG, M.F.D. (1975) 'Curriculum change: Limits and possibilities' *Educational Studies* No. 1, pp. 129–138.
58 APPLE, M.W. (1979) *op. cit.*; GOULDNER, A.W. (1976) *op. cit.*
59 GOULDNER, A.W. (1976) *op. cit.*, pp. 49–50.
60 HARRIS, K. (1979) *Classroom Knowledge* London, Routledge and Kegan Paul.
61 POPKEWITZ, T. (1979b) *op. cit.*, p. 20.
62 CONNELLY, F.M. and ROBERTS, D. (1976) 'What curriculum for graduate instruction in curriculum?' *Curriculum theory Network* No. 5, pp. 173–189.
63 GIROUX, H.A. See Chapter Four.
64 POPKEWITZ, T. (1978) 'The latent values of the discipline-centred curriculum in social education' *Theory and Research in Social Education* No. 5, pp. 41–60.
65 ANYON, J. (1979a) *op. cit.*
66 APPLE, M.W. (1979) *op. cit.*
67 FREIRE, P. (1973) *Pedagogy of the Oppressed* New York, Seabury Press.
68 GREENE, M. (1978) *Landscapes of Learning* New York, Teachers College Press.
69 BROWN, C. (1978) *Literacy in 30 Hours: Paulo Freire's Process in North East Brazil* Chicago, Alternative Schools Network.

70 EDELMAN, M. (1977) *Political Language: Words that Succeed and Policies that Fail* New York, Academic Press.
71 LASCH, C. (1977) *Haven in a Heartless World* New York, Basic Books.
72 BLEDSTEIN, B.J. (1976) *The Culture of Professionalism* New York, W.W. Norton.
73 EDELMAN, M. (1977) *op. cit.*
74 POPKEWITZ, T. (1979c) *op. cit.*
75 WILLIS, P. (1977) *Learning to Labour: How Working-class Kids Get Working-class Jobs* England, Saxon House.
76 GREENE, M. (1979) 'From the Lincoln Center Institute: A Summary of Talks' A series of speeches presented at the Lincoln Center Institute, July.
77 GREENE, M. (1978) *op. cit.*, p. 70.
78 RICOEUR, P. (1974) *Political and Social Essays* Athens, Ohio University Press.
79 ADORNO, T.W. (1969) 'Scientific experiences of a European scholar in America' in FLEMING, D. and BAILYN, B. (Eds.) *The Intellectual Migration: Europe and America, 1930-1960* Cambridge, Mass., Harvard University Press, p. 53.
80 GIROUX, H.A. See Chapter One.
81 SHARP, R. and GREEN, A. (1975) *op. cit.*, p. 590.
82 YOUNG, M.F.D. (1971) *op. cit.*, p. 24.
83 I am indebted to Ralph Page for helping me work out this idea.
84 GREENE, M. (1978) *op. cit.* p. 59.
85 EISNER, E. (1979) *op. cit.*, p. 17.
86 HUEBNER, D. (1975) 'Curriculum language and classroom meanings' in PINAR, W.F. (Ed.) *Curriculum Theorizing* Berkeley, Calif., McCutchen.
87 GRUMET, M. (1978) 'Curriculum as theater: Merely players' *Curriculum Inquiry* No. 8, pp. 37–64.
88 PINAR, W.F. (1975) *op. cit.*
89 DOW, G. (1979) *Learning to Teach, Teaching to Learn* London, Routledge and Kegan Paul.

# Author Index

# Index

Coward, R. and Ellis, J. 111
Cremin, L.A. 1, 32
Critcher, C. *(see Clarke et al)*

Dahrendorf, R. *(see Adorno et al)*
Dale, R., Esland, G. and MacDonald, M. 111
Dallmayr, F.R. and McCarthy, T.A. 60, 61, 125
Debord, G. 110
De Leon, S. 140
Dewey, J. 1, 3, 11, 146
Dolbeare, K. 126
Donald, D. 38
Douglas, M. 33
Dow, G. 162
Dreeben, R. 73, 88, 109
Dreitzel, H.P. 35, 61, 87, 88, 140, 160

Edwards, R. 110
Egerton, J. 140
Eggleston, J. 33, 109
Eisner, E. 32, 109, 161, 162
Ellis, J. *(see Coward and Ellis)*
Elshtain, J.B. 31, 35, 86, 87, 88, 95, 110, 126, 139
English, F.W. 52
Entwhistle, H. 86
Enzenberger, H.M. 34, 60
Erben, M. and Gleeson, D. 110
Esland, G. *(see Dale et al)*
Ewen, S. 41, 60

Fay, B. 60, 61
Fay, M. and Stuckey, B. 86
Feinberg, W. 5, 32, 48, *(see also Bredo and Feinberg)*
Feinberg, W. and Rosemont, H. 89
Femia, J.V. 35
Fenton, E. 62
Ferrarotti, F. 160
Fever, L. 34
Fleming, D. and Bailyn, B. 162
Foucault, M. 35
Fox, T. and Hess, R.D. 53, 62
Franklin, B.M. 32, 161
Freiberg, J.W. 32, 125, 160
Freidenberg, E.Z. 110
Friedman, J. 61
Freire, P. 3, 30, 35, 55, 62, 67, 68, 78, 84, 87, 89, 117, 126, 127–139, 140, 141, 161
Freud, S. 129
Fromm, E. 65

Gadamer, H.G. 33
Garfinkel, H. 33
Gartner, A. 86
Gebhardt, E. *(see Arato and Gebhardt)*
Geertz, C. 26, 35
Giddens, A. 17, 20, 33, 34, 107, 111

Gintis, H. 91, 109 *(see also Bowles and Gintis)*
Gintis, H. and Bowles, S. 110
Giroux, H.A. 2, 3, 4, 60, 62, 109, 111, 126, 162
Giroux, H.A. and Penna, A.N. 60, 62, 126
Gitlin, T. 34
Gleeson, D. 109
Goffman, E. 110
Goldman, L. 125
Gordon, M. and MacDonald, J. 111
Gorelick, S. 76, 87, 88, 110, 140, 160
Gouldner, A.W. 25, 33, 34, 51, 61, 62, 137, 140, 154, 160, 161
Gower, R. and Scott, M. 87
Grace, G. 88, 105, 111, 160, 161
Gramsci, A. 4, 17, 22, 23, 25, 26, 30, 31, 34, 35, 39, 94, 110, 133, 140, 148, 149, 160
Graubard, A. 33, 86, 87
Green, A. *(see Sharp and Green)*
Greene, M. 55, 62, 76, 88, 126, 156, 161, 162
Greer, C. 1 *(see also Shiels and Greer)*
Gross, R. and Gross, B. 65, 86, 87
Grubb, W.N. and Lazerson, M. 109
Grumet, M. 158, 162 *(see also Pinar and Grumet)*

Habermas, J. 9, 21, 32, 34, 50, 60, 61, 137, 138, 139, 140 *(see also Adorno et al)*
Hahnell, R. *(see Albert and Hahnell)*
Hakken, D. *(see Andrews and Hakken)*
Hall, S. *(see Clarke et al)*
Hall, S. and Jefferson, T. 35
Halsey, A.H. *(see Karabel and Halsey)*
Hammersley, M. and Woods, P. 35
Hamilton, D. 34
Harold, B. 86, 87
Harris, A. *(see Skilbeck and Harris)*
Harris, K. 154, 161
Harrison, F.R. 62
Hegel, D. 114, 115
Heller, A. 17, 35, 62, 121, 126
Henderson, B. 9, 32
Hess, R.D. *(see Fox and Hess)*
Hickman, W.I. 47, 61
Hoare, Q. 87, 88
Hogan, D. 33, 97, 110
Holly, D. 14, 33
Horkheimer, M. 45, 46, 61, 140
Horkheimer, M. and Adorno, T.W. 87
Howard, R. 89
Hoyles, M. 87
Huebner, D. 158, 162
Husserl, E. 45, 61, 129

Illich, I. 79, 91
Israel, J. 160

164

# Subject Index

accountability 47–48, 105
alternative schooling 63
assessment 84, 145

bureaucracy 10, 55

capital (accumulation of) 6, 28
capitalism *(see also education & capitalism)* 4,
    15–16, 19–20, 22–23, 31, 41, 64, 95, 144
    American 1
    contradictions of 29
    development of 6
classroom constraints 50, 105–108, 153
consumption 6, 21, 40, 41
correspondence theory 69–71, 78, 91–93,
    95–100, 103, 105, 109, 145
credentialism 2
culture 8, 17, 27, 28, 94, 96, 130, 147
'cultural capital' 3–4, 28, 40, 71, 77–78, 82,
    97, 102, 105, 108, 123, 131, 134, 136,
    149, 155, 158
curriculum, 28–29, 50–51, 94, 97, 113, 120,
    122, 125, 145, 147, 149–150, 153–154,
    159
    content of 7, 97, 99, 100
    development 37, 49, 52, 119, 136, 150
    as ideological language 3
    relevance 38, 39, 47
    social functions of 2–3
    students centred 30, 31, 123, 124, 125,
        134, 135, 156, 157
democracy 1, 3, 31, 99, 143
    as social control 7
deschooling 63
dialectics 114–125, 157
division of labour 2, 30, 85, 92, 106, 108,
    131–132, 135, 144, 153

education
    American 1–3, 10
    autonomy in 25, 58, 70, 100, 144
    and capitalism 2, 10, 64, 71, 73, 91, 93,
        95, 102

change in 63, 72, 79–86, 93, 96, 98,
    104–105, 107, 108, 118, 119, 121, 122,
    123, 124, 125, 127, 128, 132, 133, 134,
    135, 136, 138, 145, 156, 158
control of 70, 99–100, 107
critique of 80, 103, 127–128
    as 'emancipatory' force 3, 7, 32, 57, 122,
        124, 146
    managerial models of 10–11, 56, 92, 100,
        150
    political 22
    and social class 13–15, 18, 28, 31, 67, 70,
        74, 75, 77, 79, 80, 91, 92, 93, 94, 97,
        105, 106, 135, 145
    and social control 1–3, 5–7, 13–14, 18–19,
        22–24, 26, 28–29, 31, 37–38, 40, 56–58,
        64–66, 70–73, 78, 80, 94, 95–98,
        100–102, 104–106, 119–121, 123,
        129–130, 133, 134, 136, 138, 143, 149,
        152, 159
    as social equalizer 1–3
    technical aspects of 5
    theories of 5, 12
    and work 13, 69, 70, 74, 85, 92–95,
        98–100, 135
educational goals 51–52
empiricism 43–46, 48, 50–53, 56–57, 77,
    151, 153, 157
ethnomethodology 12

family the 13, 69, 70, 94, 99, 101, 149
free school movement 12, 30
functionalism 2, 3, 5, 13, 14, 71, 72, 91, 96,
    102, 129

gender 28

hegemony 3, 7, 8, 15, 16, 18, 22, 23–26, 28,
    29, 42, 72, 95–97, 99–101, 103, 131,
    147–150
    'cultural' 47, 71, 74, 94, 99, 130, 136
    'ideological' 40, 98, 102, 104, 136

# Index